Daniel Taylor

...ment
A Guide to
Critical Thinking

Argument

A Guide to Critical Thinking

Perry Weddle

California State University, Sacramento

McGraw-Hill Book Company

New York St. Louis San Francisco Auckland Bogotá Düsseldorf
Johannesburg London Madrid Mexico Montreal New Delhi Panama
Paris São Paulo Singapore Sydney Tokyo Toronto

ARGUMENT
A Guide to Critical Thinking

1 2 3 4 5 6 7 8 9 0 D O D O 7 8 3 2 1 0 9 8 7

This book was set in Times Roman by National ShareGraphics, Inc.
The editors were Jean Smith and Barry Benjamin; the cover was designed by John Hite; the production supervisor was Milton J. Heiberg.
R. R. Donnelley & Sons Company was printer and binder.

Library of Congress Cataloging in Publication Data

Weddle, Perry.
    Argument.

    Includes index.
    1. Reasoning. I. Title.
BC177.W43   160   77-11001
ISBN 0-07-068961-X

For C.D.W.
and O.B.W.

Contents

Preface

This book is designed to encourage the democratic art of thoughtful, articulate discussion. It attempts to help its readers think out their own ideas and those of others. It should prove useful to students of rhetoric, composition, and debate, and should aid journalism students in improving their reporting of scientific and economic news. It complements the formal logic provided by a university-level general education course in logic. And it should aid the general reader, for its guiding principle is the question, "What skills do educated citizens need in order to handle the argumentative raw material which confronts them daily?"

Such raw material has shaped the book's narrative, much of which centers on wire service stories, editorials, letters to the editor, street wisdom, and TV. But discussion cannot be confined to such material, for not all argument is either hucksterism or political rhetoric. The thinking that underlies life's important decisions is contemplative, or at least ought to be. Accordingly, the book touches some very basic matters—religion, human action, history, causation, art, and the theoretical foundations on which argument rests. May the material reflect the world which suggested it, and not some fantasy picture. May the reader not find many arguments like:

What you bought yesterday you eat today.
Yesterday you bought raw meat.
So you eat raw meat today.

A youngster compared to some, that example has appeared in dozens of logic books since the eleventh century.

The author of a book such as this inevitably grapples with the question of how far to accommodate the subject's rich ancestry. On the one hand, it is possible to ignore that ancestry, starting over, in effect, from scratch. This approach makes considerable sense because the subject to which we are heirs—the subject sometimes called "informal logic"—consists of a marvelous hodgepodge of overlapping, often misleading, only partly understood, excessively negative material gathered over a period of more than 2000 years from sources who were attempting widely different things for many different audiences.[1] On the other hand, ignoring tradition not only omits much of real value but also leaves readers ignorant of approaches and lore which, for better or worse, are cited by educated people. Therefore, this book attempts to follow a middle path. It makes use of its subject's ancestry where that ancestry makes perfect sense or where educated people could benefit from being able to recognize it.

The book is organized perhaps somewhat untraditionally, partly to avoid the impression that scientific, technical, and inductive thinking differs fundamentally from every other kind of thinking. Although the book contains no section on formal deduction, it does note deductive arguments wherever they are found. Though it contains no section on the uses of language ("How many pieces are there in a pie?"), it does try to foster the art of arguing objectively and the art of exposing the tear-jerking, back-patting, mud-slinging, and deck-stacking lingo so dear to propagandists. Though it contains no section on scientific method, it does discuss how to assess media interpretations of scientific findings, and it reviews how to conduct experiments which can affect such matters as which brand to buy, what variety to grow, or which practitioner to patronize. And though it contains no section on probability, the book does cover probability matters encountered in daily life—election projections, opinion polls, economic indexes, and the like.

The book does not ignore terminology but attempts to deemphasize it. Though scores of traditional terms are explained (may they be for *de*coding, not for *en*coding, vocabularies!), more forceful common expressions duplicate most of them. More importantly, careful explanation is invariably better than categorizing and name-calling.

No discourse can be worth much that does not encourage its readers to apply and develop its ideas. This book contains three types of sections to facilitate comprehension, application, and independence. First, each chapter has one or more "Quick Checks," a series of short, straightforward problems, with answers or suggestions, which will enable readers to develop and gauge comprehension on their own. Second, each chapter contains a

---

[1] For an amusing, tough-minded synopsis of that portion of the subject called "informal fallacies" (a subject with which to some extent the present work deals), see the first chapters of C. L. Hamblin, *Fallacies,* Methuen, London, 1970.

section "Examples and Comments," which is intended to foster the arts of discussion, critical judgment, and patient, orderly explanation. About a third of the problems are commented on in order to suggest various ways to continue with the remaining problems. The examples range from ones calling for straightforward answers to ones where the sensible reply will be, "I don't know; here are some possibilities." (To be lost intelligently takes no small skill.) Third, each chapter contains a section called "Applications," which tries to narrow the gap between the "on-paper" world and the world as it really is. The three sections also encourage independent research, the pooling of knowledge, and the desire to deepen or challenge the book's ideas.

Above all, everything is intended to be *discussible,* to bring individuals constructively together. Since this book aims to develop skill at assessing any argument, its own arguments must themselves always be considered fair game. Topics too complex or controversial for the space devoted to them have not been avoided. All sorts of opinions have been ventured, most of them safe and clearly right, others unorthodox and not clearly right. Everything lies open to attack or defense. Have at it.

Perry Weddle

Argument
A Guide to
Critical Thinking

The Realm of Reason

The brouhaha at home plate after a batter is hit by a pitch; a spat between Punch and Judy; a donnybrook—these are all arguments, but not in the sense of the term which concerns us. This book deals with sweet reason. It deals with arguing *over* something, yes, but in the sense in which arguing is *giving* arguments, not in the sense in which arguing is squabbling.

Reason and emotion are sometimes depicted as strict opposites. To speak of opposition exaggerates the difference between them, which more closely resembles the difference between means and ends. "Are there not soporific dreams and sweet deliriums," asks Logan Pearsall Smith, "more soothing than Reason?" There are. But if we need soothing, then it is *reasonable,* if they are not harmful, to seek such dreams and deliriums, and to do so efficiently. Logic, reason, and straight thinking are tools, our most important tools, for attaining what we want, and for evaluating what we think we want.

ARGUMENT MECHANICS

A simple *argument,* or piece of reasoning, consists of a *conclusion* and a *premise* or premises. The conclusion is that which is or seems to be supported, the premise or premises that which support. Consider the following:

> I smell bacon frying. Somebody must be up early making breakfast.

> We're a good bet to win this week. We have the better weight, speed, ball handling, and experience.

> It's either at school or at home. It's not at school. You figure it out.

> My friends support the bond issue by more than 2 to 1. Therefore, it's bound to pass.

Each piece of reasoning makes a claim and tries to support it. Support may be indicated by context alone, as in the second and third examples, or by such words as "must be" and "therefore," as in the first and fourth examples. That a conclusion is immediately coming may be indicated by such terms as "so," "hence," "it stands to reason that," "thus," "it follows that," "therefore," and "accordingly." That a premise is coming may be indicated by such terms as "because," "since," and "for the reason that." Everyday arguments usually depend on a premise (or premises) or the conclusion being supplied by the audience. The conclusion in the third example being too obvious to state, the arguer prefers to leave it unstated. In the fourth example, knowing that the audience considers the arguer no fool, the arguer does not bother to add "and my neighbors typify those who will vote in the bond issue election."

Arguments may be simple—a single conclusion supported by one or more premises—or they may be complex. Complex arguments contain many premises supporting a conclusion or conclusions which in turn form premises for a further conclusion or conclusions. In the following segment from a county council meeting, notice the variety of simple arguments.

> Yes, we could consider a site outside of downtown, as was suggested last week. However, it has become clear to me that the disadvantages of such a move far outweigh the initial cost savings that were mentioned, as well as the undoubted improvement in downtown congestion. City Hall, the city and county jails, law enforcement facilities, and more are downtown already, between 9th and 10th on J. With them downtown, building the new courthouse out in the boondocks makes no sense.
>
> The southwest corner of 9th and K has also been suggested. True, besides 8th and J it's really the only viable site downtown. But building there would mean tearing down the Frauenfelder Mansion, the only really fine example of gothic revival architecture in this part of the state. The experts consulted say the Frauenfelder can't be moved. So even if we could get a demolition permit, to destroy that landmark would be unconscionable.

Though not as choice as the Frauenfelder site, the 8th and J location has much to recommend it. The present structures on the site are of no consequence—one is unoccupied, and Ev Newberg of Newberg's Hardware, who owns the whole property, is about to retire. In other words, we could get the site fairly cheaply and at no human sacrifice.

The conclusion, that the new courthouse should be built at 8th and J, gets supported a number of ways. One set of reasons undermines the "outside downtown" alternative (which in turn has its own supports). Another set undermines the "9th and K" alternative (which in turn has its own supports). And a third set supports the "8th and J" case (which means overcoming still further arguments against that site).

Most arguments make both an internal and an external claim. The external claim is that the premises are consistent with fact. Careful arguers will have answered such questions as, "Are all of my premises true?" "Have I overlooked any critical details?" "Have I assessed the situation correctly?" The internal claim is that the premises hook up with the conclusion. "Given the premises," the claim goes, "the conclusion must be true." Put another way, the internal claim is, "If the premises are true, the conclusion cannot be false."[1]

Arguments in which the internal claim is correct are said to be *valid*. These two are valid:

Felicia is taller than Hortense, and Hortense is taller than Sybil. Obviously, Felicia is taller than Sybil.

X will not occur unless A. Y will occur only if B. Neither A nor B can obtain unless C. C is impossible. Hence, X and Y will not occur.

One knows these arguments to be valid without being familiar with the facts of the case. One can assess the internal claim in the first argument, for instance, without knowing who or what Felicia, Hortense, and Sybil are—they may be steam locomotives, philosophers, or something else entirely. Variables such as A, B, and C, as in the last example, would fit as well. One can assess an argument's internal claim simply by attending to terms. We know here what "is taller than" means. We know that the proper names designate whatever can have height. We know the rules of English syntax,

---

[1] Arguments making the internal claim are sometimes said to be "deductive." These supposedly contrast with "inductive" or sometimes "nondeductive" arguments. Suitably filled out, however, most good "inductive" or "nondeductive" arguments turn out to meet the requirement for deductiveness—that the conclusion is contained in the premises. Thus the athletic argument would go: "*Any* team with the better weight, speed, ball handling, and experience will win. *Our* team has the better weight, speed, ball handling, and experience. Therefore, our team will win." So, without worrying about the intricacies involved, I have ignored the distinction between deductive arguments and the others, and hence the idea of deduction itself.

and how to judge when and what kind of inference is drawn. For the internal claim, that is all we need.

Arguments with incorrect internal claims are said to be *invalid*. Consider:

> All *A*'s are *C*'s. All *B*'s are *C*'s. Therefore, all *B*'s are *A*'s.

Whatever *A*'s, *B*'s, and *C*'s are, the fact that two groups both happen to be something or other fails to guarantee that the first group contains the second. All Albertans being Canadians, and all British Columbians being Canadians, scarcely implies that all British Columbians are Albertans.

Arguments can be evaluated more completely by assessing their internal and external claims together. A *sound* argument is a valid argument (there's the internal assessment) with true premises (there's the external). An *unsound* argument is a valid argument with one or more false premises. This argument is unsound:

> Octogenarians are people in their eighties. President Carter is in his eighties, so President Carter is an octogenarian.

Perhaps it needs to be added that unsound arguments (or invalid arguments for that matter) may *happen* to have true conclusions, although the foregoing example does not. If I reason that all nitrates are soluble in water, so potassium nitrate is soluble in water, I will have a correct conclusion, but from a false premise (nitrates of silver, lead, mercury are insoluble in water). I will have arrived at the truth not by sense, but by luck.

Quick Check

This is the first of a number of "Quick Checks"—straightforward self-evaluations, with answers, enabling readers to gauge and improve comprehension. Do each problem, or at least a sampling from each lettered list. (Problems designed to develop skills which require resourcefulness and perspective appear later, in the sections entitled "Examples and Comments" and "Applications.")

A Let the letters *W*, *X*, *Y*, and *Z* stand for independent clauses or declarative sentences. In each of the following, which is the conclusion?
1 Since *W* and *X*, *Y*.
2 *W*, because *X* and *Y*.
3 *W*. *X* and *Y*. Hence, *Z*.
4 *Z* being ruled out, *X*, since neither *W*, nor *Y*.
5 If *W*, *X*, and *Y*, then *Z*.
6 If *X* then *W*, and if *Z* then *Y*. Either *X* or *Z*. So either *W* or *Y*.
7 *W*. Why? Well, *Z*.
8 *Y* only if *Z*. *Y*. So obviously, *Z*.

9   Y will not be the case unless W. And W is impossible because X. You draw the conclusion.

10   If W then X, and if X then Y. So if W then Y.

B   Assume the following to be valid arguments. Supply the missing (implied) part of each.

1   Anyone who knowingly carried an unauthorized pistol onto an airliner is guilty of a felony, so this woman is guilty of a felony.

2   It doesn't sound plausible to me either, but it's true. I read it in the *Times*.

3    $c^2 = a^2 + b^2$. $a = 3$. $b = 4$. $c = ?$

4   If a major earthquake occurs, the dam upriver may well burst, and there's a distinct possibility of a major earthquake in this century. If the dam bursts, this city will survive a major catastrophe only if it has an articulated evacuation plan and an effective means of carrying it out, two things this city does not have. A major catastrophe must be avoided at all costs. Is there any doubt about our course of action?

5   Of *course* it's a reptile, dummy; it's a turtle, isn't it?

6   Look, Mac, this bar goes 3 to 1 for the Democrat, see? So *Chicago* goes 3 to 1 for the Democrat. It's that simple.

7   Unfortunately, we can give the award to only one restoration, and we have five strong candidates. Of those, regardless of price category, 1825 P and 807 Thirteenth really are slightly better than the other three. Of the two "finalists," 1825 P is in a lower price category. Therefore the award should go to 1825 P.

C   True or false?

1   A valid argument must have a true conclusion.

2   No sound argument has a false conclusion.

3   A valid argument may have false premises.

4   In a valid argument if a premise is false the conclusion will necessarily be false.

5   In a sound argument the conclusion is necessarily true.

6   In an invalid argument the conclusion is necessarily false.

7   In an unsound argument both premises and conclusion may be false.

Answers

A   (1) Y; (2) W; (3) Z; (4) X; (5) Z; (6) "either W or Y"; (7) W; (8) Z; (9) "Y will not be the case"; (10) "if W then Y."

B   (1) This woman carried an unauthorized pistol onto an airliner; (2) Anything in the *Times* is true; (3) 5; (4) We should get an articulated evacuation plan and an effective means of carrying it out; (5) All turtles are reptiles; (6) Chicago goes the way this bar goes; (7) The award should go to the best restoration, regardless of price category, with ties being broken by selecting the lower price category.

C   (1) F; (2) T; (3) T; (4) F; (5) T; (6) F; (7) T.

ARGUMENT ECOLOGY

It would be shortsighted to discuss anatomical details of everyday arguments without also discussing arguments environmentally—that is, such matters as who the arguers are, what their intentions are, who the audience is, and more. Environmentally speaking, arguments consist of four elements—the *argument proper,* the *reasoners,* the *issue,* and the *point.* Since the topic of argument proper has been discussed, let us turn to the other three.

Reasoners Sometimes argument persuades, sometimes it explains, and sometimes it clinches what is already believed or known. Persuading, explaining, clinching are *for* someone. So an argument can be viewed as having two segments—the *en*coding and the *de*coding, the argument and the audience. Arguments invite the audience into their arena: "Hear me out," "Consider this," "Come let us reason together," and the like. *Dialogizomai,* the New Testament word for reasoning, nicely parallels our words "dialogue" and "dialectic": reasoning is give-and-take.

None of this is to say that argument cannot proceed in solitude. We reason to ourselves constantly and constantly judge that reasoning. Nevertheless, the acid test of reasoning's significance will be public. Compare thinking to yourself of an ingenious design for a perpetual motion machine to actually inventing a perpetual motion machine. It is not for nothing that patent offices require working models. Whether or not you have designed a perpetual motion machine depends on public, objective tests, not on your imagination alone. The audience thus forms an essential part of the reasoning process.

The Issue The issue constitutes the setting in which the give-and-take occurs. It is not one side or another of an exchange, nor even the exchange as a whole. The issue can usually be expressed in a phrase beginning "whether": "Whether the President has committed high crimes and misdeameanors." "Whether this nematode infestation justifies the use of poison gas." "Whether screen passes effectively counteract the red dog defense." In other circumstances the issue may be simply a topic to discuss (Presidential power, pesticides, the red dog defense) or an end to be achieved (how to restore the system of checks and balances, how to eradicate nematodes, how to stop the red dog defense from devastating our team's offense). The issue may be as narrow as a specific question or as broad as a general range of subjects.

Sometimes the issue will be set formally—a question posed, a challenge to what has been said, an indictment, an agenda item. On other occasions the issue, not necessarily the less clear, will arise unmentioned out of the situation. A custodian's having become trapped in a heating duct poses no occasion to discuss race relations or fashions. Even the daily noontime argument every spring at a Gary, Indiana, steel plant (just to take an example of another type) contains an issue. The discussion arises spontaneously and may ramble leisurely from White Sox pennant hopes, to so-and-so's perpetual sore arm, to so-and-so's hitting. The dialogue boasts no agenda, no chairperson, no parliamentary procedure. Like most argument, it doesn't need any. Yet were even this loose-jointed argument banter to be switched suddenly by one of the participants to questions and comments on the stock market, or to some other favorite topic, then symptoms of disruption would undoubtedly occur—protestation that "We're not talking about that," or a polite but grumbling change to the new topic, or the beginnings or cementing of a reputation on the part of the interrupter for being not exactly with it, or for having a thing about the topic introduced. Even loose-jointed argument banter is jointed.

Of course, disputes do arise occasionally in which the issue is not clear. Several issues may compete or coexist. And sometimes the goal of a discussion may, or should, be to *discover* the fruitful issue. At other times the issue will be confused, the participants arguing at cross-purposes. The value of being skilled at recognizing the issue, or lack of one, in a dispute would be difficult to overestimate. Good thinkers have developed the disposition to ask, "Just what is at issue here?"

The Point of Argument   Besides reasoning, reasoners, and issue, argument has a point. Argument is purposive, its primary point being to establish useful fact. This should be no mystery, the general superiority of fact over falsehood being obvious. William James writes:

> If I am lost in the woods and starved, and find what looks like a cow-path, it is of the utmost importance that I should think of a human habitation at the end of it, for if I do so and follow it, I save myself. The true thought is useful here because the house which is its object is useful. The practical value of true ideas is thus primarily derived from the practical importance of their objects to us.[2]

None of this is to say that reasoning cannot be used to support falsehood, or be for nothing—scholastic and barren. The claim only concerns reasoning's primary purpose. Let me explain by parallel. The institution called the checking account rests on a trust, mostly taken for granted, that checks (and their backing) are good. Were we to lose this trust we would also lose the institution. Nobody would cash or honor checks. In this way the notion that all or even a significant fraction of all checks are no good is at bottom contradictory. Good checks must be normal, and the workings of the checking account are to be explained in terms of the norm. Now with arguments something similar holds: It must be normal that reasons are real reasons for their conclusions, and that conclusions are true. It must also be

---

[2] William James, *Pragmatism,* Meridian Books, Inc., New York, 1955, p. 134.

normal that argument goes somewhere near to where people expect it to go, and that that somewhere is useful. Similarly, the workings of argument, like those of the checking account, are to be explained in terms of the normal, in terms of good argument, good reasoning. Fallacious reasoning can then be seen to deviate from, and to parasitize, that norm.

GOOD REASONING

Let us notice some quite general characteristics of that norm, of good reasoning, of sound argument practice. (1) Good reasoning is *from fact.* (2) In good reasoning the premises are *independent* of the conclusion. (3) Good premises and good reasoning are *relevant.* (4) The premises in good reasoning *adequately support* their conclusion. (5) In good reasoning, the premises are *more accessible* than the conclusion. (6) Good reasoning *goes somewhere.* (7) Good reasoning, sound argument practice, is *open.*

From Fact   I once assumed that since a can contained no gas, the can would not explode when burned. I burned the can, which did not explode but turned out to have contained gas. Although my conclusion that the can wouldn't explode when burned was true, my premise that the can contained no gas was false. I was lucky. Now since luck is notoriously fickle, we need to reach the truth more reliably. We need to *establish* the truth. Obviously, this must be done from fact, not from falsehood. Of course, simple internal validity is necessary, but in the realm of reason it is soundness that counts. In ordinary circumstances people who have argued validly but from false premises often get criticized as if their internal cases were faulty: "Just a minute, your argument doesn't hold water; you've got your facts all mixed up . . ."

Plenty of good and poor reasoning does proceed from hypothetical facts the truth of which may not be known: "*If* virtue is knowledge then virtue can be taught, and . . ." "*Assuming* that Ray acted alone, then such and such would have occurred, and . . ." Other reasoning proceeds from probabilities: "Since you have about an even chance of being convicted on either count, I'd say it'd be best not to get your hopes up." "Your chances of drawing an ace now are 1 in 26. Therefore, you'd best fold." Hypothetical reasoning establishes no more than hypothetical facts, and probability arguments establish no more than probabilities.

Premises Independent   For a man widely accused of general crookedness to vouch for his own honesty, to claim that he was not a crook, would be ridiculous. Good reasoning proceeds *from* reasons *to* conclusion. The honesty illustration offers a simple case in which the strength of premises (the vouching) depends on the conclusion (the honesty). Admittedly, the example is transparent (though con artists constantly work this deception on the defenseless), but its transparency is not necessarily typical. The case stands at one end of a continuum many members of which would tax the powers of the subtlest thinkers. Ways in which arguers attempt to sneak support for their reasons from their conclusions will be discussed in the next chapter under the heading "Begging the question."

Premises and Argument Relevant In a good argument, although the premises must not depend on the conclusion, the reverse is certainly not true. The conclusion must depend on the premises. Irrelevance is one common form of nondependence. A customer writes:

> Dear Consumer's Hotline: Two months ago I bought an air conditioner from my Maelstrom dealer. The machine works okay, but hot weather is over and I need money. Maelstrom is a very big company and I am just a little guy. I should be able to return the machine for a refund, but Maelstrom refuses. Can you help?

Since the purchase agreement would have implied nothing about the weather, or about the seller's or purchaser's relative financial strength, this customer has no argument: case dismissed.

In the air conditioner example, although the premises did not bear on the conclusion, the conclusion at least did bear on the issue, the question of whether the customer should get a refund. Good argument addresses the issue. In some arguments the premises presumably bear on the conclusion, but the entire argument bypasses the issue. A politician charged with graft may adduce solid evidence to support the conclusions that his wife does not wear a fur coat and that he is a veteran. However strong the politician's arguments might be, the arguments quite miss the issue—those charges of graft. Ways in which premises miss conclusions, and arguments miss the issue, will be discussed in the next chapter under the headings "Ignoring the issue" and "Smokescreen."

Premises Adequately Support Conclusion Relevance is not enough. Conclusions in good arguments exactly reflect the strength of their premises. Premises meriting a "certainly" would get a "certainly" conclusion or its equivalent. Premises meriting something less venturesome, such as "probably" or "possibly," would get that. Beautiful arguments can even be built on inconclusive premises. Such arguments weigh and summarize the evidence masterfully. Their arguers exercise the art of *withholding* conclusions—as fine an art as the fine art of drawing them. They will conclude: "Given the evidence at hand, this matter cannot yet be decided." Indeed, in situations in which everyone is concluding left and right, the showing of pro exactly to balance con, or the sizing up of a situation as inconclusive, or an analysis revealing that crucial but as yet unobtainable evidence has been overlooked, will be immeasurably more valuable than any conclusion one way or the other.

Premises More Accessible than Conclusions This requirement makes sense because so much argument amounts to explanation. To argue, to explain, is to unfold the unknown, unclear, or unaccepted, in terms of the

known or better known, the clear or clearer, the accepted or more accepted.
Notice the way a loan officer's argument/explanation displays details for a
couple who have inquired about financing a house:

> Now since both of you are veterans, your best bet would be a VA loan. These
> are loans guaranteed by the federal government. They're superior to conven-
> tional loans because first of all they end up costing you less. Second, they are
> assumable, meaning that if you ever decide to sell, anyone, veteran or not, can
> take over the loan. Third, they can be paid off early without additional charge.
> Finally, you can take longer to pay off the loan.

The case is made fairly, without unnecessary technical lingo.

The requirement that premises be more accessible than conclusion may
have exceptions. The argument, "A horse is an animal, so a horse's head is
an animal's head," is obviously sound. The demonstration proving that
soundness, however, will take concepts, skill, and subtlety much beyond
anything it takes to appreciate the original argument. And then there are
those devilish children's questions, such as about where sugar goes in iced
tea. The phenomenon is usually elementary, its explanation complicated. In
such cases the proper response may be not to explain or argue at all. ("It
dissolved" would be a good answer to a small child's question about the
sugar.) Ways in which arguments violate this requirement by indulging in
needless technicality and pseudo jargon will be discussed in Chapter 3 in
the section on argument style. The topic of useless precision will be discussed in Chapter 4 in the section on the uses of statistics in argument.

Reasoning Goes Somewhere   Reasoning which ignores this characteristic invites charges of evasion, sterile pedantry, rambling, or in extreme
cases, madness. Does the following excerpt from a news conference have a
familiar ring?

Q   Senator, could you please outline for us your views on southern Africa?
A   Sure. My position on southern Africa is very simple. I think that our concept as
a nation, and that our actions, have not kept pace with the seriousness of the
situation. And therefore our actions there are not completely relevant today to the
reality of the magnitude of the very real and profound changes taking place in this
vital area of the globe.
Q   Senator, what does that mean?
A   Just what I said.

The question-and-answer continues in this vein for several minutes. Now
imagine what would become of reasoning if reasoning, or even news confer-
ences, were *typically* like this one! Various ways in which arguers avoid
going somewhere will be discussed in Chapter 3 in the section on argument
style.

Argument's Climate Is Open   The goal is the truth, but if reasoning
sometimes goes awry, thus missing the truth, then good argument must be
as open as is consistent with what might be called the "maximization of

correction" principle. The probability of the whole truth emerging from a controversy generally increases when all sides can get their opinions aired. Exceptions to the principle will be defensible on grounds that not limiting such opportunity would clearly decrease the possibility of the whole truth emerging.

Certain practical applications of the maximization of correction principle are interesting: for example, the fairness doctrine, the doctrine of "equal time," under which if one candidate or side in an election gets free electronic media exposure, the opponents can demand equal exposure. Something like equal time is rational policy, clearly, but in what form? Any policy produces its own climate. The current policy seems to delay obvious candidates from announcing formally, and may actually discourage healthy debate: well-known candidates may keep silent electronically in order to deny less well-known candidates free media exposure. The networks complain that they cannot cover front-runners in depth because other candidates would demand equal depth. And how far should equal time extend? A charge may merit a rebuttal, but many a rebuttal containing unsupported charges or doubtful information itself merits further comment. And to whom should equal time extend? To third, fourth, tenth party candidates? To unrecognized or nonaligned individuals? Somewhere along it, such a continuum would become confusion-generating, not truth-generating. On the other hand, a vicious circle in which a viewpoint is denied media exposure because it lacks popularity, and yet is incapable of achieving popularity because it cannot get media exposure, is to be avoided.

Such matters call for theoretical clearheadedness and experience. When weighing openness against a clear definition of all possibilities, it is probably wise to err on the side of openness. Having watched the emperor parade in his new clothes, anybody who was anybody discussed the qualities of garments too gossamer to be perceived by sight or touch. For the sake of truth it was critical for that little child—unqualified, unrecognized—to have been heard.

Now, with the foregoing principles in mind, let us examine some arguments in action.

Examples and Comments

Each chapter's "Examples and Comments" section consists of a number of pieces detached, or constructed as if detached, from the real world. (Context can usually be deduced from internal evidence, or from supplied hints, such as "Editor" for a letter to the editor or "[PNS]" for a wire service story.) The pieces usually, but not necessarily, reflect material from the chapter (though some attempt at review is made in the pieces in later chapters). About the first third of the pieces in each section are commented on. (So as not to imply that there is only one way to skin a cat, more than one type of approach and more than one degree of thoroughness have usually been adopted.) The remaining pieces are left for readers to comment on or to discuss. Some may be fairly easy, and some the opposite of easy.

Directions: Where the following are arguments, for each one: (1) state the issue; (2) paraphrase the argument, identifying premises and conclusion; (3) comment, noting the argument's strong points and suggesting lines, if any, along which it might be improved. Where the piece seems not to be an argument, simply comment briefly.

1 "The suspect," mused Inspector Wolff, "will have to leave town driving south. If the suspect leaves town he can leave only by plane, bus, or automobile. Since he knows that he can be recognized, he would not chance buying a ticket. For the same reason he cannot leave town driving north or east. He'd know that the toll collectors on the bridges along those routes will be on the alert."

Comment *Issue:* How to catch the suspect or how to prevent the suspect from slipping away.

Conclusion: The suspect will leave town driving south.

Premises: Possibilities are: "drive south," "plane," "bus," "drive north," and "drive east." "Plane" and "bus" are ruled out by danger of recognition at a ticket counter, "north" and "east" by that danger at a toll booth.

Evaluation: Wolff's structure, the process of elimination, is valid. There remains the question whether or not Wolff's argument is sound. The way he has sized up the situation looks suspicious. Has Wolff exhausted the real alternatives? What happened to "west"? Must the suspect leave at all? Why can't the suspect leave by private plane or boat?

2 "*Editor:* I am writing about the outlawing of fireworks on the Fourth of July. Ever since I can remember, the Fourth has been a time of celebration. Young children especially have looked forward to this day on which they wave sparklers in the air and laugh with joy when their Piccolo Petes whistle. With proper supervision fireworks are safe. Must they come to an end?"

Comment The issue here is whether or not fireworks should be legal. The writer obviously concludes that they should be, on grounds that fireworks appropriately celebrate the Fourth, that they please children, and that with supervision they are safe.

Clearly, the grounds are relevant; any reasonable case for outlawing fireworks would need to show those grounds to be outweighed by something else. The author does need to strengthen her case by continuing, if she can, to meet objections, as she has begun to do in mentioning safety under supervision. She needs to address the question of the difficulty of supervision, for instance, and the questions of fire hazards, accidents in spite of supervision, equally satisfactory ways to celebrate, and the like.

3 "*Editor:* Thanksgiving is the time of year to reap a joyful harvest by counting our blessings. Children are blessings. Their angels always see the face of God, and they generously share their visions with all who open their hearts to them. Our material blessings vary with the individual, but each generation seems to have more than the generations before. Faith is a blessing that sees even our troubles as reflections of the beauty of nature's dark skies, against which autumn's bright colors contrast all the brighter. Thanksgiving Day itself is a blessing—our country's unique gift for bringing joy to those who revere it."

Comment   Unless injected into a context where the writer ought to be sizing up the facts (in which case it would be a Pollyanna-like blindness to bad conditions), this piece is not an argument. It more closely resembles exercises such as pledges of allegiance or official prayers. Such performances, although they may produce the same states of affairs that arguments produce, do not pretend to give reasons for them. (Is this piece subject to an alternative analysis?)

4   "In testimony before the Senate Small Business Committee, Dr. Natalie Shainess, noted psychiatrist, has suggested that advertising has been particularly harmful to women. In support of her contention, Dr. Shainess zeroed in for the committee on that ultimate absurdity of contemporary marketing, the feminine spray deodorant, for which there exists no affliction except an artificially induced fear of social rejection. Worse, there seems to be evidence linking the use of such sprays to more than one real affliction. Next, it was suggested, we'll probably be offered a product to cure *those* afflictions! Advertising, Dr. Shainess continued, has cheapened human relationships by suggesting over and over to women that happiness with *him* can be attained simply by buying various gimcracks and potions. Particularly degrading, she finds, is advertising's promotion of the cult of youth, which suggests day in and day out that after age 40 a woman is worthless."

Comment   The issue here is the psychological effects of advertising, or perhaps more narrowly, advertising's effects on women. On one reading, the conclusion could be said to be that the Shainess analysis is true—based on Shainess's doctorate and her being a "noted psychiatrist." Alternatively, one may see not Shainess's authority but her *argument* as establishing the conclusion, her conclusion that advertising has been particularly harmful to women. This conclusion Shainess supports by highlighting one glaring abuse, feminine sprays, and two classes of harmful beliefs caused by ads— that products alone confer happiness, and that the only desirable state is youth.

Although Shainess's testimony seems cogent, at least two lines of questioning (which may have been considered in unreported testimony) ought immediately to come to mind. First, what of advertising's alleged *benefits?* Surely feminine-spray-type campaigns don't typify *all* campaigns. Second, is advertising *particularly* harmful to women? Doesn't the "gimcrack and potion" cure-all, the cult of youth, etc., hit men equally? (Think of the way hair-care products, razors, "muscle" cars, colognes, etc., are purveyed.)

5   "Americans who doubt the value of the swine flu vaccine should put those doubts aside and get their shots. At the price of a little time and possibly of a mild reaction for a few hours, anyone can be at least partly protected from what could be a devastating illness. Equally important, by taking the vaccine, each of us can help contribute to the prevention of a worldwide pandemic by nipping this kind of broad outbreak in the bud.

"No deaths directly attributable to flu vaccination have ever been recorded. Much concern has been expressed over the deaths of some chronically sick people soon after they received the vaccine. This, in itself, is no cause for alarm, because about one death among 10,000 old people occurs each day. In no instance reported to date has a cause-effect relationship been found between vaccination and death. Any healthy adult can take the vaccine safely, with very little risk of incurring even a sore arm."

6 "Look," said Malcolm, "if we try the south face, it'll be two o'clock before we can cross that steep slope. The snow will be so soft we'll be sinking in up to the waist, not to speak of the possibility of avalanche."

Rap stared east. "Yeah, I know. The thing is, the only other way up is straight ahead. I've been that way. There's a chimney that looks good until you get most of the way up. Then the whole top half of it's schist, and steep. You'd have to be Superman to get all the way up. Besides, it's late in the year; the sun's angle is low enough that the crust on the snow will hold, if we go the other way."

"Well, I don't like it, Rap, but you've been here before. Let's get going."

7 "Most of us are not telling the public that there is relatively little the police can do about crime. We are not letting the public in on our era's dirty little secret: that those who commit the crime which worries citizens most—violent street crime—are, for the most part, the products of poverty, unemployment, broken homes, rotten education, drug addiction and alcoholism, and other social and economic ills about which the police can do little, if anything.

"Rather than speaking up, most of us stand silent and let politicians get away with law-and-order rhetoric that reinforces the mistaken notion that police—in ever greater numbers and with more gadgetry—can alone control crime. The politicians, of course, end up perpetuating a system by which the rich get richer, the poor get poorer, and crime continues." (Robert J. Di Grazia, Boston Police Commissioner, as reported in *Parade,* Aug. 22, 1976.)

8 "Morality Protest. By most standards, Representative Robert Leggett has led a highly unorthodox life in recent years. Few variations in personal behavior are any longer capable of causing raised eyebrows, but having two families may be one of them.

"In an editorial recently appearing in The *Bee,* the Santa Rosa Press Democrat suggested that Leggett's morality could reasonably be construed by voters to disqualify him from holding office.

"Naturally, voters may use any criteria they wish in casting their ballots. Yet, there is something in the spirit of democracy that insists that people vote responsibly, that political decisions be based on political principles. The voters will do a disservice to themselves and to the nation if they indignantly elect the Republican to the office.

"It is reasonable to chide Robert Leggett for his carelessness with secret documents; it is less reasonable to condemn him for his audacious personal habits because they are not our own, and it is folly to elect his clearly inferior opponent as a morality protest." (Lt. Col. Robert Denham, USAF, ret., *The Sacramento Bee,* Aug. 22, 1976.)

9 "The duties of all public officers are, or at least admit of being made, so plain and simple that men of intelligence may readily qualify themselves for their performance; and I cannot but believe that more is lost by the long continuance of men in office than is generally to be gained by their experience. I submit, therefore, to your consideration whether the efficiency of the Government would not be promoted and official industry and integrity better secured by a general extension of the law which limits appointments to four years." (Andrew Jackson, first message to Congress.)

10 "Our governor spoke out clearly and honestly on the dictate of his conscience regarding the death penalty in California. I find this a very refreshing change from all too many public pronouncements by our elected officials.

"Now comes a storm of criticism because his views are different than the majority. We don't need to look far in our national experience to find instances when the majority was quite wrong.

"I didn't help elect a governor who had to count noses to determine what his next idea should be. I had hopes for a man of principle and high ethics. Now I find he has courage to advocate his beliefs." (Harry T. McCallum, *The Sacramento Bee,* Jan. 14, 1977.)

11 "When a child has felt the sensation of pain from touching the flame of a candle, he will be careful not to put his hand near any candle; but will expect a similar effect from a cause which is similar in its sensible qualities and appearance. If you assert, therefore, that the understanding of the child is led into this conclusion by any process of argument or ratiocination, I may justly require you to produce that argument; nor have you any pretense to refuse so equitable a demand. You cannot say that the argument is abstruse, and may possibly escape your inquiry; since you confess that it is obvious to the capacity of a mere infant." (Hume, *An Enquiry Concerning Human Understanding,* sec. IV, part II.)

Applications

The sections entitled "Applications," the book's shortest sections, but by no means its least important, have two broad purposes. First, they counteract the artificiality of lists of examples selected less on naturalistic than on pedagogical grounds. Valuable though the effort may be, rummaging around in such lists resembles hunting Easter eggs—one *knows* that the situation has been set up so that one will find what one is expected to find. Real-world material, on the contrary, is rarely isolated from context and rarely related to what one has just been thinking about. Only sometimes is it brief, and only sometimes does it resolve neatly. To assume a carry-over from lists to the real world would be naïve. Second, the "Applications" sections try to tap a bit of eduction's great pooling potential—the opportunity for students to contribute to each other's knowledge and development. Part of learning to think well is learning a wide variety of specialized skills and informational details, and many people's experience will have given them such expertise. It would be wasteful not to tap this expertise. Some of us have military, homemaking, business, or law-enforcement experience; academic majors in economics, science, or English; familiarity with some form of bureaucracy. All such expertise will come in handy, especially in the "Applications" sections of chapters which follow.

Directions: Either as an individual effort or in committee, attempt one of the following. (Where the problem involves collecting clippings or photocopies, save the material for future use.)

A Drawing on material from Chapter 1, produce your own "Quick Check," administer it to a group of colleagues, and evaluate the results.

B Produce your own brief "Examples and Comments" section, selecting material from your experience—for example, from letters to the editor, from editorials, from issue-oriented advertising, from the literature of religious, political, environmental, consumer, natural-foods, or related movements. Comment briefly on each piece, drawing where possible on material from the chapter.

C Construct a short essay which completes, or counters, this chapter's brief thoughts on the fairness doctrine ("equal time," p. 11) or on the point of argument (p. 7f).

D In this project "take them as they come." Using letters to the editor and/or the editorial page of a given edition of a newspaper as raw material, for each piece: (a) describe the issue (or unclarity about the issue); (b) give the conclusion, if any; (c) note any especially strong or weak points.

E If one of the author's comments sets you thinking or raises hackles, or both, write an essay subjecting the comment to careful assessment.

Chapter 2

Fallacy

Thus far we have emphasized argument mechanics and not argument evaluation. We have emphasized argument principles and not argument pitfalls. Now let us reverse emphasis by considering a number of such pitfalls, and, especially, how to avoid them and how to handle them. Let us take for this chapter's motto William James's observation: "To study the abnormal is the best way of understanding the normal."

The terms *fallacy* and *non sequitur* ("it does not follow") fault any argument. "Fallacy," however, really identifies a particular argument as a member of a type of bad arguing. A fallacy is a bad *way* of arguing. More fallacies have been named than flowers of the field—many of them not necessarily bad ways of arguing at all! And there exist so many alternative, by no means exclusive, species of fallacy that almost any bad argument qualifies as more than one. Although this book ignores much of the traditional terminology and does not intend to introduce new (there is enough name-calling already), and instead tries to treat arguments individually, still, educated people ought to be familiar with the more frequently encountered species.

Let us look, then, at some of the ways in which the principles of good argument noted above get violated, doing so under two broad headings. An arguer may *oversimplify*—distorting the facts by making them simpler than they actually are. Then again, an arguer, intentionally or not, may lay down a *smokescreen*—incapacitating thought by diversion. The categories included under these broad headings overlap considerably and give only a sample of the countless varieties of argumentative devilishness, many of which will be examined in later chapters.

OVERSIMPLIFICATION

Not only must good arguing make facts bear on the issue, it must do justice to those facts. To neglect significant or potentially significant facts is to oversimplify. Let us look at a variety of oversimplifications, each of which occurs frequently not only in the practices of arguers inclined to employ cheap shots but also in the thinking of all of us. Since the following categories, mostly traditional, exhibit family resemblances to each other, it would be good practice to try to fit an example into categories other than the one claimed for it. More oversimplifications will be discussed in later chapters.

Improper Questions By far the usual case is that the questions we deal with have answers. The problem, given a question, is to get the answer. That questions usually have answers produces in us a disposition to look for the answer without considering the question itself. Normally, this disposition is harmless, but not always. Arguers sometimes illegitimately trade on it in order to manipulate opinion, and not infrequently people pose improper questions to themselves. Confronted with a sticky question, therefore, remember this advice: When in doubt, suspect the question.

Any question, including the so-called "innocent" question, expresses what (with a little stretching) could be called assumptions. "How much did you pay for that hat?" expresses a considerable amount about what its asker believes. Among other things the asker believes that it is a hat, that it was purchased, with money, by the person being addressed. A question which oversimplifies by ignoring that one or more of its assumptions may be false, would be improper. The arguer's trick of asking a complex question is called "many questions" or "complex question." Consider the classic, "Have you stopped beating your wife?" The question's form suggests a "yes" or a "no" reply, yet either reply would commit the respondent to a presumably false assumption—that the respondent had been beating his wife and has now stopped, or that the respondent had been beating his wife and is still beating her.

Provided that the false assumptions packed into them are recognized, complex questions are easy to counter. One may be able to attack the question by *dividing* the question, and then denying the false assumption:

for example, "You are right that I have a wife, but I have never beaten her in my life." Alternatively, one may be able to reject the question: for example, "The question is ridiculous; I'm not even married." Gertrude Stein, on her deathbed, was asked, "What is the answer?" Her famous rejection of that question, her dying words, were, "What is the question?"

Questions sometimes have built into them an unwarranted framework which can lead to unsatisfactory results. The problem of air pollution sends some people off asking the question, "How can we clean up automobile exhaust emissions?" The question assumes that the best solution to air pollution lies in cleaning up exhaust when in fact other approaches may be better suited to the problem or necessary for its control. What about smog's industrial component? What about non-internal-combusion power, mass transit, clustering housing with industrial facilities, making home environments more desirable, and so on? Suspect the question. The utility executive who bad-mouthed wind as a viable source for generating electricity was probably right. Given our energy needs, however, the question being asked, "Is wind a good source of electricity?" was too narrow. Whereas electricity is high-level power, most energy needs are low-level. Wind may be a good source of low-level power. If we accept the utility company framework we could end up writing off a valuable resource.

False Dilemma   Related to the many questions of oversimplification is the phony either-or, the false dilemma. As people tend to answer a question before examining the question itself, so they tend to choose either the "either" or the "or" option without examining the pair of options itself. They take one horn of the dilemma or the other. Normally, this will be logically unobjectionable, since the dilemma will be true in that it will present a genuine pair of options. "We must go either left or right" fairly represents the case in which people want to proceed and the road forks. If the people do not necessarily want to proceed, or if the fork contains an unnoticed third branch straight ahead, then the same dilemma will be false. If we take one horn or the other, we will not have acted on the facts. The professor who replied that "We have a choice between giving into student demand and teaching what students want, or standing firm and teaching what needs to be taught," in not setting out all the possibilities, attempts to channel us into the second alternative. She oversimplifies by ignoring obvious possibilities—obvious, that is, if we retain the presence of mind to consider what they are.

Like complex questions, false dilemmas once detected are easy to counter. One rejects the entire pair, perhaps then formulating a broader range of options or another range of options altogether. Choosing a new option is called "going between the horns" of the dilemma. Rather than becoming impaled on either the "either" or the "or" horn, one escapes between them. Seeing the trick, a 4-year-old, when asked, "Do you want a cookie or some milk before you go to bed?" countered with, "I want both, and I'm not going to bed at all!" (The trick, notice, poses a false dilemma in the form of a complex question.)

The false dilemma occurs not only in the repertoire of the trickster but also in the thinking of the honest and subtle. Speaking of an impasse in an argument between two mathematical geniuses, the philosopher Frank P. Ramsey has remarked that "In such cases it is a heuristic maxim that the truth lies not in one of the two disputed views but in some third possibility which has not been thought of, which we can only discover by rejecting something assumed obvious by both disputants."[1] Although discovering that "third possibility" may take gifts beyond those of the run of humanity, it by no means always does. And to develop the healthy habit of thinking in terms of there being such third possibilities scarcely requires such gifts.

Sometimes indistinguishable from the false dilemma is a device called "poisoning the wells," in which the opponent gets the "choice" of drinking at one of two or more wells, all but one of which the arguer has unfairly tainted, usually by name-calling or caricature. At one point a few years back, President Nixon gave the nation the "choice" of, on the one hand, "an immediate and precipitate withdrawal of all American forces from Vietnam without regard to the effects of that action" and, on the other hand, his own way. But even those who favored "immediate and precipitate withdrawal" (and they formed only one part of a whole spectrum of people seeking withdrawal) did not favor such action "without regard to the effects." Quite the contrary. It was an assessment of precisely those effects which led many of them to their positions.

Straw Man In the previous example we have, too, a favorite technique of certain arguers, including many who should know better, called "knocking down a straw man" or, sometimes, a "straw man" argument. When attacking a general position there can be no excuse, other things being equal, for not attacking the position's strongest version. Instead, the straw man argument attacks what may *look* like the position, but what is really only a simple version, or only part of the position, or a ridiculous exaggeration. As in the following:

> *Editor:* The outrageous ruling against public schools holding father-and-son or mother-and-daughter parties is what you can expect if the Equal Rights Amendment is ratified. Half our armed forces and police would be women. There would be no more men's and women's restrooms. Once HEW can figure out how to manage it, men will be required to give birth to half the babies. Pennsylvania should rescind the ERA.

[1] Frank P. Ramsey, *The Foundations of Mathematics and Other Logical Essays,* Harcourt, Brace, New York, 1950, pp. 115–116.

Since the Equal Rights Amendment means no such thing, the author has only produced the illusion of an attack. Nor is the straw man ruse confined to the argumentatively inexperienced. Numerous advanced degrees did not keep a trustee from arguing as follows against tuition-free education at a state university.

> Opponents of tuition argue that since our state benefits from well-educated university graduates, it should pay for higher education through taxes. This is ridiculous. Our state benefits also from a well-fed, well-housed, and healthy population. But this does not mean that we should pay all the costs of everybody's food, housing, and health care.

By isolating one argument from the rest of the opponents' qualifying arguments, the trustee misrepresents their case. Paying for everyone's food, housing, and health care may be "ridiculous." But if it is, that has no bearing on the question of whether it is ridiculous to pay a fraction of the education costs of 10 percent of the population for about 6 percent of their lifetimes. Raising the specter of the welfare state here unfairly exaggerates the opponents' position.

There is, however, a difference between exaggerating a position and carrying a position to its logical conclusion. Had the opponents argued solely on the principle that the state should support *whatever* benefits society, which they did not do, the trustee would not have been unfair to attack their argument by showing their principle to lead to ridiculous consequences (supposing that it did). Although he would not be demolishing their conclusion (which could perhaps be defended in some other way) nor establishing his own, he would be doing something legitimate.

To show a position to be self-refuting, or to lead to untenable consequences, is to create a *reductio ad absurdum*: accept the argument (temporarily) and show that on its own grounds the argument is reduced to absurdity. Fairly used, the *reductio ad absurdum* is unobjectionable, indeed valuable. In Plato's *Theaetetus,* for example, Socrates considers the theory that absolutely everything in the universe is radically changing, in both place and state. Taken at face value, Socrates notices, the theory can amount to no more than the illusion of a theory. It can't even be stated, for the very words of the theory would not have the same meaning from one moment to the next. The theory cannot even be uttered, for the meaning of their terms would, as he puts it, "be escaping in the change." And so "the maintainers of the doctrine have as yet no words in which to express themselves," and indeed could never get any. Socrates makes use of the fact that airy generalities often apply to themselves. In this case self-reference seems also to produce a self-refutation.

Like Socrates, the careful thinker weighs generalities not only against fact, but also against themselves. As with the flux doctrine, this test of self-reference occasionally finds them wanting. For example, among the brighter members of virtually every introductory philosophy class will be a student who maintains, "There are no absolutes; everything is relative." A reply like, "Are you *absolutely* sure?" seems not unfair. The reply not only points out that the thesis must be modified but also drives home the advice to scrutinize one's own pronouncements.

An effective but little used variant of the *reductio ad absurdum* is the *infinite regress,* a maneuver which undercuts an attempted explanation by showing that it systematically must leave something else unexplained. In attacking the explanation that what accounts for intelligent behavior is something "inside the skin"—whether mind, brain, or whatever—B. F. Skinner considers an explanatory film from a television psychology documentary:

> The viewer learned, from animated cartoons, that when a man's finger is pricked, electrical impulses resembling flashes of lightning run up the afferent nerves and appear on a television screen in the brain. The little man (inside) wakes up, sees the flashing screen, reaches out, and pulls a lever. More flashes of lightning go down the nerves to the muscles, which then contract as the finger is pulled away from the threatening stimulus. The behavior of the homunculus [that little man] was, of course, not explained. An explanation would presumably require another film. And it, in turn another.[2]

Skinner's point here is that it will not do to explain intelligent behavior by positing intelligent entities. The question of *their* intelligent behavior, as the infinite regress shows, would be at least as puzzling as the question of *our* intelligent behavior. (In citing Skinner's argument with approval, incidentally, I do not mean to imply that automatic response to pain is not a strange subject matter with which to illustrate something about intelligent behavior.)

Stereotyping   Think, on the one hand, of "people on welfare," and, on the other, of crippled Mr. Adams down the block or of the abandoned mother of three across the street. Think on the one hand of "the Arabs," and on the other of Danny Thomas or of Omar Sharif, or even of Sirhan Sirhan. In general our malevolent side exercises itself less with individuals and specific proposals than with groups and ideologies. Arguers frequently trade on this weakness. Instead of confronting opponents as individuals, the stereotyper gives them labels, types them, puts them in pigeonholes, thus making use of the various associations which the labels evoke. Your opponents may *be* liberals, say, or hippies, or hard hats, but very likely they have interesting ideas or lovable traits of their own, ideas or traits which, if you

    [2] B. F. Skinner, *Contingencies of Reinforcement: A Theoretical Analysis,* Appleton, New York, 1969, p. 222.

attack the label rather than assessing them individually, never get examined. Stereotyping can be used to elicit favorable conclusions, too. The principle is the same: substitute prejudice for judgment. Any time friends or foes get characterized as "the *x*'s," beware. Are they really that homogeneous a group? Maybe they are, but one can prove or disprove it only by looking.

A related form of detail suppression has been dubbed by Madison Avenue "projecting an image." Forget what your product *is*, and project a simple fantasy picture instead. If your candidates are chain-smoking, alcoholic, foul-mouthed, adulterous, self-serving atheists, never mind. Have them flatteringly photographed attending church with the adoring family. Never show them taking drink, drag, or drug. Publicize them walking through a few ghettos to show their deep concern (in politics all concern is deep), and to show them philosophers—film them strolling in deep contemplation by the womb-dark sea. (And don't forget the dog.) Even though facts contrary to the image may be common knowledge, people resist thinking in any terms but those of the image.

More than a few fortunes have been made by being skilled at replacing one image with another. Filter cigarettes, now by far the most prevalent sort, formerly claimed only a tiny fraction of the market. Research had shown that heterosexual men, then the great majority of smokers, would not touch filter cigarettes, which were regarded as effeminate. Philip Morris performed a masterful sex-change operation on filters, however, capturing the lucrative masculine market with its famous Marlboro campaign featuring real tattooed, weather-beaten cowboys. Nothing specific was said about the cigarette. Nothing needed to be.

Once recognized, stereotyping and related oversimplifications are easy to counter. Remember the advice given in *King Lear*: "I'll teach you differences." Emphasize the *variety* which the oversimplification ignores; and since a psychological barrier as well as a logical barrier must be overcome, it may be necessary to risk oversimplification by temporarily projecting a counter image. For example:

> When Riley speaks of "the women's libbers," as he calls them, he paints a picture of strident, justice-be-damned monomaniacs. He forgets the majority. He forgets the millions of Betty Fords that give the movement its strength.

It is high time we asked, "Are image-projecting and similar Madison Avenue gimmicks really logic or reasoning at all, let alone good or poor logic or reasoning? In such matters, after all, no attempt has really been made to argue. Nothing has been reasoned about candidate or product. All we get are sets of associations." The objection has merit. In that we are given no reasons and, possibly, no pretense of reasons, to judge such types by logical criteria could be said to be inappropriate. (A biplane towing a

Pepsi-Cola banner is not bad arguing, for it is not arguing at all.) On the other hand, with the typical image projection, people get sent off in new directions on the basis of pictures (each the equivalent of 10,000 words) plus a few lines of copy. If many people *think* that they had been reasoned with, or *act as if* they had been reasoned with, then the result is the same as if they had been reasoned with. Practically speaking, therefore, it is probably best to continue as if the context were one in which reasons ought to have been given, and to risk charges of naïveté by continuing to ask, "Wait, where are the reasons?" "Sure he's a Southerner, but *what's his record* on racial issues?" "Do you *really need* an iron tonic at 35?" (Let alone at 60?) "Okay, big labor favors the bill, but *what does the bill do?*"

Half-Truth   The simple truth is, the truth is never simple. Someone obliged to tell the whole story who tells less than the whole story, while implying that all has been told, commits that form of lying called half-truth. A sheriff has been compiling records, including fingerprints, of all who attended a trial of members of a radical underground group. When ordered by a federal court to destroy those records, the sheriff invited the media to observe the destruction of the files. In implying that he had complied with the court order, however, the sheriff was not telling the whole truth, since he neglected mentioning that before depositing them in the shredder he had had the files copied. (Half-truth is, of course, not half of the truth but none of it; "truth," goes a Yiddish proverb, "is the safest lie.") A witness who supplies less than 100 percent of the evidence he or she is able, and asked, to supply (witnesses swear to tell the whole truth) would be guilty of this form of deception. So would a researcher who reported data favorable to a hypothesis while failing to report data to the contrary, or who failed to report having neglected areas where contrary data might be found. Someone who argues one side of an issue when under the obligation to *weigh* the various sides commits that form of half-truth called *special pleading*.

Precisely when someone has the obligation to tell all or to weigh all sides is a question of some interest. What of the advertiser who purchases the space to make a pitch? What of scientists bought by a corporation to do its bidding? What of the lawyer hired to defend a client, or of the district attorney in the case? And so on. Sketching what seems to me the beginnings of an answer, I will leave the reader to take it from there. (Or from somewhere better.)

In a court of law, when an attorney need not volunteer details which would hurt a client's case, the attorney cannot be accused of special pleading. The courtroom situation being an adversary situation, detrimental facts, if any, will get mentioned, since the other side has equal chance and will surely take it. Courts provide for something like equal time, dialectical openness being thus preserved.

Now what of paid advertising? If company Exco purchases space to tell you about its product, then can Exco be accused of special pleading if it does not mention the competition, the size of last year's profits, and so forth? It's Exco's space to do with as it wishes, we may think, free speech and all. Compare this to the courtroom. What makes arguing only one side of an issue unobjectionable in court is the adversary system. Counter evidence, and hence the real truth, has a chance. And with paid advertising something like such a system would exist, too, given a truly free market, ample advertising space, and even distribution of advertising funds. The trouble is, a truly free market does not really exist. Typical markets are dominated by three or thirty companies, each of which realizes that it is best to avoid potshots at the others. And consumer-oriented advertising scarcely exists. Hence, no adversary, no equal time. As with all propaganda the result is people being misled, or left in the very uncertain clutches of good luck. The brewery which touts its can recycling program fails to mention the environmentally better system of using returnable glass bottles. The timber giant heralding its tree farming program, in failing to mention the miniscule scale of those operations compared to its clear-cutting and virgin forest operations, misleads the reader of its ads into believing the corporation to be environmentally benevolent. Half-truth even in paid advertising is as objectionable as it is anywhere else.

Black/White Thinking   There are two sides to every question, right? Wrong. We so frequently divide things correctly into pairs of opposites that we can fall into the trap of proceeding as if every field were exhausted by a pair of opposites, "black" and "white." We argue, "It's not A so it's B," or, "The more A the less B," where A and B are not the only possibilities. (Black/white thinking thus shares territory with the false dilemma.) If there *were* only communist societies and free societies, then if a society weren't communist it would be free, and vice versa. For better or worse the world is not that simple. And arguing as one member of Congress did that "Of course Brazil is a free country; it's not communist, is it?" is to succumb to oversimplification. The same mistake occurs in the following: "Not a Republican? Then you must be a Democrat." "A career is a nice choice for a girl, dear, I'm sure, if you're not getting married." "Unlike factual judgments, such as about the color of that chair, or the age of the Chief Justice, judgments of quality in the field of art cannot be made according to an objective standard; therefore, such judgments are purely subjective."

Items get sold sometimes with a version of the black/white deception in which the hucksters mention not the item's merits but the competition's alleged demerits, relying on the hearer to draw the faulty inference that the item advertised must be good. "Contains no scopolamine," to judge from a recent ad, seems to be the chief virtue of one of the popular sleeping aids, nothing else being said about the product—one feels like replying that neither does strychnine. The chief selling point of some candidates seems to have been that they were *not* involved in the political corruption of the Nixon administration. Others sell themselves simply as not being part of the Washington establishment. So what; neither was Hitler.

Appeal to Ignorance Argument environment is usually one of less-than-complete knowledge, the increase of knowledge being, after all, the point of arguing. Occasionally, someone will trade unfairly on this lack of knowledge. The arguer will appeal to the general ignorance as to the answer, relying on a kind of black/white thinking in trying unfairly to shift the burden of proof to the other side. The maneuver has been called "the fallacy of the aggressor" or *argumentum ad ignorantiam.*[3] The arguer uses the other side's inability or unwillingness to prove that a thesis is false as evidence that the thesis is true. Or vice versa. One poor soul cites "the government's stubborn refusal to release the truth about flying saucers" as proof that saucers exist. But flying saucers either exist or don't exist regardless of what the government does or does not do. Only the illusion of reasons has been produced. In similar fashion proponents of the notion that the world was created according to the letter of Genesis have argued that since opponents cannot prove that the account is false (the world, as Bertrand Russell has noted, could have been created complete with fossil and other "evidence"), therefore the Genesis account is true. This is ridiculous. Anticreationists might equally well argue that since the Creationists can't prove *their* contention, therefore the Genesis account is false. Indeed, that appeals to ignorance turned around "prove" the opposite shows the faultiness of the style of reasoning.

Another version of the technique trades on the unwillingness of public figures to answer unflattering gossip or charges, as the following editorial fragment illustrates.

> The story which appeared last month in these pages documenting the governor's extramarital liaisons raised considerable protest. We were accused of being "greedy scandalmongers who would publish doubtfully authentic photos of the state's highest official."
>
> Well, it's been several weeks since our story appeared. If the Governor's Office can manage to respond overnight to a little girl who wants to complete her autograph collection, surely it could muster the vast resources at its dispos-

---

[3] *"Argumentum ad x"* is modern Latin for an irrelevant or faulty appeal to *x* in order to get a conclusion accepted. *Argumentum ad hominem* (attacking the arguer) and possibly *argumentum ad captandum vulgus* ("grandstanding") are the only such terms which seem to retain any currency. The "argumentum ad" tradition will be ignored, since the phenomena it labeled claim equal or superior expressions in plain language: *argumentum ad superbiam* (spiritual pride) is "flattery," "snow job" or "buttering up"; *ad baculum* or *ad metum* (force or fear) are "might makes right"; *ad populum* is "playing to the gallery," "projecting a favorable image," "fear-mongering," "jingoism"; *ad verecundiam* (awe) is exploiting "hero-worship" "status transference," etc.

al to deny the allegations contained in our story. The fact that it has not done so speaks for itself.

The Governor's Office's "failure" to respond to the charges is understandable.To respond to them would be to dignify them. The mere association of a public figure with unsavoriness tends in the public mind to link the figure to the unsavoriness—a sad comment on the level to which many citizens have let their responsibilities slide. Silence from the Governor's Office does *not* "speak for itself."

Appealing to ignorance gains its convincingness from outwardly similar cases where such reasoning is quite in order. Where methods of proof are accessible, cut-and-dried, and someone who has every motive to prove a claim attempts to prove it and fails, *then* that the person cannot prove the claim true does constitute grounds for considering it false. The student who insists that his tape recorder has been left in his professor's office is shown wrong by an exhaustive fruitless search of that office. The place is small, tape recorders are large, stationary, and obvious. All possible hiding places can be exhausted. It is when all possibilities cannot be exhausted, or when there is unwillingness, that fruitless attempts fail to prove the opposite.

Appeals to ignorance cheat because where there is ignorance as to the exact truth, the burden of proof belongs on whoever steps off of noncommittal ground. Until a search has been made, the burden of proof in the tape recorder matter lay on either side. Whoever pressed either the "it is" or the "it is not" side would be justly required to back the claim. After a fruitless search, however, the burden, supposing there was a question, would have been on the student. Barring evidence to the contrary—evidence which it would then be the student's responsibility to produce—argument, fact, knowledge lies on the professor's side.

With burdens of proof a sort of "conservative" principle seems to govern. Walking along a street in the old part of town, Jay asks, "Did you know this sidewalk is not really solid?" Surprised, Kay asks, "What do you mean, 'not solid'?" Kay's "What do you mean" is well taken. Because cement sidewalks are typically solid, Jay's position, not Kay's, needs the proof. Solid sidewalks are normal. We have been getting by fine with the normal. Changing our views on cement sidewalks would mean changing our lives, something which our "conservative" natures see no point in doing for no good reason—hence the demand for good reason. Such demands constitute the burden of proof.

Our "conservatism," then, shapes the demand for proof. We don't want trouble for ourselves, or we realize, other things being equal, that change is unreliable, or, typically, much ado about nothing. Such "conservatism" backs pleas for or defenses of a number of practices. For example, the law demands that before general introduction, new medicines be proved both safe and effective; we do not want to be guinea pigs. And if that law is just, then on the same grounds the pleas would seem to be justified to extend the "safe and effective" requirement to other substances introduced into our bodies and into the environment. Similar attitudes put the burden of proof on the prosecution. Accusation, like the claim about the sidewalk, is relatively disruptive, or unusual, and like the introduction of untested drugs, more chancy and perilous than not acting. Again the burden lies with the unorthodox, not with the orthodox.

Begging the Question   Earlier we noted that in good argument premises are independent of the conclusion in the sense that support or acceptance of the premises must not come from the very thing the argument is trying to establish. An argument which depends partly or wholly on its conclusion is sometimes called a *petitio principii,* Latin for the commoner term, *begging the question.* Begging the question comes from ancient debating practice. Apparently, a debater would normally "beg" the opponent to grant certain premises. To attempt to beg the very question to be resolved, then, would be illegitimate. The old meaning still partly fits. We say that people have begged the question when they ignore glaring objections to their way of proceeding. In a context in which the findings of Freud, let us say, were in serious question, it would be inappropriate to base points on those very findings.

Ways in which an argument's conclusion can be used wholly or partly to shore up its premises can be obvious or subtle. One sneaky way involves concocting a string of premises in which the string, itself insufficient to sustain the conclusion, ultimately receives support from the conclusion. Such reasoning is called *circular,* like that of a teenager caught with a case of beer in his car: "Well, officer, if you don't believe me when I say that I'm of age, here's my driver's license. If you don't trust that, here's my draft card. The draft card's genuine. You can take my word for it." This is about as simple as circular reasoning gets. The boy's word is questioned. The word is backed by the driver's license. So far we have a straight authority argument (see Chapter 4), except that then the driver's license's authenticity is questioned. So the license is not taken as authority. Neither is the draft card. So what ends up "backing" the card? Precisely what was questioned in the first place, the boy's word. In this rather obviously fallacious example, the circle is tight, consisting of only three elements. With the number of elements multiplied, circular arguments are often much less obviously fallacious. Many arguments have only an element of circularity. This makes the circularity less obvious. A theory, for example, may be defended by a journal edited by someone married to the theory's proponent. To appeal to the journal to back the theory would be circular to the extent that the relationship could affect the result. The exact extent probably being difficult to ascertain, it would be advisable for someone who knew of the relationship at least to supplement the journal's defense with more independent testimony.

Consider something maybe less obvious. Religious people have often claimed that the order and the majesty of the universe shows the existence of an all-good, all-powerful, all-knowing God. To such claims it is natural to reply with reminders of that range of natural conditions, seemingly equal and opposite, which seems to show, if it shows anything at all, that there is not such a God—such conditions as pestilence, parasites, earthquakes, avalanches, hurricanes, conditions which sometimes go under the heading of "natural evil." Could an all-good, all-powerful, all-knowing God permit these? To this reply sometimes comes the defense that the conditions mentioned only *seem* bad to us because of our limited viewpoint—that in reality natural evil is really a good component of a greater overall picture. Now regardless of the soundness or unsoundness of the original argument, doesn't this defense beg the question? Earthquakes, pestilence, and the like are "horrible," "disastrous," "calamitous." Such terms exactly fit. To deny the application of such terms, one must resort to a framework against which all the suffering and death is seen to serve a greater purpose. That is, in order to make the "proof" go, one must rely on the very notion which one is trying to prove, namely, God. In other words we have here only the illusion of defense.

An allied technique produces a phony look of premise independence by smuggling in a stacked deck. One university sets its faculty salaries "objectively" through comparison with those paid by a group of comparable institutions. Many faculty at this university did not realize that when the "comparison" institutions begin paying higher salaries, their university quietly switches its comparison to others paying less, and, Surprise! the salary picture looks pretty good. As one faculty member put it, the "objective" criterion is about as objective as a rubber yardstick which stretches to exactly the dimensions of whatever it "measures."

When a conclusion is a theory or a deduction according to a theory, one way to stack the deck is to formulate the original problem in terms of a framework presupposed by the theory. And if the theory is in question, a theory to be proved, then setting up the problem that way will beg the question. A magazine article defending traditional sex roles will illustrate. This article contends that women, not men, are the real source of social stability and continuity; that women are more suited for child-rearing and homemaking than for careers; that in order to keep them on the job, men ought to be paid more than women. These startling conclusions are all placed by the author or editor in headline form before and through the text.

One looks to the text, therefore, for independent support. What the text supplies, however, is a story about how, evolutionarily, the differences came about. Now although the story is plausible, it is not more plausible than several others one could dream up on a rainy afternoon. The story receives no support. And since the conclusions come in terms of the story, we have as yet no real argument.

In yet another sort of question-begging there appear to be premises and conclusion—an argument—yet the "premises" and "conclusion" amount, in different language, to forms of each other. I have heard it maintained that capital punishment should be abolished "because it is not right for the state to continue its policy of putting humans to death for crimes they have committed, no matter how horrible." Now what does that "because" do? "Capital punishment should be abolished" could not be *supported* by what follows the "because," since it *is* what follows it. The form *"p because p"* only mimics good argument.

Quick Check

A   Appropriately resist the following, by rejecting, for example, or dividing the question, by going between the horns, or by giving further possibilities.
1   You didn't support my candidacy; why are you so against me?
2   You're not one of those spoiled, lazy college kids, are you?
3   Do you prefer to become a "contributing member" at $25 or a "sustaining member" at $50?
4   Look, if Sue couldn't make the height limit (you have to be over five feet four) then Sue must be shorter than five feet four.
5   Have you given up your annoying habit of answering every question with a question?
B   In the following questions, dichotomies, and dilemmas, pinpoint the assumptions which ought to be examined.
1   How far can one sail before falling off the edge?
2   The city must reduce spending or continue overburdening the homeowner.
3   "The great powers still must determine the kind of role they are to play in the Middle East, whether they are to revert to power politics or to undertake to advance and enforce a compromise peace through the United Nations." (J. W. Fulbright, U.S. Senate.)
4   The goal of our researches will be to uncover the occurrence in the subject's early childhood which caused him to have such fear of heights.
5   It remains for us to account for the manner in which the observation of equal objects imparts to us our idea of equality.
C   Try a little name-calling. Where the following are deficient, are they so because of self-reference, question-begging, stereotyping, an appeal to ignorance, because they knock down a straw man? Are they candidates for an infinite regress, do they exemplify special pleading or half-truth, do they engage in black/white thinking, or what?
1   "No medical evidence or scientific endorsement has proved any other cigarette superior to Sussex." (Advertisement.)

2   "Everything which exists exists in quantity." (Attributed to Lord Kelvin.)
3   "If the earth is in a void," asked Apu, "why does the earth not fall when
     everything else falls?"
          "The earth does not fall," answered the guru, "because it is supported
     upon the back of a great tortoise."
4   " 'For example' is not proof. If you ask my Uncle Shel a question about any-
     thing—cancer, love, politics, you name it—he always tells a story about one of
     the people he knows 'down the store,' as he says. As if that store were the
     whole world!"
5   "Let's face it. It's one of two things: stop or smoke Real. I smoke Real, the
     low-tar, low-nicotine cigarette. Think about it. Shouldn't your brand be Real?"
     (Advertisement.)
6   Were the Tenure Committee's motives honorable? Thus far not one shred of
     evidence has come to light—and there has been ample time—to indicate the
     least bit of good faith. And thus it becomes little more than folly even to
     entertain the suggestion that its motives could have been anything less than
     pure.
7   After 3000 years of asking the question, "What is knowledge?" we must admit
     in all honesty that we do not yet have any real idea what it is.
8   Regardless of what laws, churches, liberation groups, and so forth say on the
     subject, the plain fact is that it is not right to terminate a human pregnancy
     voluntarily, whatever the circumstances. For this reason abortion cannot be
     justified.
9   If you don't trust Capital's figures, talk to Zeeburg. Zeeburg's been around. If
     you don't trust Zeeburg's figures, go to the Census Bureau. That's where ev-
     erybody gets their information.
10   "*Editor:* Are you a Commie Lover? Would you pardon Benedict Arnold for
     desertion? Would you let those deserting scum back into our country?"

Suggestions and Answers

A   1   "I'm not 'against' you at all, I simply thought J had more experience."
     2   " 'College kid,' yes; 'spoiled,' yes; 'lazy,' no."
     3   "I prefer to become an '*honored* member' at no charge."
     4   "No, Sue could be exactly five feet four."
     5   "Have you given up your annoying habit of asking people if they've 'given
     up their annoying habit' of this or that?"
B   1   That there is an edge, out there, that one can fall off of it, by sailing.
     2   That the homeowner is presently overburdened, that reducing spending will
     relieve the overburdening, that alternative sources of revenue are unfeasible.
     3   That the great powers ought to play any role at all, that they had been
     playing power politics, that there is no alternative to peace except power poli-
     tics, that any peace must be a compromise, that it must be advanced and
     enforced through the United Nations.
     4   That the subject has a fear of heights, that it is hidden, that it is extreme
     ("such"), that the fear was caused, by an occurrence, in his early childhood.
     5   That the idea of equality is imparted, by observation, of equal objects, that
     the process is accountable.

C   (1) appeal to ignorance; (2) deficient because of reference; (3) candidate for
     infinite regress; (4) deficient because of self-reference; (5) false dilemma; (6)
     appeal to ignorance; (7) deficient because of self-reference; (8) question-beg-
     ging ("*p* because *p*"); (9) question-begging (circular); (10) many questions.

SMOKESCREEN

As noted earlier, in the brief remarks on relevance, the issue in dispute can
appear to be addressed when in fact it is not being addressed. Let us review
some sources of such deception.

Ignoring the Issue   Inherited from ancient debating practice, the term
ignoratio elenchi means literally an ignoring of the opponent's *elenchus,* or
argument. Used rather more loosely nowadays, the term could be said to
designate any argument the premises of which (presumably) do bear on the
conclusion they attempt to support, but which bypasses the issue. An *ignoratio elenchi* can be identified by more appropriate terminology: "not answering the question," "phony issue," "smokescreen," "diversionary tactics," "red herring," "leaping the issue," "irrelevant argument," and the
like—together, of course, with what beats any terminology: a careful explanation of just how the argument fails to meet the real issue. The following
letter is typical.

> *Editor:* Every time a killing takes place somebody jumps on the bandwagon
> and starts hollering "strict gun laws." If someone would come up with how
> many people are killed with guns and how many with automobiles, you would
> find out it's not the gun that kills. It's cars and licensed drivers that kill more
> people than people with guns.

Even though the issue here is gun control, an issue which is itself not often
carefully defined, that issue, even in its vague form, is here missed. Yes, cars
and drivers kill. So do fires, speedboats, and blowguns. The issue is not
automobile control. Gun control could have been, should have been, addressed.

But missing or dodging the issue is not confined to the argumentatively
unskilled. Those with million-dollar media budgets may indulge in the same
practices, usually deducting the costs as a business expense to boot. Imagine coming across a magazine displaying the corporate logos of about fifty
firms which sell gasoline. The copy reads:

That's a "Monopoly"?!

> This "monopoly" gives everybody and his brother a piece of the action. Of the
> thousands, yes thousands, of American oil companies, the biggest has only
> *one-twelfth* of the national gasoline market.
> If that's a monopoly, it's the most unmonopolistic monopoly in town.

Its other faults aside, this argument fails to meet the real issue. It states a

case against a retail gasoline monopoly. But that's not the issue. The movement to break up big oil companies has not primarily been concerned with
gasoline. It has been concerned with vertical integration of the big oil companies, and with their horizontal expansion into other energy fields. Right
or wrong, critics fear a "Big Oil" stranglehold on home heating oil, natural
gas, coal, petrochemicals, electricity, and nuclear energy. And why, they
ask, even in the oil business, does Big Oil need to explore *and* import *and*
refine *and* make fertilizers and plastics *and* pump gas?

A related move, which is sometimes irrelevant, is to address not the
issue but the principle. Instead of assessing the proposition itself, a union
official opposed a statewide initiative election-reform proposition by attacking the state's entire initiative system. But in the absence of an attempt
to show how a "no" vote attacks that system (an attempt which would have
been unconvincing) the official's line of arguing was quite irrelevant. The
proposition, not the system, was the issue of the moment.

Diversion also sometimes occurs not by addressing the larger issue but
by elevating a subissue. Someone milks an existing issue much beyond its
rightful claim to attention in order to divert attention from the real issue. In
my opinion, the "prisoner of war" issue so emphasized by the U.S. Government in its last two wars was a prime example of such a distraction. In the
late stages of America's Vietnam involvement, one would have thought
from listening to the press and the administration that the entire war had
been fought to free the prisoners. But prisoners are an inevitable part of any
war. They are taken by all sides in a conflict, their numbers are relatively
small, and the atrocities to which they are subject are often minor compared to those being suffered by the populations still engaged directly in the
conflict. Moreover, American prisoners of the Korean and Vietnam wars,
being mostly pilots, were unlike many in those populations. They were not
innocent victims. They had volunteered to carry out the missions which
resulted in many of the worst atrocities. But chiefly, prisoners of war are
incidental, not essential, to the real issue, the war which created them, the
ending of which dissolves them as a problem.

Acting Rationally   One pervasive source of reasons not addressed to
the issue is, to put it rather archaically, subversion of reason by the pas-
sions. That biology, culture, instinct, and emotion powerfully shape actions
goes almost without saying. They shape reasonable behavior as much as
unreasonable. In order to be well rested for a long drive to visit a sick
relative, one must get enough sleep the night before. This may mean passing
over unpleasant dinner table remarks and topics in order to avoid a di-
gestion-disrupting row with the family. The rational course of action here
subordinates other functions and feelings (natural conscientiousness, family
resentment, digestion, sleep) to reason. The trip is more important than a

good row, no matter how tempting. Frequently the order gets reversed; such functions and feelings overcome reason. Possibly this latter is the natural order. "Appeal to reason," advertising theorists used to say, "and you appeal to 4 percent of the human race." But that something is natural by no means implies that it is good. For if the goal of an action is good then we have the obligation, other things being equal, to pursue that goal *rationally*. Writing of the emotional urges which motivate action, George Orwell in his essay "Notes on Nationalism" expresses clearly the proper attitude:

> They are part of the makeup of most of us, whether we like it or not. Whether it is possible to get rid of them I do not know, but I do believe that it is possible to struggle against them, and that essentially is a *moral* effort. It is a question first of all of discovering what one really is, what one's feelings really are, and then of making allowance for the inevitable bias.[4]

Although Orwell has primarily political action in mind, his comment obviously holds as well for other types of action. If it is important to visit a sick relative then getting there safely dwarfs getting one's two cents worth into a family squabble. Avoiding such a squabble is a moral effort. And avoiding purchasing a wasteful appliance, electing a bad senator, or choosing the wrong lifestyle, is a moral effort, too.

The Morality of Nonrational Methods   Ever since it was employed by the legendary mother of us all, appealing to the nonrational in human nature has been a favorite form of behavior modification. What is an intelligent attitude toward such appeals? When, if ever, is their use reasonable or moral?

Clearly, nonrational methods can be used for good ends as well as for evil—for fighting littering, promoting charities, combating syphilis, as well as for creating epidemics of prejudice, making the rich richer, or encouraging petty selfishness. And clearly there exist circumstances in which nonrational methods are preferable—as when the bootcamp sergeant bellows an obscenity in order to frighten a recruit who has foolishly raised up during a belly-crawling exercise in which bullets are being shot overhead. What, then, is wrong with the nonrational appeal? A united campaign may be sold solely on nonrational grounds ("Every good guy gives") or it may be sold on its merits. Financially the results may be identical. Morally they are not identical. Other things being equal, we owe others control over their lives, and control is what a nonrational pitch usually denies. It denies control in several ways. First, it denies information upon which to make intelligent decisions. Without such information good decisions will have been reached by chance, a most unreliable guide. Second, even granted that a good deci-

---

[4] *The Collected Essays, Journalism and Letters of George Orwell,* Harcourt Brace Jovanovich Inc., New York, 1971.

sion has been made in response to a pitch, what assurances exist that the decision will *remain* good? Unlike the nonrational decision, the rationally made decision is flexible. If and when times and circumstances invalidate the old reasons, new reasons come to the fore, and a new decision can be made. Finally, of course, the nonrational pitch can be used to modify behavior for the worse as well as for the better. "Every good guy gives" can be used to support a poor cause as well as a good cause.

What follows discusses various ways to bypass the reasoning process, to jump directly to a conclusion from instinct, emotion, or prejudice. It also discusses techniques which put reason at the service of emotion. Many of the techniques, transparent to most of the people most of the time, are enshrined in ordinary speech, in countless terms and expressions—"flag waving," "ballyhoo," "might makes right," "scare tactics," "buttering up," "bandwagon," just to name a few. That the techniques are obvious and widely recognized, however, does not mean that they may not be at work subtly and unrecognized in the thinking of the honest. Nor does it mean that it is easy to be articulate in exposing the techniques, when used illegitimately, to those exploited by them. Therefore, let us consider a few in some detail, in the examination of the first ones forming principles which apply to others or to all.

Appeal to Pity   One well-known device used to leap the reasoning process is the appeal to pity. Someone who attempts to arouse pity or some other emotion in order to influence a conclusion may or may not be arguing relevantly. In a relevant appeal, the issue, by its nature one which arouses sympathy, will be presented with a force proportional to the issue's claim to consideration. The appeal avoids "milking" the issue. If an agency which proposes to lessen child starvation heightens its pleas for funds with photos showing a starving child in all his wretchedness, this maneuver will surely arouse emotional responses. Well and good. Part of moral persuasion, after all, does involve thrusting others' moral lapses into their faces. The children's wretchedness *is* the issue; the funds elicited are to eliminate that wretchedness. Therefore the emotional appeal is at least relevant. (Whether sufficient, or strong, is another matter.)

Appeals to pity, like other subrational appeals, achieve irrelevance by either the type or the degree of their appeal. They either fail to touch the issue at all, or else they "milk" the issue, "lay it on thick" by inflating an otherwise relevant factor beyond its claim to consideration. With either, the result is the same. A firm hiring crane operators for urban renewal may sympathize with an otherwise qualified applicant who has become subject to fainting fits, but his plea that he should be hired because he has been unable to get work in order to support his children, though it may touch the hearts of his prospective employers, fails to touch the real issue, the question of whether the operator ought to be one of those hired. The way an appeal to emotion achieves irrelevance by blowing up an otherwise relevant issue all out of proportion might be illustrated by the following: Defenders of Presidents sometimes emphasize what extreme hardship the person in office must bear, the implication being that true humanitarians will acquiesce in the President's policies, or mute their criticisms, in order to spare the poor victim further suffering. This is ridiculous. We are born, or learn, to take the suffering of every single person seriously, at attitude which in close-to-home, simple circumstances is unarguably right. But not all circumstances are simple or close-to-home. In the argument before us we have, on the one hand, the possibility, and only the possibility, of hurting the feelings, and at the very remotest of endangering the sanity or life of one individual, the President, who has sought office knowing full well its extreme rigors and who has withstood the extreme rigors of lesser offices. On the other hand, we have policies which directly and significantly affect the well-being and life itself of millions and billions of people: to borrow a sentence from David Hume, "Does not the great disproportion bar all comparison and inference?"—an irrelevant appeal to pity.

Appeal to Vanity   Many arguments prey on our natural vanity. Everyone has seen arguments like the following.

> You were probably born with a bigger share of intelligence than most of your fellow men and women . . . and taught how to use it. And you appreciate the difference. You aren't ashamed of having brains. You enjoy using them. That's why *The Hundred Greatest Classics* belong in your home.

The issue is introduced by the seller: whether you, reader of this middle-brow publication, would be well advised to buy a set of these classics. Now what could a good case for buying be? The desirability of the knowledge contained in them might be spelled out, or the feasibility of someone of average intelligence mastering it. The economy of buying the set over buying the books individually might be stressed. The trouble is, no such point, though relevant, would be very convincing. Nearly everyone wants to have the material, but hardly anyone wants or is able to undergo the prolonged, intense labor of acquiring it. A small *part* of it, maybe, in which case buying the works individually would make more sense. And what of the public library, cheap editions, borrowing from friends, until one's capacity and determination have been ascertained? So instead of rational argument we get a snow job. The pitch simply butters us up and then asks us to buy.

Could an objection be made that since sets of classics, encyclopedias, and boxed editions of famous authors are in fact directed at and bought by individuals primarily to enhance personal prestige, a pitch directed at their desire for prestige is not irrelevant? In such an objection we see a healthy sign, the attempt to clarify or redefine the issue. In questions of relevance this is sometimes exactly the right tack. Is it the right tack here? An ad for luxury automobiles which explains how such an automobile will enhance its owner's prestige would be, however objectionable on other grounds, quite to the point. Prestige is one reason for owning a luxury automobile. According to market research it is why families buy sets of classics, too. The book ad, however, fails even to argue for prestige enhancement. Instead it simply butters us up and asks us to buy.

Appeal to Gregariousness   Our natural gregariousness provides a fertile field for issue subversion. "Everybody's doing it" tends to carry people along, whether the "it" be loving one's neighbor or stoning paraplegics. We are inclined to buy "America's largest selling bourbon," or to feel guilty about buying a cheaper brand, though in the pitch nothing gets said about quality. We tend to forget that while in numbers may lie strength, in numbers seldom lies complete good sense. And numbers don't answer the critical question: "Why this brand over its competitors?" Something may be largest-selling because its promoters spend millions to boost sales beyond those of equivalent or better, and perhaps cheaper, brands. As it was once put: "If you can build a lousy mousetrap and spend $10 million advertising it, the world will beat a path to your door."

None of this is to suggest that there might not exist circumstances in which popularity would be relevant. The authority of numbers may offer some sorts of safety and assurance. "America's largest selling bourbon," for example, couldn't be grossly harmful in small doses and must be moderately pleasant. Or knowing that a candidate is the party's best vote-getter may be good reason for preferring that candidate in a primary election over a more competent candidate with a better program whose chances of getting elected are slim.

One correlate of people's gregariousness is their inclination to boost self-esteem. Many a pitch plays on hero worship, snobbism, the desire to be so young, so fair, so debonair. We all want to be sociable, or negotiable, or lovable, with the skin "you love to touch." Knowledgeable people, the story goes, buy a certain medium-priced blended whiskey, and buy it by the case. The ads show liveried chauffeurs, Rolls Royces, Park Avenue addresses, the psychology being to propel us from our wealth/prestige fantasies directly to the liquor counter without our having passed through any reflection whatsoever. That the product may or may not be good or desirable could from such a diversion never be gleaned.

Another familiar sort of status transference is the hero endorsement. An actor well-known from his TV role as a crusading young doctor is seen plugging a popular headache remedy. A football hero associates his name with a brand of dietetic beer. One ex-astronaut compromises his name with a plug for toothbrushes. Another runs for office. Had such people claim to expertise (which is possible), their testimony could be weighed according to criteria used to evaluate any argument from authority. Advertising testimonials, however, lacking usually even the pretense of expertise, fall more neatly under the present heading, the irrelevant subrational appeal.

The negative side of our gregarious urges gets worked at least as much as the positive. Fear of losing popularity or friendship motivates many a pitch, dozens of coined terms from which have stuck in the popular vocabulary: "halitosis," "B.O.," "dishpan hands," "morning mouth," "the frizzies," "ring around the collar" and so on. Many products don't meet actual needs, they meet potential needs which are then created by advertising. It is amusing when traveling abroad to observe the attempts to convince Indonesians of the offensiveness of body odor, or Spaniards of the horrors of bad breath.

Appeal to Popular Prejudice Playing on culturally induced fears, likes, and aversions has won many an election, sold many a vacuum cleaner, provided support for many a war and even for a few periods of peace. These techniques claim various titles—"grandstanding," "demogoguery," "jingoism," "playing to the gallery," and in a few circles, *argumentum ad populum* or *argumentum ad captandum vulgus.* Each generation, each group, has its pets and bugbears. Billions have been spent exploiting and reinforcing the myth that healthy people must have their daily bowel movement. The mere mention that something will "destroy millions of germs that swarm into your mouth with every breath and attack teeth and gums" likely evokes a Pavlovian "Good!" response without our pausing to reflect that all those germs may not need exterminating. Items touted as "more powerful," "new," or "whiter-washing" probably get similar responses without our pausing to reflect that more powerful may also mean more dangerous, that new may also mean more expensive and shoddier, or that whiter may also mean sooner worn out. Advertisers insult women's intelligence with the news that women have "come a long way, baby," and that with this progress naturally they'll be smoking modern or special, or gutsy cigarettes, or cigars, though the advertisers must hope that their audience fails to notice that "a long way, baby" seems to be a silly millimeter or more not toward liberation but toward an early grave.

And for the political scoundrel, shallow patriotism, far from being a last refuge, becomes a vanguard. That the Russians are doing something seems reason to some Americans without further reflection whether it is worth doing, for pushing chess, for giving our Olympic athletes economic free rides, or for spending further billions on weapons of doubtful effectiveness. That the Carthaginians were doing something seems to have had about the same effect on the early Romans.

Appeal to Subconscious Motivation   Some appeals attempt to exploit us by using psychological theories of subrational motivation. A stir was created a few years back by a technique called subliminal advertising. In a feature film or related presentation a message would be repeated over and over in units of such short duration that the recipients were unaware of having sensed any message at all. For example, the word "popcorn" would appear in single-frame units throughout a film. Although the units could not be seen as the film played, the message supposedly registered subliminally (below the threshold of perception), resulting in increased popcorn sales. Despite considerable publicity this technique's effectiveness at motivation remains at least inconclusive. And in any case the technique is rather far removed from the realm of argument. Like candyshops reversing their ventilation fans, like bars providing free pretzels, or like a half nelson, subliminal advertising, even though quasi-verbal, made no attempt to give even the illusion of being argument.

Attempts to exploit the insights of clinical psychology have frequently done otherwise. A whole school of advertising, known as Motivational Research (MR) sprang up behind the theories of Freud, Jung, and their followers. MR's basic tenet could be summarized: "Don't appeal to the rational mind, appeal to the subconscious." Instead of selling soap on the theory that people buy soap in order to get clean, MR sold soap by tapping everybody's supposed subconscious desire to return to the warm, primeval safety of a mother's womb. Ads depicted a smiling woman luxuriating in a warm, sudsy, steamy bath. (Nothing was said about the quality of the soap.) Instead of selling salt by touting price, convenience, or resistance to caking, MR sold salt with a campaign built around people's supposed subconscious motivation by loading its ads with overt and hidden reminders of generation and fertility—pictures of erect ears of corn, or ripe soft fruit, and the like. Instead of selling automobiles on rational grounds, MR sold them and even designed them as symbols of male sexual prowess. (Examine hood ornaments, for instance, on cars of the 1950s.)

The success of some MR campaigns is undoubted, though whether specifically MR features or other factors achieved the success could be questioned. In many cases MR people also happened to have been advertising whizzes. Was it really subconscious motivation which sold that soap? Freud or no Freud, a warm bath, after all, is very pleasant. In this sense the soap ad and many of its MR brethren differ not at all from other emotional appeals. Moreover, did MR ads sell products? People may have been attracted or stimulated by the appeals to their subconscious (demand for frameable reprints of the salt ad series was reportedly very high), but whether the appeals sold products better than other techniques remains open to question.

Although the influence of MR on advertising may have peaked, anyone reading current ads psychoanalytically may be rewarded (assuming, that is, that one has some addiction to the pop in mass culture, and a high tolerance for bad taste). Some ads require no acquaintance with psychoanalysis to decipher, as anyone who has reflected on Linda's invitation to "come on and fly me" will surely realize. Making the Freudian connection between flying and copulation is not really necessary; the invitation exploits the male sex drive overtly as well as subconsciously, and thus can be classified along with that large category of persuadings which attempt to use Eros to blindfold our rational natures.

Other ads may require a bit more familiarity with psychoanalitic lore to decipher. One television ad for cameras shows a father photographing his preteenaged daughter in her new party dress. The scene is rustic, all idyllic innocence. Or is it? Those gyrations look suspiciously like courtship behavior. "Is this just our dirty mind at work?" we ask. It turns out that it is not, for after the pitch about capturing those fleeting moments (or whatever the cliché is) fathers everywhere are reminded that "before you know it she'll be somebody else's girl." Behind this ad is the psychoanalytic claim that there exists an unconscious sexual bond between father and daughter, a bond to which the father jealously clings. Subconsciously, fathers are supposed to react, "Somebody else's girl? Oh, my God! Get that camera today!" without stopping to reflect whether a camera is needed, or whether that brand will serve their needs better than some other. Here is a related pitch, this time with the sexes reversed. An ad for boys' T-shirts in one of the homemaking magazines reads, "His wife will buy him T-shirts that don't shrink—will you?" and is accompanied by a photo of a walled garden in which stands a cute little girl, archetypal temptress, offering a little boy—yes, folks!—a candied apple. (The only thing they have left out is the snake!) Now if the market contains brands of T-shirts which shrink, then touting shrink-resistance would be sensible. It is not relevant, however, to prey on the Oedipal rivalry between mothers and their potential daughters-in-law. The shirts merit buying or not buying on their qualities, not on a mother's jealousy. More narrowly Freudian is the recent attempt to exploit the alleged female phenomenon which Freud, who imagined that every woman feels slighted by nature, called penis envy. This alleged lack one enterprising pen promoter seems to be attempting to remedy, with a slim-line version, thrusting out at us from rather dignified advertisements but under the slogan, "Every woman should have one of her own!" Enough said.

A list of emotions, instincts, and prejudices exploited by persuaders would be very long. But the principle in all such exploitations is always the same—let the heart or the guts, not the mind, do the work. One more nonrational faculty worth mentioning, though, is humor. If the speculators are right about the evolutionary function of humor being the avoidance of violent physical confrontation, then one can see how humor can have come to be used for the avoidance of argument confrontation too. As administrators, diplomats, and politicians know so well, where reason fails a joke comes in handy. Humorous ads seem especially effective at avoiding discussion of the product or issue. Perhaps we should be thankful; what could be duller than a "straight" commercial? Bears are more fun than an argument for beer, and cougar kittens more entertaining than details about mileage and horsepower. Let us enjoy then, only let us not forget.

Examples and Comments

Where arguing along the following lines is inadequate, explain what is wrong, not only using material from this chapter but especially using common sense. Where the issue has been missed, state what it seems to be. Where the arguer has oversimplified, indicate in what way the facts are more complicated than the arguer has taken them to be. (Again, although the first examples have been done in order to suggest ways to proceed, the adequacy of their comments should be considered too.)

1 *"Editor:* The founders of this country learned, the hard way, that as government increases, liberty decreases. They fought a war over it; they overthrew their government. The reason government is the opposite of liberty is that, of all mankind's institutions, only government is permitted to use brute force. No church, labor union, business, or charity is allowed to back up its decisions with a gun. But government is allowed that privilege."

Comment Black/white thinking: the more government the less freedom, and vice versa. This simple dichotomy neglects that in some cases government seems to preserve liberty. (Think of governmental enforcement of the Bill of Rights, think of antitrust laws, of national defense, etc.) It also neglects the fact that nongovernment often destroys liberty. (Think of how unfree we'd be under rule of tooth and claw, or with unbridled cartels or only Mafia-type institutions.) The author needs either to abandon the dichotomy by conceding numerous sorts of exceptions (much strengthening the case thereby) or show by defending the dichotomy (though this would seem hard) that the seeming exceptions are not exceptions.

2 " 'Phony Issue, Artificially Inflated.' National Urban League Director Vernon E. Jordan Jr. . . . met with newsmen October 26 in Los Angeles where he described busing as a 'phony issue, artificially inflated.' He added that Americans are in the heat of a period of failing to face up to national problems, and said the promises made to minorities in the 1960s have not been realized in the present decade."

Comment As reported, Jordan's is no argument, it is just a charge. The charge attempts, though, to redefine the issue. And *if* Jordan can now show that the busing controversy has led to people "failing to face up" to the real racial problems—economic discrimination, plain prejudice—then he will have shown the busing controversy to have been a red herring.

3 "Another original advertiser at this period was Richard Tanner, who was trying to revolutionize the art of writing. Apparently the public clung to the quill, distrustful of Tanner's claim that his steel pens were 'the noblest invention of which mankind can boast.' So Tanner . . . assured his readers that the stripping of geese, as practised in Lincolnshire and Cambridgeshire, was a reproach to civilization. He swelled on 'the streams of empurpled dye, and the half-expiring contortions of these birds,' and asked: "Cannot the science of writing be improved without inflicting such violence.'" (E. S. Turner, *The Shocking History of Advertising,* Michael Joseph Ltd., London, 1965.

Comment Clearly, Tanner appeals to pity. The question remains, did he do so irrelevantly? Surely the plucking of geese was not all *that* horrible. If it were, then Tanner's point is well taken and his ardor part of the story. If not, then Tanner is just another in that long line of tear jerkers for profit.

4 "Here's some straight talk. Nobody but nobody pays higher interest than Central Savings. In fact, banks pay a good deal less. And no one has ever lost a penny at Central. Insured by an agency of the federal government. Save at the highest. Save at Central." (Advertisement.)

Comment This pitch is fine for distinguishing Central from banks. However, in implying that Central significantly betters other savings and loan associations, the piece tells a half-truth. Central could mention daily compounding, free services, friendliness—if it has them—not all of which all savings and loans can claim.

5 "How are we going to get every citizen to buy American in order to do his part to help stabilize the dollar?"

Comment This question contains several suspicious assumptions which need to be thought through before the question can be answered: that the dollar needs stabilizing; that foreign consumer goods are a principal cause of instability; that buying American will help, etc. This is an appeal to blind patriotism too. (None dare call it nationalism, or chauvinism; those are something afflicting the other guy.) Although it may be good to support domestic industry, it is not *automatically* good to support it. For instance, will buying American cause capital to be squandered on wars or investments which siphon dollars abroad?

6 "What type of reader does *Playhouse* reach? A young guy who's always in the limelight. He's the guy with choice seats on the aisle and a smashing girl on his arm. He's a man who takes the lead others follow. Facts? *Playhouse* reaches over 2,700,000 adults who purchased legitimate theater tickets in the past year. That's two out of every five male theatergoers in the U.S.: better than 1 of every 2 under 35. Want a bigger box office for your product? Put it stage center. Put it in *Playhouse*. (Advertisement.)

Comment Since it emphasizes that *Playhouse* readers are young and have money to spend, two points of prime concern to the space buyers to whom the ad is addressed, this pitch is basically relevant. The ad is guilty of some oversimplification in the form of image-mongering: get that "handsome, sought-after" image etched on the buyer's consciousness and the buyer may forget about the stay-at-home slobs and others in *Playhouse*'s readership. Also, the statistics seem suspicious: how does *Playhouse* know how many of its readers purchased tickets? Survey results on such matters are unreliable (see the section in Chapter 5 called "Survey Psychology"). Does buying a legitimate theater ticket (and how is "legitimate theater" defined?) make one a theatergoer? And does ticket-buying translate into buying the sorts of products which potential *Playhouse* space buyers purvey?

7   "If the remaining tapes contained no incriminating evidence, you can be sure that Nixon would have been the first to release them. So from the fact that Nixon has not released those tapes we can rest assured that they do indeed contain things which are incriminating."

Comment   We may not "rest assured" that the tapes contain incriminating material. Whatever we may have thought of Nixon's reasons for not turning over the tapes, they were not totally insane reasons. The burden of proof here still lies with the prosecution. The proper conclusion from our ignorance in the situation should still be, "We don't know."

8   "Felicia Munoz. Age: 37. Profession: Conductor. Hobbies: Painting, attending concerts. Profile: Vigorous; chic; exciting; conducts with a sure command of her music and her musicians. Scotch: Robbie Burns." (Advertisement.)

9   "Test drive a Svenska II and help the National Ski Patrol. Between now and April 15th. We'll make a donation to the National Ski Patrol. We think it's a good way of helping this nonprofit organization of 25,000 dedicated volunteer skiers. We build Svenska II with features no skiers should be without. Like front-wheel drive, four-wheel disc brakes, and rack-and-pinion steering."

10   "The feminization of the American male. Many men's fragrances make you smell like a bunch of lilies. Or fresh fruits. Or vanilla ice cream. Ascot makes a tough cologne, with the clean, fresh, masculine bite of spice. Ascot, *because a man shouldn't smell like a woman.*" (Advertisement.)

11   "When asked whether military limousines would carry a flock of military brass to the Army-Navy game, the Pentagon answered with a solemn no. The Pentagon failed to mention, though, that then-Defense Secretary Melvin Laird had arranged at public expense to haul 180 guests to the game in six special train cars crammed with food, booze, and setups. Laird's guests were serenaded by nine strolling Navy musicians who provided mood music."

12   "But the simple truth is, O Athenians, that I have nothing to do with physical speculations. Very many of those here are witnesses to the truth of this, and to them I appeal. Speak then, you who have heard me, and tell your neighbors whether any of you have ever known me hold forth in few words or in many upon such matters. . . . You hear their answer. They are silent. And from what they say of this part of the charge you will be able to judge of the truth of the rest." (Socrates in Plato's *Apology.*)

13 "The nonpolitical, objective nature of Soviet psychiatry has at last received the defense it has for so long been without. A. V. Snezhnevsky has written a masterful set of articles. Though writing for *Izvestia,* a party organ, the author is not himself a party member. Rather, he is chief psychiatrist of the U.S.S.R. Ministry of Health and secretary of the Academy of Medical Sciences."

14 "Doomed to suffer and die simply for human vanity. Baby harp seals are so beautiful that humans wish to wear their fur. Each spring the migratory seals form two herds, one in the St. Lawrence Gulf, the other off the coasts of Newfoundland and Labrador. Then, each year Canadian and Norwegian sealers come with their clubs. The pups cannot get away—less than one week old, they are too young to swim. Most never do. The pups are *clubbed and skinned before their mothers' eyes.* The pelts are destined to become luxury furs and leather. Only continued forceful public opposition can stop this insane killing. Write the Canadian and Norwegian ambassadors *today.*"

15 "Suppose someone replies that theism is a kind of belief that does not need justification by evidence. This means either that no one cares whether it is correct or not, or that there is some other way of checking that it is correct besides looking at the evidence for it, i.e., giving reasons for it." (Michael Scriven, *Primary Philosophy,* McGraw-Hill, New York, 1966, p. 99.)

16 "Looking for an ordinary job? Don't look here. Our jobs don't require experience; they *give* you experience. You'll be *paid while you learn.* Our jobs include free medical and dental care, food and housing, a 30-day paid vacation every year, and a good salary. Many jobs offer you one kind of work. We offer you a choice of training in *hundreds* of good jobs. And if you qualify, we'll guarantee your job training *in writing.* Finally, many jobs give you a chance to work for a company. Ours give you a chance to work for *your Country.* Call Army Opportunities." (Advertisement.)

17 "Let's be realistic," said the politican to the police officer. "Can you conceive of a criminal organization so enormous, so organized, so secret, so powerful that it can do what it likes, not only here but in the United States? . . . Put it this way: Can you tell me of one trial that has ever produced proof of the existence of a criminal association called the Cosa Nostra, which actually arranges for and carries out crimes? Has a single document ever been found—I mean real written evidence—any sort of proof, in fact, of a relationship between criminality and the so-called Cosa Nostra?"

18 "According to strict behaviorism all so-called psychological goings on—intention, memory, pain, desire, etc.—we ascertain solely by observation of the agent's behavior. Fine, only what of the observer's *own* supposed observation? Ascertainment of that would require another observer, and *his* observation would in turn require another, and so on, *ad infinitum.* Which shows that as a psychological theory pure behaviorism cannot even get off the ground."

Applications

Directions: Try either **A** or **B**, and one more from the remaining lettered sections.

A Where the following terms suggest strong stereotypes, briefly delineate the stereotype. Then neutralize it by emphasizing variety, or perhaps by projecting a counterimage.

inner city	Frenchman
multinational corporation	Jew
Made in Japan	Miss America
alcoholic	insurance broker
Texan	deer hunter
communist	jock
gay	farm worker

B Supplement the list in **A** with terms from your own experience. Then supply delineation and neutralizing, as above.
C Derive and defend a useful principle or principles around which to structure the material in the "Oversimplification" section. For example, certain fallacies are errors of presumption—presuming a question is settled when it is not (question-begging), presuming a false part of an improper question, or presuming that a universe is exhausted by only two possibilities. (Another possibility: dichotomizing.)
D Trying for variety, collect a dozen (or half dozen) pitches from printed media. Do the job with flair, searching out the tawdriest, the most offensive, the most reasonable, the subtlest clippings possible. Then comment on their relevance, adequacy, and factuality.
E Using your experience, and chiefly the material in this chapter, construct your own "Quick check." Try it on colleagues or friends.
F Formulate thoughts which complete, or counter, one of this chapter's sketches of:

  1 Where in a dispute the burden of proof lies (pp. 27–28)
  2 Public policy toward advertising (pp. 38–41)
  3 When an arguer has the obligation to weigh, and when to advocate (pp. 24–25)
  4 The morality of nonrational methods (pp. 34–35)

Chapter 3

Language

Not only *what* one says counts, but *how* one says it. The language in which something is expressed can mean the difference between truth and false-hood, between boredom and fascination, between pique and persuasion, between failure and success. This chapter samples linguistic matters which affect argument. Chief among these is the twisting of meanings in order to doctor results. The chapter also contains a section on argument style and a section about the effect on reasoning of certain ideas concerning definition.

ARGUMENT LANGUAGE

If the central purpose of reasoning is to establish useful fact, then good reasoning will be *clear,* and it will be *objective*: what can't be followed can't lead anyone to fact; what is unobjective leads *away* from fact. An arguer's style conveys that clarity and objectivity. Like most argument skills, good style does not spring up overnight. Very few famous writers have not thought about style their entire careers. But one need not have haunted the marketplace of ideas for years in order to *begin* to develop good habits.

Therefore, with the aim of heightening stylistic consciousness as it pertains to argument, not teaching style, let us proceed under two main headings—"Clarity" and "Objectivity."

Clarity   Presenting a case well means not only stating the case but also caring that the case be grasped: clarity is an indication of the arguer's good faith. Though being clear is a skill of detail, not of principle, it is helpful to cultivate the following habits: needle details; seek simplicity; expose structure.

Needle Details   Redundancy turns dedicated servants into bureaucrats. To exorcise this demon, force logic into the details of argument language. Be alert when an editorial complains that "the Spirits lost their fourth consecutive game in a row out of the last four games played." Nonsense like that assaults us daily. Since "consecutive" *means* "in a row," what is "in a row" doing there? The writer might as well have added "cha-cha-cha." Worse, the writer compounds the redundancy, for what is "out of the last four games played" but "their fourth consecutive game"? The sentence should have ended at "game."

In themselves such slight breaches of logic mean little, But like the buckets brought by the sorcerer's apprentice, they can multiply on those who lack the trick of stopping them. Look at this passage from a seminar report on poverty issued by the august American Academy of Arts and Sciences. The poor, according to the report, have "a set of pursuits outside the occupational sphere which provides direct and immediate emotional or physical gratification, and a quest for stimulating inner experience characteristically involving strong drink." The report, which goes on like that for pages, *could* have said that the poor fill their spare time with booze, sex, TV, etc. That would have been too easy, and too obvious. Instead, the poor's pursuits provide "direct" *and* "immediate" gratification. Now what distinguishes something direct here from something immediate? The second adjective, in other words, adds only hot air. Similarly, what does "inner" add to "experience"? What would "outer" experience be? And since the subject is boozing and the like in the first place, what does "stimulating" add? "Emotional" and "physical," too, make it look as if the seminar had discovered something. They had not. Those terms, if they mean anything at all here, are contained in the ideas of watching TV, having sex, and getting drunk. Relieved of hot air, this passage amounts to a platitude. Worse, its verbosity obscures what looks suspiciously like an elitist stereotyping.

Many absurdities pass as clichés. People don't point to their record these days but to the "pretty good *track* record." What does "track" add? Similarly, what is the point of "very real"? "There is a very real possibility that swine flu will break out simultaneously in every state" says only that there is the possibility; "in a very real sense we have a conservative backlash" says only that we have a conservative backlash. And watch those "nature" and "character" descriptions. Material "of a confidential nature" or "subversive in character" is simply confidential or subversive. Talk about "the nature" of love, or of juvenile delinquency, sounds deeper than talk about love, or juvenile delinquency, but is not—except that those who use "nature" seem to feel less obligated to supply facts. Then we must not forget that mouthful so dear to the Watergate Hearings cast. Except for a phony air of precision, how does "at that point in time" improve on the honest word "then"? Not only Watergaters have fallen victim to verbal idiocy, however. It's not six o'clock any more, it's "in the six o'clock time slot" or "time frame" or "time period." Poor time! Next it'll be "at that point in space" or "at that level of existence."

One small warning. That the sun "went behind" a fast-moving cloud, or that someone "tumbled head over heels" may strike you as odd. Clouds pass in front of the sun, do they not? And wouldn't one tumble heels over head? But the seeming illogic in standard expressions is charming, untroublesome, and entrenched beyond assault. The thoughtless jargon of the time, useless clichés, needs the attention, not standard expressions. We could have done without WASP—has anyone ever seen a *black* Anglo-Saxon Protestant? But if I called someone as ASP I would probably not be understood.

Many terms work against a stated or implied standard. With the standard omitted the words lose their meaning. If *A* tells *B* that Sid is a good mechanic, *B* can now emphasize how good Sid is by replying, "Sid is a very good mechanic." *B*'s "very" has a standard to work against. Without such a standard, words like "very" add nothing. "This is a very good choice" equals "This is a good choice." Yet some people cannot resist adding that "very," "quite," "extremely," "rather," "intensely," or whatever their favorite happens to be. Some people have no friends, only "very dear" friends, including the ones met only once. (Remember that boy who cried "Wolf!"?)

Failure to notice omitted standards accounts for a whole family of current expressions. What, for example, distinguishes a packaged soup from a *pre*packaged soup? Was the latter packaged before it was packaged? We have prepaid subscriptions, preplanned strikes, prerecorded cassettes, even (the doubly redundant) preplanned strategy. Then of course there's "advance planning." Maybe the "advance" distinguishes that planning from the planning which goes on during or after!

Seek Simplicity   A hatter designing his shop sign in the shape of a three-cornered hat bearing the words *Rene Prinet, Hats Made and Offered for Sale* was reportedly advised by Benjamin Franklin to omit all words except the name. The hat made them redundant. Franklin was right. In persuasion, as in architecture, less is more. The use of "jawbreakers," (big obscure words) rarely gets a conclusion across effectively—as the following Victorian exercise, by showing what *not* to do, well illustrates.

> Eschew conglomerations of flatulent garrulity, jejune babblement and asinine affectation. Defenestrate platitudinous pomposity, polysyllabic profundity, psittaceous vacuity and ventriloquial verbosity. Sedulously shun rhodomontade, pestiferous profanity, prurient jocosity. Embrace clarified conciseness, compacted comprehensibility, coalescent consistency and concentrated cogency.

Amen. Forthright, plain terms convince, not jawbreakers from Latin or Greek but "four letter" derivatives from Anglo-Saxon. "Odd jobs," as that poverty report *could* have put it, says it better than "a versatile pattern of income acquisition." Not only do four letter words say it better, they are democratic. They do not talk down. And they do not hide the truth, a point which Walter Raleigh stated beautifully: "If you talk non sense in Saxon, you are found out at once."

Scientism, the feeling that nothing counts unless couched as science, clouds much writing. The poverty report quoted above notices that the poor have "a versatile rather than restricted pattern of work involvement entailing predominantly nonspecialized physical labor." Now Americans on the economic bottom, last hired and first fired, do go from lousy job to lousy job. But everybody knows that already. Replacing "job" with "pattern of work involvement," do we progress? The word "pattern" implies that a further regularity has been discovered. None has. And although the term "work involvement" resembles quantitative technical terms like "optical density" or "surface tension," no quantity has been measured. We have trappings, but not substance. One might as well have dressed an ape in a lab coat and called him scientist. (And again, notice how obscurity cloaks what might go challenged if expressed in plain English. Why are the jobs "nonspecialized"? Is it because you don't have to go to graduate school to be qualified? But being a good custodian or street worker requires as much specialized skill as anything else.)

Expose Structure

> Dammit, Krause, first you tell 'em what you're going to say. Then you say it. Then you tell 'em what you said. Now don't come back until you do *that*!

The renowned anthropologist who rejected a graduate thesis with these words may have overstated, but he was not far wrong. Good argument, like good architecture, reveals its structural elements so that *what* is being said and *how* it is being supported lie open to the consideration of all. And by revealing duplication and omission, structuring forces any arguer to be simple and complete. The following typify devices by which presenters of complex arguments have revealed the structure of their cases:

1 In this paper I argue that X ought to be abandoned. Proponents of X maintain that a, b, c, and d. Points a and b I argue to be false. And although c and d are valid points, neither singly nor together can they offset e.

2 Damage from non-x is moderate and reparable because a, b, c, and d; damage from x is incalculable because e and f. Therefore, non-x.

3 From what one reads in the press the issue here is x. A, for one, has stated x_1. B has maintained x_2. Maybe so, but the "x-ers" overlook that a, b, and c. No, the real issue is not x but y.

4 So far we have considered three arguments for x, none of which was convincing. Let us go on now to examine two more of a different sort, arguments d and e.

5 Although the question of x cannot be settled now, the time when x is settled cannot be far off because p and q. Therefore, we should be preparing now for the time when x is settled. If x is settled pro, then a and b will occur. If x is settled con, then c and d. Now a and b mean that we should y, an easy and harmless thing to do in advance with small benefits of its own even if x is not settled pro. So we should at least y. If x is settled con, then c and d mean that we should z. Unlike y, z is disruptive and expensive, and should not be done in advance. But we should have *plans* ready for z, if needed.

Objectivity   A well-argued case not only persuades its friends but also attracts the uncommitted and the unfriendly. Nothing alienates the uncommitted and the unfriendly like provocative language. Calling policemen pigs or calling liberals communist dupes, or fascists, never served but to alienate, a direction opposite to that of reasonable argument. Compare the following letters to the editor.

> *Editor:* Congratulations on your sensible position on American draft-dodgers, deserters, and expatriate cowards. Human parasites such as these have merited, and received, the contempt of all loyal citizens of all nations. Aside from a small amount of concern from immediate relatives, only maudlin sentimentalists have responded to their "cause." Let Canada, Sweden, etc., keep these dregs. Doubtless they have more respect for this American riffraff than we do. Until they humbly atone for their transgression against loyal Americans, let our draft-dodgers, deserters, and self-exiled cowards become "men without a country."

> *Editor:* We have a free country. We have laws. If you steal, the law says you must be punished. For service to our country there are noncombatant alternatives. If a person chose to leave this country to avoid the draft, it was his free choice to evade the law. But if he wishes to return he should stand trial. He still has a free choice and we still have our valid laws.

Instead of producing reasons, the first letter's author paints friends in friendly terms ("loyal citizens," "sensible position," etc.) and foes in unfriendly terms ("cowards," "maudlin sentimentalists," etc.). In so doing the author convinces no one and polarizes friends from foes. By contrast, the author of the second letter avoids name-calling or gratuitous praise, relying instead on an argument which is, whatever we ultimately think of it, thoughtful and to the point. The second author has a chance of winning over foes. Terms of praise and fighting words are not the only things of which the careful arguer must be wary. Many words in themselves convey approval or disapproval—they have a positive or negative connotation—and need to be wielded carefully. This topic deserves detailed attention.

Connotation   Certain terms, called *pejorative,* tend to trigger aversion or avoidance. Others, called *honorific* or *commendatory,* tend to evoke favorable responses. *Euphemisms* replace pejoratives or offensive plain terms. Now I would maintain, despite what sometimes gets said on this subject, that pejorative and commendatory terms belong in argumentation. If a stockbroker's or a candidate's performance has been fabulous, or an environmentalist's tactics sleazy, well, then they have been just that, and whatever the emotional accompaniments, fair assessments will call spades spades. However, pejorative and honorific terms fit in careful arguing *only* where their use is justified: that is, in conclusions or derivations from conclusions. Otherwise they amount to the name-calling or gratuitous praise we saw above in the letter to the editor.

Perhaps it needs to be added that certain terms never belong in argument: those which are always abusive. "Fighting words" induce fighting, not reasoning; they induce wrath rather than truth. It may be descriptively accurate to call a person's tactics sleazy; it is never merely descriptively accurate to call a person a kike.

Euphemism, unlike pejorative and commendatory terms, is a valuable, sometimes perhaps necessary, ingredient in all parts of argument. Like social pleasantries and ceremonies, euphemism lubricates the wheels of society. Bartenders finesse drunks, radicals gently suppress the excesses of aging comrades, executives let each other down easy. Teachers do not tell parents that their darlings are stupid or are brats. Legislators do not call their constituents a great beast. Euphemisms allow the robust, the plainspoken, and the rude to interact with the sensitive, the innocent, and the genteel without anyone going off in a huff. Honestly used, euphemisms, like white lies, promote objectivity by quashing disagreement over trivia in order that attention may be focused on significant business.

Less than honestly used, euphemisms cloak inaction or what might be corrected if left exposed, or they hide unpopular action from those who need to know. One of the more euphemized subjects is economic depression. The word "depression" was once itself a euphemism for the then standard terms "panic" and "bust." As happens with many euphemisms, time, usage, and reality diluted "depression's" euphemistic strength to the point where "depression" was nearly as pejorative as the terms it replaced. What next but to make a distinction and invent a new term? From "panic," then, we went to "depression," and from "depression" to "recession"— which is any depression smaller than the Great Depression. Since "recession" now has nearly as bad a name as "depression," officials will do anything to avoid it. Hence we have "softness in the economy," a "downturn," a "dip," a "rolling readjustment," or (as a recent commerce secretary put it after the GNP declined for the third successive quarter) "a little sideways waffling." Bureaucracies are euphemistical heavens. It's not an instrument of mass human destruction, it's an "antipersonnel weapon," a "daisy-cutter," a "nuclear device," or an "Operation Ranch Hand." It's not old-age insurance, it's "Social Security." It's not antisecrecy legislation, it's a "sunshine law." Even the antibureaucrats with their "sunset laws" may be less "anti" than they imagine.

Parasitizing Connotation Let us look now at some of the numerous other ways in which arguers use connotation to influence results. Whatever is "natural," "organic," "analytical," or "structured" is usually being commended. We like what is "new," "creative," "dynamic," "original," "unique," "real," "positive," "objective," "commonsense." Situations would be difficult to imagine in which someone was scolded for being "practical," "clear," "scientific," or "precise." Sometimes the approval implied in such terms gets transferred to topics and conclusions where it does not belong. This can occur a number of ways.

One of these ways is the creation of an "ism" or "ology" or the like from a commendatory term. And although the resulting movements range from the most respectable and profound to the most kooky and fraudulent, it is difficult not to believe that they draw some of their appeal and at least the shallower of their adherents from the names themselves. The "great society" and the "creative society" of the 1960s, despite their promising titles, turned out to contain very little out of the ordinary. And suppose that Logical Positivism had been called Logical Negativism (the latter perhaps a more accurate title). Likewise, Objectivism or Scientology or Transactional Analysis by any other name just would not sound as sweet. Could a corporation like Interpersonal Dynamics or Scientific Associates be a "paper corporation"? Could Concrete Solutions be a Mafia front? Or take pragmatism, the philosophy (at least in popular interpretations) of practical action. Everyone wants to be practical, yes, but without previously understood goals the advice to be practical is perfectly empty. Depending on viewpoint *anything* can be practical, from forgery ("it's easy money, you've got to live") to ascetic monasticism ("for theirs is the Kingdom of Heaven").

Commendatory terms sometimes play a related trick. Though normally occurring as approval, none *has* to occur as approval. The trick involves transferring the approval to where it does not belong. Generally it is good to behave rationally. But it might be right to criticize a participant behaving rationally in an encounter group session for not opening up. Analogously, it might be right to criticize an actor playing the role of a scatterbrain for being too commonsensical. By means of this usually-but-not-always characteristic, commendatory terms sometimes lead their hearers to look favorably on what the term is applied to, even when the term adds nothing favorable. That a job applicant is described as "extremely creative" sounds positive. But is it necessarily positive? It would be unwise to count creativity a point in favor of hiring a dispensing pharmacist, or someone in charge of firing nuclear missiles.

Future historians of language will undoubtedly enjoy our obsession with the word "natural." Food items, sprays, laxatives, vitamins, shampoos, and the most unlikely concoctions get touted as "natural," "country," or "organic." This hype seems automatically to recommend them to some. They fail to reflect that "natural" does not equal "good." For example, is that "natural," "organic" raw milk tuberculin-tested? Tuberculin bacillus, don't forget, is also natural, and organic. So is death.

Then there is the other side of the coin. If one's product is "natural" or "organic," the competition's is "artificial" or "imitation." But artificial or imitation items may not be inferior at all. Artificial abrasives, artificial pigments, and countless other products have proven superior to their natural counterparts. Furthermore, terms like "natural" and "artificial" are relative. An artificial x can be seen as a genuine y. Millions have been spent to convince governments not to require the word "imitation" on labels. It's not imitation cream, it's coffee creamer or whitener, not ersatz mayonnaise but honest-to-goodness salad dressing, not fake bacon but real country breakfast strips.

Another disapproval trigger is the word "chemical" (a word which seems almost naked without "harsh"). Since all material, good or bad, is chemical, is not the negative connotation misplaced? Consider these two lists:

Ingredients: Natural texturized vegetable protein, toasted bread crumbs, dehydrated parsley, tomato flavor, sodium citrate, monosodium glutamate, disodium inosinate, and disodium guanylate.

Ingredients: Wheat flour, water, butter, eggs, honey, salt, lactic acid, cyanocobalamin, pyridoxamine phosphate, retinol, alpha-tocopherol, napthoquinone.

Neither product sounds very appetizing. But do you *know* what's in the products? One would not only have to be a chemical whiz but have kept up on medical research in order to say which chemicals are harmful and which not. (The second product I invented myself simply by appending the chemical names of certain vitamins found in ordinary food.) The epidemic of new substances introduced since World War II certainly supplies grounds for caution, even for alarm, but not for panic. We need our wits about us more than ever.

Another technique for parasitizing connotation, a kind of question begging, involves smuggling in a viewpoint or conclusion by means of the very language in which something is expressed—what might be called "framework" language. Take a term like "consciousness raising" (or my phrase, "heightening stylistic consciousness"). The term "consciousness raising," which propagandists everywhere would be proud to have invented for their own schemes, suggests a direction—"up," from worse to better. Yet what is described as "consciousness raising" (or heightening) may or may not raise consciousness. That is a matter to be decided by observation or insight—by argument—not by terminology alone. The same could be said for what is described as "progress," "liberation," "development," and others. And again, notice that the positiveness or negativity depends on the observer's point of view. One side's "liberation" will probably be the other side's "enslavement." One person's "development" may be another's "despoilment." As one native in the cartoon says to the other, "Here come the representatives of the overdeveloped nations."

An interesting negative framework word is "pollution." The term carries a strong connotation which, in lieu of giving reasons, arguers may unfairly try to tap. Raw sewage, smog, oil slicks—these are pollution, everyone will agree. Their harm is obvious. But when someone calls a person's *children* pollution, watch it! Yet, from one viewpoint too many children in the world are harmful to future generations. But that dangerous viewpoint would have to be convincingly *argued first* (and it is hard to see what a case for it could be) before the extension of "pollution" could be justified. Calling children pollution is of course an extreme, the sort of thing which people resort to in moments of exasperation or during periods of elitism or self-deception. (It was a favorite term of those whose racial ideas included the suppression of non-Aryans.) Not extreme, but still suspicious is the extension of "pollution" in the popular mind in all sorts of new directions, often without benefit of argument. "Thermal pollution" from nuclear plants seems legitimate; the harm has been clearly demonstrated. "Visual pollution," on the other hand, is not obviously harmful. To cite two recent cases, where is the pollution, really, in a yard full of wrecked cars which, after all, serve a valid recycling function? And where is the pollution in a hot dog stand in the form of a gigantic dachshund? Why hide the wrecking yard any more than hide a building's steel skeleton with hunks of marble? Why deny the hot dog chain its heraldic device any more than deny hair stylists their barber poles or the county courthouse its American flag? Since the term "pollution" in such cases seems to cover up what amounts to a personal opinion, its employment without argument seems illegitimate.

A bit of framework language which has done incalculable harm is Herbert Spencer's phrase "survival of the fittest." The word "fit" usually commends; we think of "physically fit," "fit to hold office," and so forth. Yet in Darwin's theory of evolution, which Spencer was supposedly expounding, "fittest" really boils down to, would have to be defined as, "*actually do* survive." There is no implication of "*ought* to survive." In this sense "fit" may come to characterize weak, otherwise unadaptable species with no more of an ability to survive than a resistance to hydrocarbon pollution or cosmic radiation. Next century, lichens or cockroaches may be the "fit." The unsophisticated or malevolent have seized on the phrase in order to further their own ends. Knowingly or not they have stolen the moral connotations of "fit" for whatever seems in their schemes to be worthy. They have tried to use Darwin's theory to back programs of eugenics, as reason for not correcting deplorable social ills, as support for encouraging a dog-eat-dog economics, and so forth.

A favorite trick to avoid commitment consists in using framework comparative terms while neglecting to supply any basis in relation to which the comparatives compare. The president of one university urges it to "move forward" and "not turn back." Fine, but depending on one's orientation, "forward" or "back" could be *any* direction. The Mideast oil-producing nations announced that their policy on exportation of crude oil to the West will be, stealing a phrase of Eisenhower's, "flexible but firm." Thanks a lot. *How* flexible? "Flexible but firm" could cover anything. Notice, too, how commendatory glitter but not substance has been borrowed from "forward," "flexible," and "firm." And in the slogans of politics—for example, that of the candidate who promised us "tough-minded compassion"—the same can be seen.

The trick seems to be especially effective when worked with a "sandwich" of pejorative comparative terms—two excesses enclosing what, by contrast, looks like the golden mean. "We mustn't overreact," says the politician, "but then again neither must we do nothing." Without specifying what overreacting and doing nothing (or "underreacting") consist of, the words, because they cover virtually anything, convey nothing but the illusion that commitment has been made. They and their like might be called the Goldilocks ruse: "Not too hot, not too cold, but just right."

Quick check

A   Insofar as this "bureaucratese" can be deciphered, cut it down to size.
1   Actuarial science.
2   Broad in character and scope.

3 Educational experience.

4 Meaningful interpersonal dynamics.

5 Avocational pursuits outside of the occupational sphere.

6 Effective utilization of all resources.

7 Criterion referenced analysis.

8 Maximally optimized consultative inputs.

9 Exhibits an aggressive pattern of behavior characterized by tendencies toward upward vocational mobility.

10 Prescribe future courses of action to effect desirable results.

11 Fair and equitable advice and counsel.

12 At this present moment, my memory can form no recollection of that incident.

13 In this modern world in which we live today.

14 Open to everyone regardless of age, sex, color, creed, religion, or national origin.

15 In the last crisis situation she did not panic, but rather cooly reacted by keeping her wits about her and not losing composure.

B Supply for each of the following at least one pejorative equivalent.

1	fastidious	**6**	associates
2	persistent	**7**	child
3	willowy	**8**	education
4	labor leader	**9**	military action
5	high density neighborhood	**10**	American

C Supply for each of the following one or more euphemistic equivalents.

1	fat	**5**	drunk
2	insane	**6**	kill
3	toilet	**7**	lazy
4	old (people)	**8**	spying

D Each of the following is or once was euphemistic. Try to supply one of the originals.

1	insane	**5**	incursion
2	toilet	**6**	alcoholic
3	perspiration	**7**	credibility gap
4	homosexual	**8**	Department of Defense

E When a speaker uses the following to describe something, what framework do the words suggest?

1 the extra-large size

2 a retreat for overpaid executives

3 a mere 500 words

4 special interest group

5 a form of sexual perversion

6 admits that he was there

7 could use behavior mod therapy

8 victim of governmental meddling

9 at intensive care rates

10 a highbrow publication

Suggestions

A   (1) insurance; (2) broad; (3) school, learning, etc.; (4) good meeting, relation-
    ship, etc.; (5) hobbies; (6) efficiency; (7) objective study; (8) best advice; (9)
    bucking for promotion; (10) prescribe, advise; (11) good advice; (12) I forget,
    I do not recall the incident; (13) today; (14) open to everyone; (15) in the last
    crisis she acted coolly.

B   (1) fussy, picky; (2) stubborn, pigheaded; (3) skinny, emaciated; (4) union
    boss; (5) slum, ghetto; (6) cohorts, accomplices; (7) brat; (8) indoctrination,
    brainwashing; (9) aggression, invasion; (10) Yanqui, Gringo, paleface.

C   (1) heavy, obese; (2) bananas, bughouse, loony; (3) potty, powder room; (4)
    elderly, senior citizen; (5) tipsy, pie-eyed; (6) put to sleep, terminate with ex-
    treme prejudice; (7) unmotivated, underachiever; (8) surveillance, intelligence-
    gathering.

D   (1) mad, lunatic; (2) crapper, jacques; (3) sweat; (4) bugger, sodomite; (5)
    invasion; (6) drunkard, sot; (7) chronic lying; (8) War Department.

E   (1) it is larger than the normally large (larger than at least three-fourths of the
    sizes); (2) executives are too highly paid; (3) 500 words is paltry; (4) the group
    does not seek everyone's interest (or the general welfare); (5) it is improper (or
    unnatural or abnormal); (6) he shouldn't have been there; (7) she isn't "right"
    some way—behavior mod will help; (8) the person was blameless—the govern-
    ment acted improperly; (9) the care exceeds normal care; (10) it is more cere-
    bral than most.

TRADING ON WORDS

The validity of an argument such as, "A whale is a mammal; hence a dead
whale is a dead mammal," depends on every term being just as it is. The
argument, "A whale is a mammal; hence a dead whale is a common mammal," would be invalid. In any valid argument at least one term or its
negative must be repeated. Now if a shift of meaning were to take place
between the first occurrence of a term and the "repetition," we would get a
non sequitur, just as we did when what should have been the repetition of
"dead" was changed to "common."

Logicians give the name equivocation to the illegitimate switching of
meanings in midargument. Sometimes a conclusion which employs a term
in one sense will appear to be based on premises which turn out to use the
term in another sense. A letter to the editor once shocked its readers with
the complaint that in the dormitories under construction at the state university, men and women were going to be living together. One's picture of
cohabitation and orgy, which was the intended effect, turned out to be
unjustified by the evidence, that men and women would indeed be living
together—on sex-segregated, alternate floors of a high-rise. With the equivocation on "live together" exposed, the argument is easily seen to be a non
sequitur. In a related sort of equivocation, two or more reasons which together would clinch a conclusion if a term in them were used uniformly
throughout seem acceptable only because the term is not used uniformly. A

philosopher once argued against the existence of space as follows: (1) "Take any two bodies; if anything separates them it would be space"; but (2) "space, as we know, is nothing"; and (3) "if nothing separates two bodies they would be together, with no space between them." The argument tries to have it both ways. If we believe premise 2 it is because we read "nothing" as "no matter"; reading it as "no distance" we would reject it immediately. If we believe premise 3 it is because we read "nothing" as "no distance"; reading it as "no matter" we would reject *it* immediately. But if the conjurer can sneak the two meanings past undetected, he will have "won" his point.

Maybe no argument as transparent as the foregoing two will show that the well-manipulated word is quicker than the mind. (Obscured by its original terminological jungle, however, the latter argument was far from transparent.) More convincing, though no less silly, is the high-turnover retailer's perennial ploy, one version of which runs: "XYZ Foodstores earns less than 1½ pennies on each dollar of sales. Not much, is it?" The implication is that XYZ makes small profits. Malarkey! The perpetrators of this version really perform two conjuring tricks at once. First they get us to focus on one tiny sale ("1½ pennies"), on, say, a shopper buying a dollar box of detergent, from which XYZ makes 1½ cents. Our inclination is to think of the 1½ cents. This shifts attention away from XYZ's profits, which run to many millions. This first trick is a form of equivocating on relative terms, about which more will be said later. The second conjuring trick, the argument's major thrust, gets us to believe that 1½ percent profit on sales is "not much." The arguer knows that we will think of 1½ percent *per year*, measly by any standard. But a 1½ percent profit on sales reveals nothing about profit per year. With its high turnover the grocery business does well despite a "low" per sale profit. To illustrate the principle involved let us simplify: Item x costs a chain $1; they sell it for $1.01. They rake off 1¢ and reinvest their original $1 in another x; sell *it,* rake off, reinvest, sell, rake off, and on and on. If they can repeat the sell-rake off-reinvest cycle fifty times a year, say, they will have earned $.50 on their original $1, a phenomenal profit, while their profit is still "less than 1½ pennies on each dollar of sales." In other words profits on sales of itself reveal nothing about annual profits on capital investment (which for supermarkets, incidentally, in a recent year averaged 12½ percent).

Equivocating on Relative Terms   This type of equivocation involves changing standards of comparison in midargument, a mechanism well demonstrated by the jingle, "A Sophomoric Philosophy":

> The more you study, the more you know,
> The more you know, the more you forget,
> The more you forget, the less you know,
> So why study?

(The second stanza goes, "The less you study, the less you know," etc.) Though its rhetorical-question conclusion may be true, the argument obviously fails to prove it. In equivocating on relative terms the trick is to combine statements each of which contains a relative term (in this case "more" and "less"), while shifting the implied base against which the term functions. Some of those "mores" are more than others and some of those "lesses" are less than others. In general the more you forget the less you know, but only against a stable base. Forgetting a considerable amount of a large store of knowledge, as compared to forgetting a considerable amount of a smaller store of knowledge, will normally net more knowledge. To simplify, imagine a 20 percent overnight forgetting rate on unfamiliar French verbs. J learns 20 and quits. K learns 200. At 20 percent loss, K will still be ahead by well over 100 verbs, even though having forgotten 10 times as many as J. The more you study *and* forget here, the more you know.

Here are some variations on the theme. A university regent plumping for the instituting of tuition argued: "A person with a college degree earns on the average about $150,000 more in his lifetime than a high school graduate. A tuition charge of $500 a year would thus still be quite modest." This is the trick of spiriting in a big amount in order to make the item under consideration seem small by comparison. (The "1½ pennies" maneuver did the reverse, making a big amount seem small.) Since the regent mentions no post-graduation payback scheme, the $150,000 figure, against which the $500 fee is supposed to be "quite modest," is irrelevant to a student's ability to cough up $500 per year before graduation.

After the Republicans' poor showing in the 1964 presidential election (if an example may be excavated from recent history), spokespersons were consoling their comrades with an argument which went like this: "The Republican Party is more successful than many people realize. In the recent election many many more people voted for Barry Goldwater than voted for the first Republican candidate, Abe Lincoln." This is playing with two senses of "successful" only one of which applies to elections. Victory, or perhaps percentage of the vote, not the absolute number of votes garnered, measures political success. The argument equivocates on relative terms in that success relative to the 1860 electorate is, in absolute numbers, something quite different from success relative to the many-times-larger 1964 electorate.

Finally, here is an equivocation on relative terms which shifts the base against which a percentage works. Britain's Royal College of Physicians appended to the *Report on Smoking and Health* a defense of tobacco advertising put out by the tobacco industry's Tobacco Advisory Committee, part of which stated:

Press and television advertising expenditure on tobacco goods in the U.K.. . . .
was 0.52 percent of retail expenditure on those goods whereas press and television advertising expenditure on all consumer goods and services was 0.87 percent of retail expenditure on all consumer goods and services. Press and television advertising expenditure on tobacco goods could thus be increased
two-thirds without exceeding the proportion that press and television advertising expenditure on consumer goods and services generally bears to public
expenditure on these goods and services.

The comparison is unfair. In Britain taxes on tobacco goods amount to
about 90 percent of their retail price, while taxes on all goods and services
amount to about 10 percent of their retail price. So although the conclusion
that the tobacco industry's expenditure on ads is small (small relative to
total retail sales) does follow, the intended conclusion, the net effect of the
argument, that the advertising expenditures are small (small relative to another base) does not follow at all. In fact, as against sales less duty, the
usual method of calculation, the tobacco industry's advertising costs were
2.2 percent against less than 1 percent on all goods and services. (Discussion on the topic of equivocation by using different ways of arriving at a
statistic can be found in Chapter 4.)

Equivocation "by Inertia" Propagandists employ a species of equivocation designed to continue approval, or to mute disapproval, by exploiting
the lag created by what might be called semantic inertia, our tendency to
believe that terms continue to apply to just what they did formerly. In order
to hide something undesirable, the propagandist retains a familiar term
while worsening what the term covers. For example, I had taken foreign
delivery on a popular model of imported car, call it the "12." Satisfied, I
took another foreign delivery two years later, and at quite an increase in
price, on another "12," I thought. However, upon arriving I discovered a
stripped-down model with less chrome, no rear-window defroster, no side
pockets, no this, and no that. Infuriated, I asked where all the stuff was and
was told, "Oh, that's all gone into the "Super 12." The company could
bother changing the name of the jazzed-up model but not of the stripped-
down one. This sort of deception, of course, goes on all the time. California
is still bragging about tuition-free higher public education for residents. It's
true, no tuition. But residents registering in California universities have had
to pay higher and higher "incidental fees," fees which originally were incidental (almost) but which over the years have come to equal or exceed what
in other states is called what it is. Another typical example of exploiting
semantic lag involved the phrase "protective reaction," originally applied
only to a severely limited type of retaliation against individual North Viet-
namese missile sites whose radars had been tracking U.S. planes. But when
the large-scale bombing of North Vietnam was resumed in the summer of

1972, suddenly this also became a "protective reaction." Actually, however, the missions and tonnages of those 1972 raids exceeded everything since the 1968 bombing halt—in other words, some of the most intensive bombing in history.

Equivocation by Name-Change   A Chinese emperor is reported to have solved the problem of a flood-prone river called the Rampager by renaming it the Tranquil. Not only do we sometimes proceed as if along with linguistic stability goes actual stability, we sometimes proceed as if along with linguistic change goes actual change. This weakness gets exploited by those wishing to cover up unpopular actions or to give the aura of progress to inaction. Sudsy brand soap may have been okay, but *new* Sudsy seems better. The "improvement" may be only semantic. On the same principle crime has "dropped" simply by certain crimes having been declared legal. France's embargo of arms sales to Mideast belligerents, a popular policy, was costing the country hundreds of millions in badly needed foreign exchange—until the defense ministry hit on the brilliant solution of keeping the admirable policy while declaring certain nations nonbelligerents. More often, political name-changing cloaks the retaining of an unpopular policy. At one point in the long Vietnam deescalation, the American public was told that the army had given up the unpopular search-and-destroy missions. Was this progress toward ending American bloodshed? Apparently the army had given up only a term, substituting instead "reconnaissance-inforce for pacification purposes." The missions designated by this bureaucratic mouthful consisted of doing the same as the search-and-destroy missions.

Let us turn now to another aspect of the study of the meanings of terms, the topic of definition.

DEFINITION

Not infrequently writers on definition have proceeded as if defining were a matter of meeting formal requirements. The result has been unnecessary shackles or senseless artificiality, such as that which pervaded the classroom of the schoolmaster in Dickens' *Hard Times,* that notorious utilitarian, Thomas Gradgrind:

"Bitzer," said Thomas Gradgrind. "Your definition of a horse."
"Quadruped. Graminivorous. Forty teeth, namely, twenty-four grinders, four eye teeth, and twelve incisive. Sheds coat in the spring; in marshy countries sheds hoofs, too. Hoofs hard, but requiring to be shod with iron. Age known by marks in mouth." That (and much more) Bitzer.
"Now girl number 20," said Mr. Gradgrind. "You know what a horse is."

Since no child who had advanced as far as Gradgrind's classroom could *not* have known what a horse is, Gradgrind's is a hollow ceremony.

But it is not that much hollower than those countless discussions of definition built around examples such as "A brother is a male sibling." Why this
and similar statements should be trotted out as models of proper definition
is hard to grasp. Nobody defines "brother" in the first place. And even if
anyone did, nobody would define it that way, since whoever did not know
what a brother is would be most unlikely to know what a sibling is. (That
there is little point in trying to define words whose meaning is already
familiar seems to have been grasped by Dr. Johnson, who warned those
who would look for clarity in each entry in his *Dictionary* of "words too
plain to admit of a definition.")

Therefore, let us proceed to the subject where definition is natural and
healthy. Such a point, and there may be others, lies in answers to spontane-
ous questions asked by someone, perhaps a child, unable to make sense of
an unfamiliar word. Since to define is basically to explain what a term
means, let us first dwell briefly on "explain" and on "mean," two concepts
perhaps even more prone to misrepresentation than "define." *Explain:*
Good explaining puts the unclear or unknown in terms of the clear and
known. If to define is to explain, then good definition rephrases a term
whose meaning is unclear or unknown in words whose meaning is clear and
known. *Mean:* Whoever knows what a term means can variously employ
it—can understand sentences containing it and can put it to use in sentences of his own. A term's meaning is thus rather complex, something like
the sum of the various jobs at which it is found. *Define:* Definition explains
these jobs, either all of them (as in a complete dictionary), or the more
important of them (as in a short or bilingual dictionary), or those of them
which bear on the subject at hand (as in lecture-hall definitions, glossaries,
or most conversational definitions *ad hoc*). If the important thing is getting
the meaning across—that is, teaching the term's correct use—then any consideration of form and method should be judged by its ability to achieve
that end. Thus, a satisfactory definition might take the form of a wave of
the hand (as in defining "crevasse" while traversing a glacier) or a Bronx
cheer (as in defining "Bronx cheer").

Its audience is an integral part of any explanation. Definition is no
exception. Good definitions fit their audience. If at a family counseling
session a psychologist were explaining something about sibling rivalry and
someone were to interrupt, "Wait a minute, what's a sibling?" the psychologist would explain in terms something like these: " 'Sibling' is a term used
by psychologists and others to mean either a brother or a sister." Such a
definition is tailored a number of ways. Since all those present obviously
know how to employ "brother" and "sister," this definition really consists
in informing that the jobs done by "brother" and "sister" can (except for
the sex-differentiation of the more specific terms) be done by "sibling."
And since what prompted the question was the counselor's use of "sibling

rivalry," obviously no discussion of the various senses of "brother" or "sister" is necessary; nothing need be said about monks and nuns, about mankind, about blacks or fellow women, or about any other kinds of brother or sister. Context rules these out from the start. Moreover, the definition omits mentioning the extension of "sibling" to nonhuman littermates. For the purposes at hand there is no need to mention it, definitions being incomplete only relative to the needs they fail to fill. (Failure to mention it would be a lack were the definition given in, say, a psychology textbook glossary.)

Although the foregoing sketch may capture the spirit of most defining, this is not to say that it captures every bit, the term "define" being used to designate various phenomena. The following constitute some of the more frequently encountered sorts of definition—the stipulative definition, the operational definition, and the persuasive definition.

Stipulative Definition   If what a term does mean is a matter of general usage, then good definitions describe that usage. Such descriptions are called *lexical.* (*Lexicon* is modern Latin for dictionary.) What a person means by a term, however, need not be governed by what a term does mean—as long as the person explains in a generally understood way what he or she means. Such explanations are called *stipulative:* "A pace = 75 cm." "What I have in mind here by 'full employment' is 2 percent or less of the work force actively seeking work." "I use the term 'aud' to designate not just hearing, but hearing plus active understanding." In stipulating meaning one need not be governed or even guided by usage. And as long as it remains clear that a term has been defined stipulatively, the use of stipulative definition can be valuable. It can anticipate and meet ambiguity by indicating just which of several possible meanings the definer intends. Further, many existing terms cannot bear the strain we would like to exert. In such cases one modifies the old terms stipulatively, a procedure amounting to the introduction of new terms.

If stipulative definition has its uses it also has attendant dangers. Stipulated meanings can fuse with conventional meanings, resulting in equivocation. Researchers get so used to using ordinary terms in stipulated senses that when they discuss their findings publicly they sometimes leave the impression that they are using terms in conventional ways. Often, not the researcher but the press shocks or amuses us with such a mixup. "Students Learn Most from Least Liked Profs" we read in a headline. Buried in the story, if we are lucky, we discover that "learn" has been defined as the score on a mathematics exam consisting of setup equations. The net effect, unfortunately, is a conclusion about learning, an idea incomparably larger than the specialized skill actually tested. What about analytical ability, enthusiasm to continue independently, perspective, creativity, etc? (Even the learning of mathematics is tested poorly by testing the ability to solve setup equations.)

Operational Definition   A partial subclass of stipulative definition is known as the *operational* definition. Operational definitions specify meaning in terms of the procedures one goes through in order to arrive at a case: "A 'salt' is the result of the reaction between an acid and a base." "To determine the 'area of a circle' in square inches, measure from center to perimeter in inches, square the result, then multiply the result of that operation by pi." "The employee is 'authoritarian' if he answers 'yes' to five or more of the following eight questions . . ." Operational definitions can be descriptive because the lexical definitions of some terms (such as "area of a circle") do specify operations. The definition of others ("authoritarian" here) are results of nondescriptive stipulated operations. Defining in terms of operations has several good effects. First, it offers a precise way to stipulate exactly what is meant—"Of all possible ways of doing it I'm doing it *this* way." Second, it leads the audience into the activities of which the term is part—one learns more completely, more usefully, what a slugging average or a correlation coefficient is by being led through the calculation of one.

Finally, the operational definition sometimes counters the urge to *hypostatize,* to feel as if there ought to be a *something* or a *doing* which an abstract term denotes. For example, I have here a nickel. I can see its color and shape, feel its texture and hardness. But what of its *value?* Where is *that?* Value can seem mysterious, and some thinkers have denied its existence. Others have thought it to reside solely in the mind of the beholder. Still others have thought it to be somehow hidden in the object, or in some sense to be "up yonder." Such strange views come from thinking of its value as the same kind of thing as a nickel. They come from the urge to hypostatize. Explaining value operationally counteracts the urge. Instead of asking, "*What* is the value of a nickel?" ask, "*What operations measure* the value of a nickel?" What would you do, for instance, if you were a foreigner trying to determine the value of a U.S. nickel? You would observe asking prices, transactions, the making of change, the exchange of goods and services. A nickel's value, that is, is to be seen not in the coin itself, not in some weird realm or other, but in the marketplace—the activities of offering and selling.

On a more sophisticated plane the urge to hypostatize can sometimes be seen not in the deduction that there must be a something or a doing denoted by an abstract term, but in the denial of meaning to an abstract term because no something or doing can be found. Look carefully at this passage from B. F. Skinner's *Contingencies of Reinforcement:*

> Nothing is easier than to say that someone does something "because he likes to do it" or "because he has made a choice." But have we knowledge of the private life which such statements imply, or at least ought to?[1]

[1] B. F. Skinner, *Contingencies of Reinforcement: A Theoretical Analysis,* Appleton-Century-Crofts, New York, 1969.

Skinner is saying that terms of desire and choice (and other "mental" terms) really "ought" to be about the activity of something in there, a "private life." Because Skinner rightly sees that we know no such thing, he denies sense (as his question implies) to mental terms. In resisting the urge to hypostatize, Skinner seems to have fallen victim to the very assumption that underlies it. Again, the operational definition may be useful. Rather than thinking of a "private life" behind terms like "want" and "choose," think of the sorts of things you would go through in order to find out if, say, someone *wants* something. Look at a child's face Christmas morning. Or ask the person. Watch what they do with the thing, how they care for it. Offer to buy it for a song, or for a fortune. The point is simply that desire is not to be seen in a "private life" but in the entire "marketplace" of human situations. In presenting meaning in terms of doings rather than in terms of unintelligible somethings, the operational definition inclines us to see the relation between the term and those activities which give it its life.

Persuasive Definition   Definitions carry an aura of authority. Occasionally, writers and speakers parasitize this aura in order to pass opinion off as fact. They give a *persuasive* definition disguised as a lexical definition. A persuasive definition sets down not what the term does mean but what its author would like it to mean. If I were to define "trial by jury," say, as "the right which guarantees justice to every citizen by allowing him or her to be judged by a group of peers," I would, in my enthusiasm to state what *ought* to be the case, be misrepresenting what *is* the case. (Jury trials are not the right of every citizen, and though they may encourage justice they scarcely guarantee it.) I would have couched advocacy in descriptive terms. Perhaps as long as it is made clear that advocacy is going on and not description, the persuasive definition is unobjectionable. However, since persuasive definitions are so prone to misinterpretation, complete honesty would seem to rule in favor of less descriptive-seeming forms of advocacy.

Some Definition Folklore   In addition to, or following from, the misconception that lexical definition consists of following formal requirements, there exist other misconceptions about definition. Among the more widely held are the feeling that good definitions must give the common and distinctive property; that defining by example is no good; that definition must never be circular; that definition must precede understanding; that definition is a form of discovery. Each of these has been used to stifle the opposition or divert the flow of argument. Let us examine them in turn.

The Common and Distinctive Property   In Plato's dialogue *Meno,* Socrates exhorts Meno, "Since you call them by a common name . . . [give] the common nature." The assumption is natural enough: whatever gets called x gets called x for a reason, and to define is to produce that reason. Without going into the philosophical issues involved, which are considerable (the controversy is called the problem of universals), let me state bluntly that the assumption is prejudice. Its initial hold can be dispelled by observation. Like customs, words and expressions come into practice, evolve, sometimes become obsolete. The pervasive mechanism of word flux is *concatenation,* a chain-forming process by which the meanings of the habitual accompaniments of what is called by a term come to attach to the term's meaning. The term develops a series of "links" of meaning, each connected to one or more links, with no link connected to all. Take the adjective "green." Originally meaning the color of grass, "green" naturally got applied to whatever things are of not the color of grass but of a similar color—"greenish"— as in "olive green" or (as one Shakespearean playbook had it) "goose turd green." Among these things typically are unripe things: unripe grain and unripe fruits are green. The habitual association of green with unripe then became imbedded, and "green" came also to mean "unripe." From then on, green things no longer needed to be, or be like, the color of grass—as in, "Blackberries are red when they are green." Now "unripe" itself carries the habitual association of "not yet useful." Green grain and green fruit need seasoning. But so do various things not ripening biologically. "Green" eventually came to apply to them too. In this sense of "green," a barrel of white beer, a yellow pine two-by-four, and a black, brown, and white soccer team may all be green. At the end of the process the original "green" has grown to four "links"—the color of grass, greenish, biological unripeness, and immaturity. What do all "green" things have in common? Answer: Nothing. Concatenations need not be simple as in the "green" example. Links may develop off links in several directions, connecting links may become obsolete, and so on. It would be good exercise, using a good etymological dictionary, to trace linkages between the senses of familiar terms ("bank," "run," "dog," and "cardinal" might prove interesting) just to sample the complexities involved.

Insistence on there being a unique, exhaustive defining property, an essence, could be called the *essentialist* fallacy. Critics have argued that certain modern plays, and even certain Roman and Shakespearean plays, are not really tragedies since they lack one or more of the features set down in Aristotle's *Poetics* as characteristics of real tragedy. However, that Aristotle isolated the gist of the tragedy of his day (and that he did is highly arguable) scarcely implies that he also succeeded in anticipating every turn which resourceful tragedians, and with them the term "tragedy," have taken and will take.

Essentialism often makes itself felt in the form of a demand for simplicity—for a theory. A reviewer once criticized a logic book for offering no theory of fallacy. The reviewer apparently thought that everything called by the term "fallacy" can usefully, nontrivially, be subsumed under a formula. Now perhaps it can be so subsumed. But why require anything of the sort? Why not as well assume that "fallacy" can be better explained by laying it out, case by case, in all its richness and variety? The point is, whatever procedure fits best in a given case is a matter to be decided by investigation, not a matter to be decided according to a prior requirement.

Think of demanding a theory of, say, traffic accidents. Traffic accidents arise for *all sorts* of reasons—drunkenness, natural disasters, anger, mechanical failure, production cost-cutting, and on and on. Rather than a theory of traffic accidents, rather than a "lumping," so to speak, we need to emphasize the range and variety of the many things called by the term "traffic accidents." We need, as it were, a "distribution." With the many sorts of mistakes called fallacies the same holds. Fallacies seem to arise from *all sorts* of causes. And, although speculation about and testing of those causes is undeniably useful, there is no reason to expect that anything will follow from them which is not to a great extent piecemeal.

Defining by Example Is No Good   Again in the *Meno,* Socrates exhorts Meno not to list examples as a definition but instead to produce "that common nature which you designate as figure—which contains round no less than straight." But is a list really no good? If someone asked, "What is a plane figure?" would it be so bad to respond, "Well, circles, triangles, squares, ovals, pentagons, and so forth"? From such an array a person might come to understand perfectly what a plane figure is. "The sense," as Dr. Johnson remarked of some of his entries, "can be collected entire from the examples." What of the objection that since no common and distinctive property has been produced, definitions by example can be misunderstood? Indeed they can. In this regard there can be better and worse definitions by example, as well as terms and situations that are more, and terms and situations that are less, amenable to such definition. But if definition by example can be misunderstood, it shares this potential with any type of definition. Even the best short exhaustive characterization may be no better. When told that a zwitterion is "a molecule or ion with separate positively and negatively charged groups; a dipolar ion," (an elegant explanation by means of a common and distinctive property), would the average person really be that much clearer on zwitterions? What counts is not the form of definition but the effect.

Definitions Must Never Be Circular   A definition is said to be circular when the term being defined appears in some form in the definition, as in a good book on sailing which begins, "A sailboat is a boat with sails." To avoid circular definitions is good policy, as long as it is subordinate to the principle that what explains should be more accessible than what gets explained. There would be no point in telling someone that "entropic" means "of or pertaining to entropy," since whoever does not know the former would be unlikely to know the latter. But defining an unfamiliar form of a familiar term by means of the familiar term ought to be unobjectionable. Pronounced "im'pee-uss," the word "impious" sometimes causes confusion (students think it means "impish") which could be dispelled simply by defining the word in terms of its other pronounciation. And there should be no objection to defining "Shavian" as "of or pertaining to George Bernard Shaw." Nor with contemporary lexicographers does avoiding circularity interfere with good sense. For example, they would not hesitate to define the adjective "equinoctial" by using its noun form, "equinox," since "equinox" in the alphabetical listing would appear right below.

Definition Must Precede Understanding   Some people think that a person does not know what a term means if the person cannot define it. "First we must define our terms" begins many a discussion, the implication being that unless one can produce a definition one does not yet know what one is talking about. Which may be true sometimes. Understanding and being able to define, however, are different. We all know what a dog is, yet most of us would be hard-pressed to come up with an effective, complete definition. And those of us particularly good at constructing definitions might be bad at recognizing dogs and distinguishing dogs from other things.

Insistence that definition precede understanding usually stems from the feeling that vagueness and ambiguity are in the term itself and must be eliminated by precise defining. Is it *terms* which are ambiguous or vague? When the Delphic oracle told Croesus that in the upcoming battle a great army would be destroyed, it was not *language's* fault that the army turned out to be Croesus' own. It was the Oracle's fault, or, more accurately, Croesus'; no definition of "great," "destroy," or any other term was needed. What was needed was one ordinary word. Overstating, one could say that "words are neither ambiguous *nor* vague; words are used ambiguously or vaguely. It's not the word but the user."

Like so many terms, "ambiguous" and "vague" are relative, relative to the situation. A man who says to the grocer, "Give me five pounds of kumquats" is being vague *if* he wants unripe, extra-large, or canned kumquats, or any kind other than the normal. But chances are good that he does want the normal. Or he may not care what kind he gets. In fact, when our desires are less than definite, relatively indefinite language—"Give me a whole lot of kumquats," "Give me a sack of fruit," etc.—may express our meaning perfectly.

Definition Is Discovery   People sometimes proceed as if to construct a definition is to discover the hitherto unknown. This is false. Could you define the word "syzygy," say, without first knowing what syzygy is? Knowledge precedes definition, not vice versa. Definition can extend only to the limits of knowledge, no further. This is not to say that defining may not *arrange* what is already known in novel and perhaps enlightening ways. Such ways we may call discovery, and value as discovery and new knowledge. As long as it is recognized that their potential was contained completely in what we previously knew, calling such ways discovery is unobjectionable.

Examples and Comments

A Where appropriate, purge the following of unjustified connotations and verbosity, and defend your changes or retentions.

1 "Marcanera, the finest domestic parmigiano manufactured in this country."

Comment Since "domestic" *means* "manufactured in this country," the latter phrase may be omitted. "Parmigiano" should probably be changed to "parmesan."

2 "You may believe that you have finalized this project but actually what you have completed thus far is only the tip of the iceberg."

Comment "You have only begun this project" would be equivalent. "Finalized," jargon for "finished," adds a phony technical air. "Only the tip of the iceberg" *was* a vivid metaphor but has been overworked; replace it with an original equivalent.

3 "Proposition no. 1 is based on an egghead theory that if you place a limit on state expenditures your total taxes will eventually be reduced."

Comment Purge "egghead," a perjorative, stereotyping term. Otherwise, the language is straightforward and concise.

4 " 'The real thrust of this administration,' observed Chancellor Otsev, 'consists in opting where possible for programs which tend to be cost-effective in meeting this institution's missions and goals.' "

Comment "I will try to run this institution efficiently" says about the same thing. "This administration," "this office," "the Presidency," and the like frequently mask what are really *personal* decisions. "Opting for" and "cost-effective" are pseudo-technical synonyms for "choose" and "efficient." Three out of four occurrences of "tend to" add nothing. And what is the difference between "missions" and "goals"? "Thrust" and "opt" make Otsev look dynamic; is he really doing that much?

5 "The degree of interpersonal attachment between two or more organisms in a human society varies directly with the frequency of their interaction with one another."

Comment The truism, "The better you get to know people the better you like them" has been elevated here to scientific status by "varies directly." "Organisms in a human society" are no more than people. "With one another" repeats "interaction."

6 "Those who fall into the below-poverty-threshold category of economic status tend to be characterized by a level of monetary or nonmonetary recompense generally commensurate with low levels of occupational skills."

7 "According to our criterion-referenced study the optimum solution is to gradually phase out the traditional two-way pattern of traffic flow on the more impacted streets, replacing it with a system utilizing an integrated network of one-way arteries."

8 "Most programs on television have a tendency to be directed specifically either toward the young child or toward the adult instead of toward the family as a whole."

9 "He was a Yale-educated man, six feet four inches in height, eyes blue in color, and 38 years of age. These are the reasons why the electorate tended to select him. Their reasons were frivolous ones rather than worthwhile ones."

10 "In a very real sense what we have here on balance is a group of actions which are revolutionary in character."

11 "Granted we don't want to overcommercialize the Bicentennial," remarked Hanson, the chairman of the board, "but on the other hand we wouldn't want to undercommercialize it either. Let's put this idea on the stoop and see if the cat licks it up; let's run it up the pole and see if anybody salutes."

12 "The early, middle, and late childhood of offspring of parents whose occupational pursuits lie predominately in the agricultural labor area is characterized by a pattern of educational involvement marked by a minimum of formal schooling taking place in a succession of localities ranging from those of heavily urbanized nature to those which are definitely rural in character."

13 "After conferencing for a period of six hours and four minutes, the joint meeting between physician representatives and the governor's cohorts came up with a report of four pages in length which negatively critiqued the entire malpractice insurance system as it now stands."

14 *Policy Guidelines, Internship Program,* California University. "It is the policy of California University to encourage participation in an internship when such an experience is directly related to the educational goals and the career aspirations of students. To be a valid learning experience the internship will (1) enrich and reinforce the academic program of the student; (2) take place under adequate supervision; (3) permit evaluation of the experience; (4) allow the student to integrate knowledge and to apply concepts and generalizations learned in the classroom; (5) demonstrate the relationship between the university program and the world of work; and (6) facilitate wiser course selection by students. To be of value to the agency engaging the intern, the program should result in attracting a student of appropriate ability and potential into the organization as a possible future employee. An end result of the program should be the improvement of service to public or private organizations by former students who have participated in an internship."

15 "There is now no effective mechanism for introducing into the initiation and development stages of reporting requirements information on existing reporting and guidance on how to minimize burden associated with new requirements" (Survey, U.S. Office of Management and Budget).

16 "Pages 7 and 8 have been revised to provide, in accordance with a recent Executive Order, that all employees will be excused on the preceding workday when a holiday falls on Sunday. This includes any employee whose workweek is other than Monday through Friday when a holiday falls on his 'regular weekly nonworkday in lieu of Sunday' or on his regular weekly nonworkday other than his regular weekly nonworkday in lieu of Sunday" (Department of Agriculture circular for employees).

17 "Presently exhibiting characteristic manifestations of a tendency to effect a recovery from its previous low, the economy seems to be continuing its syndrome of fluctuation between periods of relative prosperity and corresponding periods of relative hard times."

B Using the ideas sketched in this chapter and elsewhere, and using common sense, comment on the following:

1 "It is preposterious, ladies and gentlemen of the jury, even to consider that Mr. Lazzarini could be guilty. I ask you: Does that look like a guilty man to you? Do you see his eyes shift? Do you see his face twitch? Do you see his brow glisten? No. What you see is not guilt. What you see is innocence."

Comment Equivocation. The attorney shifts meaning in midargument, drawing a conclusion about *legal* guilt (or innocence) from premises which hold only about the *psychological state* of looking guilty. But "he did it" and "he shows it" are obviously different.

2 "The more money you make, the more worries you have. The more worries you have the more likely you are to get ulcers. So the more money you make the more likely you are to get ulcers."

Comment This reasoning is valid if not very informative. "More" is not being equivocated on, since in each occurrence there are not really any implied standards to shift, and, of course, there is then no shift.

3

> Wittgenstein totally ignores obvious cases that conflict with his position that there is nothing common to the instances, and only the instances, to which a word is correctly applied. Consider cases such as "brother," "aunt," and "highball," where it is quite clear that, for each, there is a unique defining condition: in the case of "brother," it is that the person be a male sibling of another; in the case of "aunt," it is that a person be someone's parent's sister; and in the case of "highball," it is that something be a drink of diluted spirits served with ice in a tall glass. (Jerrold J. Katz, *The Philosophy of Language,* Harper & Row, New York, 1966, p. 73.)

Comment Doesn't Katz ignore obvious cases that conflict with *his* position? The many senses of "brother" concatenate ("brother's keeper," "lodge brother," "blood brother," etc.), with the members of no single sense sharing unique characteristics with members of all the other senses. Nor is it clear that members of the same sense of the same orthographic element (the senses being invented by lexicographers for clarity and convenience) share unique characteristics. Is it "obvious," for example, that highballs need to be served in glasses? Why not in mugs or cans? Is it "quite clear" that they require ice? Whether or not Katz turns out to be right, his confident tone here seems to derive from essentialist presuppositions. (Readers who wish to pursue the matter further should read Katz's remarks in context.)

4 "By religion I mean the Christian religion, and by the Christian religion I mean the Protestant religion, and by the Protestant religion I mean the Church of England."

5 "The less you study the less you know,
The less you know the less you forget,
The less you forget the more you know,
So why study?"

6 "PCI's Amendola Stars in Italian Puppet 'Show.' Unless the Italian working class acts at once to depose Giorgio Amendola from the leadership positions in the Italian Communist Party (PCI) there is no chance of working-class resistance to Rockefeller's plan to replay the Chilean coup in Italy. As long as this class traitor—sewage conduit of the CIA—is permitted to formulate PCI policy, Italian politics is nothing but a multi-colored puppet 'show.' "

7 "Look at it this way: Your daughter just spent $45 for second-hand jeans that a cowboy threw away. And you're still drinking ordinary scotch? Highlands, the 12-year-old scotch." (Advertisement.)

8 "This year you have a choice in the election. You've got to decide beforehand what you are going to do. You can vote for the Democratic Party (or for what's left of the Republican Party) and watch the world collapse into facism. Or you can build your own political party—the U.S. Labor Party."

9 "Formerly, U.S. companies operating abroad could deduct from their U.S. taxes income taxes paid to foreign sovereign states. Royalty payments were another matter. Only a fraction of such payments could legally be deducted. Then the companies hit on a stroke of genius. They asked their Arab associates to declare the royalties income taxes, a request which was readily granted. Result: Savings in the hundreds of millions."

10 "We do things freely—we think. We jump—but can always imagine jumping higher. We learn—but not every possible bit. We desire—but never immediately, effortlessly, fully attain what we desire. In every case there turns out to be some constraint, some 'friction' as it were, which prevents the action from being free. True freedom? Alas, were that wishing made it so."

Applications

A Quickly, unthinkingly, separate the following adjectives into three categories—"pejorative," "commendatory," and "neutral." Next, by describing a context, try to move each term into another category.

educational	old	fascist
propaganda	free	sloppy
natural	commercial	considerate
real	gourmet	aroma
good	shabby	zionist
horsey	pig	overelaborate
USDA Good	military	pseudoscience

B Research and speculate on causes of verbal obscurity (for example, naïveté; boredom; laziness; the desire to mislead; to say something regardless, to avoid saying anything; or whatever). (An interview with someone intelligent in a government agency, a university, a corporation, or the military might prove enlightening.) What direction for improving matters do the research or speculations suggest?

C Analyze for connotation an extended piece of argumentation, such as a magazine article or Sunday paper in-depth analysis. Select the piece carefully, so that you will be able to defend the use of some terms and criticize the use of others, suggesting substitutes.

D Using material on equivocation, connotation, and definition, construct, administer, score, and defend your own "Quick Check."

Chapter 4

Authority

Whoever appeals to authority reasons in effect, "It's so, because it's so according to A," where A is the authority. The term "authority" covers here not only the people or publications ordinarily considered authorities, it covers anyone or anything whose word is taken.

Appealing to authority has often been judged by its abuses. We were urged—on good authority, no doubt—to shun authority and instead to see for ourselves. To offset the abuse of authority this may have been good advice. As general policy, however, it is short-sighted, and as the vicious self-reference shows, ultimately incoherent. Often, to see for ourselves is impossible, too costly, or simply not worth the effort. Equally to the point, maybe more to it, anything called a society requires authority to perpetuate the language, lore, and institutions which form the social fabric. We could not begin to get by without reliable teachers, consultants, and, in countless instances, ordinary people. The sensible approach, therefore, instead of blanket distrust, is to nurture skills for distinguishing reliable authority from poor authority.

EXPERTS AND OTHERS

One of the commonest devices for glamorizing something is to cite eminent persons on its behalf. We're supposed to do it, or use it, because so-and-so says to, or does. Advertisements feature beloved athletes, aging film stars, "prominent New York doctors." Letterheads and full-page ads of groups seeking funds or actions sag under the weight of countless worthies. Introducers of speakers feel obliged to sweeten up speaker or speech by reciting the speaker's every accomplishment from kindergarten up. No book dust jacket nowadays seems complete without a battery of blurbs. Most of this folklore the average person probably ignores. But that shopper spoke truly who, having claimed never to be influenced by advertising, was pressed as to why she used a certain popular brand of toothpaste. "Well," she replied, "you know, you can't always brush after every meal." Actions can be swayed in ways we never suspect. Having experienced the ads, letterheads, introductions, blurbs, we do find ourselves buying a certain brand, feeling guilty for not contributing, listening less critically, or thinking, "There must be something here I'm missing."

So let us rehearse some characteristics of good authorities. When a person is cited as an authority it is wise to have developed the habit of asking questions such as: "Is it a matter for authority?" "Is the authority expert on exactly this subject?" "Is the authority well recognized?"

Is It a Matter for Authority? Almost any field contains masses of material about which the experts agree. Here appeals to an expert are happily at home. We rest content with a good dictionary's information that we have been misspelling "gauge," rely unquestioningly on the elementary chemistry learned at college, accept the testimony that the skidmarks reveal the plaintiff's car to have been exceeding the speed limit. The opinions are from knowledgeable, experienced experts relying on standard tests, and both experts and tests are uncontested. But on topics on which the experts are in disagreement, appealing to authority is usually insufficient. My chemistry teacher's undoubted brilliance and reputation in nuclear technology ought not make us automatically accept her judgment that nuclear plants are safe. Other experts of equal brilliance and reputation maintain the opposite. In areas of disagreement any attempt of the form, "It's so because A says so," can be easily countered with, "Well, so what, B says such-and-such else." In such areas the proper alternative must be either the withholding of judgment or a more direct form of argument.

Unfortunately, more direct forms of argument are frequently beyond all but less than 1 percent of the public. How can ordinary citizens possibly estimate such matters as fluorocarbons' potential to damage the earth's ozone layer, Patty Hearst's mental condition at the time of the robbery, or the advisability of oil company divestiture—examples of the countless pressing issues upon which eminently qualified experts cannot agree. Should one withhold judgment? Yes, for the nonexpert. But matters may cry for decision. To do nothing courts injustice. A few members of the scientific community have suggested a Science Court to help separate fact from exaggeration in scientific matters affecting government policy. The suggestion has merit, though the attendant dangers are also great—establishment deck-stacking and the creation of an "official position," something which many scientists find fundamentally antiscientific.

It does seem legitimate to use someone's eminence to add weight to opinions on topics about which there is dispute among experts, but only to the extent that this weight bids us to consider those opinions more carefully, and to dismiss them less readily, than those of someone without expertise. A book may be worth reading even though eminent reviewers are divided over it, or the theory of a great scientist well worth considering even though the scientist's colleagues have lined up solidly against it. Such situations usually are good places for the nonexpert to exercise that fine art of withholding judgment.

There are other ways in which a person's endorsement can be used, not to bid us blindly accept an opinion, but to do something less venturesome, or different. Famous names on letterheads or full-page ads do not mean nothing. Whether the cause is worthy may be debatable even though it is supported by this athlete or that film star, but if nothing else the legal resources available to such persons do give some assurance that the cause is legitimate. And if such-and-such political action seems too radical or hopeless of success, the very endorsement of those establishment worthies diminishes its radicalness and increases its chances.

Is the Authority Expert on Exactly This Subject?   People who have earned renown seem always to be giving opinions. Mostly it is not their fault. They are continually being asked for them, often at cocktail parties or in hotel lobbies. Some, like Albert Einstein, seem to have given them out of a humble willingness to oblige, while others seem more or less arrogant and opinionated. Whatever the circumstances, it is amazing how frequently someone eminent in one area gets cited in order to glamorize a conclusion in another area. This deception has been called the fallacy of "borrowed" authority. Race car driver Janet Guthrie may know high-performance automobiles, but she probably knows little about how to judge cigarettes or $5000 passenger cars. A biochemist who has won renown for a breakthrough in molecular genetics probably never paid much attention to fluorocarbons and could not care less about the chemistry of toxins. Even what seems to be an expert's field may turn out to be something with which the person is unfamiliar. You might think that a famous scientist would not fall for a simple illusionist trick performed with the aid of a powerful magnet in the shoe. Expertise in science, however, has on more than one occasion proved no match for an illusionist's well-executed bit of applied psychology, typically leaving the scientist speculating about how experimentally to investigate hitherto unknown forces.

The deceptiveness of borrowed authority probably derives partly from our oversimplifying the concept of intelligence. We think that with talent at one type of thinking goes talent at other types. We think that with brilliance goes good judgment, that with cleverness goes wisdom. But since for very intelligent people things have generally been intellectually easy, they not infrequently suppose that they know what they are talking about when in fact they do not. This intellectual ease can lead to shallowness. Moral: Don't be amazed, or cowed, upon hearing foolishness from the eminent.

Occasionally, an argument will appeal to authority without fully testing the authority's expertise. Large washing machine manufacturers probably have to be experts on detergent technology, but that a box of *XYZ* detergent gets included in every new washer by such-and-such manufacturer scarecely means, as the ads imply, that the manufacturer thinks XYZ the best. They have merely included the box for a fee. Similarly, the fact that "eight out of ten new homes have gas heat" shows only that gas heat is one way to heat a house, not that it is the best way. Builders of housing tracts usually do have access to the best advice around, but their interests are not the same as a homeowner's. Low unit cost, rather than efficiency, durability, or comfort, will be their major concern.

Is the Authority Well Recognized?   Citing an authority's recognition backs authority by appealing to authority. As long as the recognizers remain independent of the authority, no question is begged. Recognition broadens the base on which the authority's opinion rests. Let us review what a careful person would look for in checking the recognition of a supposed authority. In a given case to demand or use all the criteria cited below could be unnecessary. But listing them all may help to develop the disposition to bring the right questions to mind when an expert is cited, or when one contemplates making careful use of expert opinion oneself. And in many situations (e.g., filling an important post) ascertaining expertise may be crucial. Recognition can be seen in posts held, academic training and degrees, licenses, awards and grants, publications, invitations, citations and deferrals, to professional references. Possessing any combination of these in itself means very little; one must press further. Let us review them briefly.

Posts Held   Are they desirable posts, and how are they filled? Are they filled by the choice of one superior? Are they filled by a committee of experts? Are they filled by popular election, political influence, senility, default, or what?

Academic Training and Degrees What schools? Are the degrees earned or honorary? Are these schools strong in the relevant subject? How is a "good" school being judged? Is it being judged solely by the eminence of its faculty, as measured by publications and prizes (the usual yardsticks) or by criteria which bear more directly on the quality of its graduates?

Awards and Grants There seems to be the feeling—at least the media act as if they think so—that the holding of a prestigious prize (Pulitzer, Nobel, or whatever) gives its bearer special claim to attention. To offset the awe which such prizes produce, one must remember that the prizes reward *not* expertise but work done which, though important, may be in an incredibly narrow field—the discovery of sugar nucleotides and their effects on the biosynthesis of carbohydrates, say, or the championing of the liberation of Namibia. And it is not carping to note that prize committees have their pressures, sometimes rewarding a science, race, politics, or nationality which at the time seemed deserving.

Having won grants tells in someone's favor if the decisions on the grants were made by experts in the field, on the basis of competence, and if the grants were competitive. Not a few grants are awarded to the sole applicant, or to the winner in a small field of applicants most of whom were not qualified at all. Look at the scholarship list at any university. If you are the orphaned eldest daughter of a Serbian cotton farmer, wanting to major in nuclear engineering and dairy husbandry (and this is only a modest exaggeration), you may find yourself qualified for an academic free ride.

Publications A book or more in the area of expertise may be to a person's credit, though it must be remembered that books normally get published because publishers, including the well known, think that they can make money—a book on Willa Cather does not automatically make its author a Cather expert. And vanity presses will publish almost anything for a fee paid by the author. So perhaps it is best to say that in themselves books mean nothing unless favorably reviewed. This means getting reviews not by whoever happens to get assigned the book review column of the local newspaper, but by recognized experts in the field. One can consult the *National Library Service Cumulative Book Review Index*, the *Book Review Digest*, the *New York Times Book Review Index*, or similar or more specialized review indexes. The absence of reviews in the expected publications usually means that the author should not be cited as expert. And because mutual backscratching is not rare among writers, including the well known and the learned, it is desirable to guard against circularity by obtaining favorable reviews from publications in the field which represent schools of thought at odds with that of the book.

Articles The authorship of articles published in scholarly journals generally indicates expertise. The editors or consultants of these journals usually are themselves experts. One incompetent article might get past the harried editor of a good journal—as did the put-on article which appeared in one of the electrical engineering journals describing in very high-sounding technical language a "discovery" which amounted to nothing more than an ordinary resistor. But it is unlikely that several dud articles would get past. (There does exist the complication, unfortunately, that companies sometimes "plant" articles in prestigious journals with a practitioner in the field fronting as the author of what in essence was researched and written—whether well or not—by the company.) Some journals have better reputations than others, though in a given case what part of a good reputation derives from real excellence and what part simply from being well-known may be a tough matter for a nonexpert to decide. And to avoid the charge of cronyism, articles in several journals would be preferable to articles in only one. Articles in publications other than professional journals indicate expertise only in proportion to the expertise of their editors and consultants, which may be considerable or nil.

How does one go about finding articles? There exist indexes to articles in virtually every field. *The Humanities Index, The Applied Sciences and Technology Index,* and *The Business Periodical Index* are a few of the more general. There even exist indexes of indexes, Jean Spealman Kujoth's *Subject Guide to Periodical Indexes and Review Indexes* (Metuchen, N.J., Scarecrow Press, 1969) being a useful example.

Invitations Are those doing the inviting capable of making judgments in the area? Otherwise, renown may be mistaken for expertise. Also, perfectly competent invitation committees sometimes prefer provocative to "safe" speakers.

Citations It is a useful sign of expertise when one expert defers to or cites an opinion of another, as long as it is borne in mind that in every field there are those with more reputation than substance, and that they will be cited along with the more competent practitioners on topics relatively far removed from the deferer's or citer's area of specialization. Lack of citations or deferrals by experts in the area of specialization closest to the expert's, if the expert is long established, might be grounds for suspicion.

Professional References Recommendation by a person's professional colleagues can help in establishing expertise. It is helpful to know not only the professional reputation of the referer but also the rigor and honesty of the referer's standards. One university department head overstated the point in speaking of hiring candidates from a prestigious eastern university:

We took him on the basis of the enthusiastic support of an outstanding professor at Harvard. That's very important. If Princeton pushes a man, I know it means I'll have to look somewhere else. I don't trust Columbia either, or Chicago. With one or two exceptions in each department, those bastards are shysters; they'll say anything about anyone to get a man placed. There's one man at Harvard and one at Yale that I know I can trust. I won't take a man from either place without their say-so.[1]

OTHER SOURCES OF AUTHORITY

Discussion thus far having centered on the authority of individuals, let us turn briefly to some other authority sources.

Print Some people seem to feel that printer's ink is the embalming fluid of truth. This voice crying out in Los Angeles offers an example:

> The United Nations is really a scheme for the Communists to gradually take over everything. Last week's *Houston Courier* carried an article by Furleigh and Simon which underscores what many people have not dared to say: "Revolutionary Communist Marxists are using their Third World allies in an attempt to hamstring the Free World . . ."

Why the *Houston Courier*? The insufficiency of such appeals should be apparent.

Equally fatuous is the attempt to strengthen results by claiming them to have been achieved with the use of a so-many-million-dollar electronic computer. Typical is the brochure prepared by one of the major insurance companies, entitled "Can a Machine Take a Tender Look at Your Financial Affairs?" The company promises to computer-analyze a family's finances and on this basis advise them how much insurance they need. But since such calculations would not be different from those an insurance agent makes dozens of times a week, touting the computer can only be a gimmick. Since they compute according to programs supplied by people, who may or may not be overanxious to sell insurance, or expert at selling it, computers in themselves add nothing except possibly calculation accuracy. Their use may even present a *worse* picture, distracting attention from circumstances peculiar to the individual case and from the guesswork used in any data collection.

The Authority of Experience There exists quite a link between quality and experience, between reliability and time. The first units of a new automobile model will probably be inferior to units of the same model produced a year later "with the bugs ironed out;" a master harnessmaker will outperform an apprentice; and it makes more sense to trust a known firm which has been in business for years than to trust an unknown firm which has just opened its doors. But we oversimplify the link between quality and time. Does an airline's being "the world's most experienced" or a beer's having been brewed "since 1382" make it superior to the competition? Surely, learning to fly people around or to make beer doesn't take *that* long! More-

[1] Theodore Caplow and Reece J. McGee, *The Academic Marketplace*, Science Editions, John Wiley & Sons, Inc., New York, 1961, p. 153.

over, differences in quality nowadays stem largely from applications of the latest technology, not from what might have been valid ten or a hundred years ago. The original "little old winemaker" and the folks who baked those buttery-rich goodies down at Sunnybrook Farms may have made good stuff (though nothing tastes as good as it used to—and never did). But neither had to cope with today's mass volume, tight production schedules, and distributing and marketing problems. And toward a further debunking of the appeal-to-tradition argument, recall that most companies have been taken over recently by large corporations. Firms with dedicated, conservative management have suddenly found themselves part of some "quick-draw" conglomerate. Go ahead and believe, if you want, that your favorite whiskey is still made by old Clem and old Ez down in the holler, but unless you know, it wouldn't be smart to bet much on it.

Tests and Seals   Another common source for backing conclusions is the judgment of the institutions which rate or guarantee goods and services—the various seals of approval and product ratings. Properly understood, these can be helpful. Frequently they are misunderstood. A label such as "Advertised in *Life*" will be only as good as the publication's standards for admitting advertising, which probably is based on complaints from consumers, not the most reliable of indexes, so that denying such a label might be a long time in coming. In such matters one must research the individual reputation. Labels such as *Good Housekeeping's* Seal of Approval are not usually given for quality, as is widely believed, and are not awarded. The manufacturer pays for the use of the label. What it means is that the manufacturer agrees to replace the product if it is not as advertised. The Underwriter's Laboratory seal on electrical items *is* based on product tests, though it is given only for electrical safety standards having been met, not for overall quality. And the questions as to how many tests are run and whether they are run on products supplied by the manufacturer or selected from the normal channels of consumer supply should be answered.

Publications such as *Consumer Reports* do choose the products they test from the normal channels of consumer supply. Naturally, the reliability of the findings varies, depending on the product and the features tested. A great many more light bulbs can be tested than hatchback automobiles. And the testers will be in better position to evaluate some factors, such as product design, than to evaluate others, such as the rate of assembly line defects. Also, judgment will be more reliable on some products than on others. Rating electric toothbrushes is one thing, rating brands of beer quite another. Actually, however, since the tests that these organizations run are so open and so accessible, appealing to the organization as authority is unnecessary. Conclusions about a product are better left to stand or fall on the basis of the tests themselves.

Tradition and Privilege   Appeal to social tradition—"It's always been done that way"—seems enough to satisfy some people, a premise to which one ought to reply, "Do you mean it can't be done *better*?" Maybe it can't; but that's a matter for reason, not blind insistence on tradition. It is unclear, however, that blind insistence on tradition is always incorrect. When one culture seeks to impose its way of life on another, for instance, the afflicted culture may be right in resisting simply on principle. The reply, "No, these are our ways; for us they are the only right ways" may be enough. Indeed, happy impositions of one culture on another have been rare. If blind appeal to tradition seems an acceptable way of arguing in some circumstances, then in others the environmental argument might be acceptable: "But this is the way its always been, so we'd best leave well enough alone." Neither argument, however, is really totally blind. Both rely on the very unblind fact, if fact it be, that hindsight shows sticking to the status quo to be superior to what at the time seemed smart (a thesis the sufficiency of which is far from obvious).

Another interesting class of authority appeals is the pitch to heed A because A has privileged access to information. "The committee," we sometimes hear, "is relying on classified documents," or, "Only the President is in a position to get the complete picture." In my opinion, you should not believe this for a minute. Although those in power have information that is denied to the public, the public in other respects may be in the superior position. "The king has one eye," goes a wise Arabic proverb. Surrounded by flatterers, self-servers, speakers for special interests, those in power often occupy the worst position in which to get "the complete picture." Witness the strings of disastrous mistakes made by those in power. Another objection to the "privileged access" argument derives from the principle that argument's climate must be open. If those in power have "the complete picture" then let's hear it. In parliamentary democracies the burden of reasonable explanation of policies lies with the authors and enforcers. Not getting leveled with provides grounds for housecleaning.

"Backhanded" Authority Argument   Finally, let us just mention the "backhanded" authority argument, a kind of black/white thinking, which argues a position not because of who advocates it but because of who advocates its opposite: "Vegetarianism? Nah, bunch of hooey. Hell, *Hitler* was a vegetarian." Though this argument would be valid if Hitler could not possibly do anything right, one need not be a Hitler supporter to see that such a supposition about Hitler, or anyone, is wild. That argument is debunked because of who advocated it. Here is one which advocates because of who was debunked.

Last April CBS News aired a heretical program, "You and the Commercial," the most eloquent electronic statement to date on the manipulative aspects of advertising. The program's accuracy was fully demonstrated when the masters of unfairness and deceit, the advertising industry, roundly attacked the program as being "unfair and deceptive."

Nonsense! The program is good or not on its own, not because of who opposes it.

AD HOMINEM

Authority appeals argue for something because of who maintains it. Backhanded authority appeals argue for something because of who maintains its contrary, or against something because of who maintains it. Arguing *ad hominem*, on the other hand, is not to argue immediately for a definite proposition. Rather, ad hominem attempts to *undercut* someone else's claim. It attempts to do so because of *who made the claim*. Since it aims at truth, an argument demands to be addressed. Thus, whoever advocates not listening to someone's argument solely because the arguer is a convicted felon, liar, schizophrenic, Nazi, or whatever, has *not addressed the argument* and has reasoned falsely.

Ad hominem has been said to be a fallacy, and if the term is going to be used at all, maybe it is best reserved for bad arguments. But arguing "to the person" is by no means always misplaced. One of Samuel Johnson's famous rebukes puts the matter masterfully.

Nay, Sir, argument is argument. You cannot help paying regard to their arguments if they are good. If it were testimony, you might disregard it. . . . Testimony is like an arrow shot from a long bow; the force of it depends on the strength of the hand which draws it. Argument is like an arrow shot from a cross bow, which has equal force though shot by a child.

Argument asks to be accepted on its merits, and should stand or fall on those merits. Testimony asks to be accepted at least partly on the authority of its giver. So with testimony the giver *is* very much part of the issue. And thus the lack of expertise, stupidity, unreliability, etc., of givers does tell against their testimony, though not against their arguments. Other situations abound in which arguing "to the person" is appropriate. In elections, trials, employment, and the like, where the very person is the subject, that person will definitely be part of the issue.

Let us be clear that ad hominem differs from mere invective. The stream of words which pursues the automobile that has just muddied someone's new suit—abusive language *par excellence*—implies no conclusion. The curser attacks no thesis; there is no argument, no reasoning, hence no fallacy. The fallacy results from attacking an arguer in order to get a conclusion accepted, the conclusion that an arguer's thesis is wrong or unworthy of attention. Personal abuse, period, is not ad hominem. However, personal abuse which creeps into debate over *issues* can generally be taken as intended to weaken the opponent's position and so deserves classification as fallacious. For instance, consider this probably apocryphal bit of very old ad hominem:

> When Plato was discoursing about his "ideas" and using the names "tableness" and "cupness," Diogenes interrupted, "I, O Plato, see a table and a cup, but I can see no tableness or cupness." Plato replied, "Naturally, for you have eyes, by which to see cups and tables, but you have not intellect, by which tableness and cupness are seen."

Although Diogenes's objection that tableness and cupness cannot be seen may be naïve, it is a natural enough objection, calling for a straight answer. Instead, this "Plato," who would rather score a point than make one, attempts to divert the subject to the asker of the question. And although this move may have seemed good to the audience, let us hope that they had the sense to see that the question wasn't all that dumb, and especially, that it was never answered. Diversions of this type have been called *abusive* ad hominems: instead of addressing the issue, abuse the opponent. Here is the same mischief indulged in two thousand years later by the philosopher George Berkeley in *The Principles of Human Knowledge*:

> It is merely for want of attention and comprehensiveness of mind that there are any favorers of atheism or the Manichean heresy to be found. Little and unreflecting souls may indeed burlesque the works of Providence, the beauty and order whereof they have not capacity, or will not be at pains, to comprehend; but those who are masters of any justness and extent of thought, and are withal used to reflect, can never sufficiently admire the divine traces of wisdom and goodness that shine through the economy of nature.

Praise your friends, abuse your enemies. The abuse may take various forms—directed against an opponent's intelligence, sanity, family, sexual preferences, weight, or whatever. One favorite device is to poison the wells with abuse, giving the opponent "choices" all but one of which are in some way poisoned, so that the opponent will select the remaining "choice" in order to escape. Poisoning the wells with abuse, as Berkeley does, is ad hominem, as was the first sentence of an introductory philosophy text I once received, which went something like this:

> The subject called philosophy has been seen through different eyes. Some people see philosophy as good, some see it as bad, and still others see it as mysterious. The good view comes from its appreciators; the bad and mysterious views, naturally, come from those who cannot understand it.

But why can't one "understand" philosophy and see it as bad or mysterious? Like Berkeley's, this argument amounts to: "Either agree with me or suffer abuse."

Ways of trying to take the wind out of someone's sails are endless. Some people seem to think that a "Well, she could be *expected* to say that" or a "Just the usual stuff" sufficiently debunks an argument—as if being consistent were somehow the same as being foolish! Pooh-poohing offers a temptingly easy way to dismiss the other side's argument while supplying no reasons yourself. The other side's case will be seen as "utopian," "sensationalizing;" the arguer a "sentimentalist," "bleeding heart." Some people seem to think that calling something "mere" or "only" automatically demolishes it: "You're merely saying that if this park is not funded those trees will be removed." No! The person is not *merely* saying that, the person is *saying* that. The cheater should not be allowed to get away with the trick. And some people seem to think that a view's being profitable to its proponent, or the view's contrary being unprofitable, automatically tells against the view. But, of course, the view is sound or unsound on its own merits or lack thereof, not because its proponent stands to gain or lose. Here is a U.S. senator discussing the Omnibus Crime Bill of a few years back, which provided for, among other things, "no-knock" entry and preventive detention:

> I was surprised to see that the criminal section of the American Bar Association opposed this bill. I asked a shrewd old judge I know why the criminal section of the American Bar Association would be against it. He said, "Don't you know who the criminal section of the American Bar Association are? Those are the guys who defend criminals. If crime goes up by 400 percent, their income goes up 400 percent. They have a vested interest in crime, so naturally, they would oppose that bill."

And here is Gore Vidal in a *Playboy* interview:

> Contrary to his usual billing [William F.] Buckley is not an intellectual; he is an entertainer and self-publicist, and since the far right have practically no one they dare display in public, he has been able to secure a nice niche for himself as a sort of epicene Joe McCarthy.

Neither the senator nor Vidal discusses the opponents' views. Instead both rest content at sniping. While the senator draws a distinct conclusion and Vidal may not, the implication in Vidal's remark is there nevertheless: Don't take Buckley seriously.

Arguing as these men do against a position because its proponents stand to profit is one version of circumstantial ad hominem, that is, of using people's special circumstances to tell against their positions. Since little advantage accrues from the attempt to differentiate circumstantial from abusive ad hominem, let us merely note here that the attempt has been made. In invective, abuse and circumstances usually fuse anyhow, as in the Vidal passage, or as in this letter:

> *Editor*: As much as I enjoyed your article on the Frankfurt political philoso-
> phers, I must say that it is a little hard to take seriously the reasoning of these
> thinkers from Germany, a country notorious for the overelaboration of its
> cathedrals and even more, alas, for its evil ways.

Another form of rebuttal attempts to turn advice against its givers by stating that the givers do not practice what they preach. This has been called *tu quoque*—"and you, too." To parents who caution their offspring against the dangers of using drugs, the standard youthful reply seems to be, "Well, *you* use them too—tobacco, alcohol, tranquilizers, and like that." The reply misses the point. The question is whether the sorts of drugs children take are harmful, not whether the parent, or the Queen of Sheba, uses them. (Sharp readers will have been alerted here, too, to a meaning shift, from "drugs" meaning the socially acceptable ones to "drugs" meaning anything from marijuana to heroin, a shift the legitimacy of which might be worth thinking out.) On a less obvious plane notice not only the "you too" ad hominem in the following but also the author's sneaky bit of well-poisoning:

> Like Socrates 2000 years before, Galileo too was threatened with execution if
> he did not repudiate his own teachings. Socrates held firm and was executed;
> Galileo gave in and was spared. Does Galileo merit moral censure? Since only
> those can criticize Galileo who have chosen as Socrates, we may dispense with
> moral appraisals of Galileo's choice.

It is wrong to believe that a person must be morally pure in order to make moral judgments. Indeed, if one had to be pure, one could never trust one's assessments of one's own moral lapses. Self-reform would be by mechanism or chance, never by design, morally speaking a patent absurdity.

Other undermining attempts aim at a person's inconsistency, using the illusion that someone's present argument is worthless or worth less just because the person formerly took a contrary position. It used to be said of any stand of Bertrand Russell's, "Well, don't worry, next year he'll change his mind on this too," the implication being, don't pay serious attention to Russell's reasons. That he so often changed his mind, however, surely is to Russell's credit, not the opposite. Those reasons, not their author's circumstances, his history of mind-changing, cry out for consideration. However, wavering in the past, back and forth, does in general weaken *testimony*. It shows that the testimony may be less than firmly based. Similarly, having often reversed stands, a political candidate may be shown to be vulnerable to pressure, definitely a consideration in deciding whether he or she merits a vote. In answering an argument, however, neither past change nor past wavering really matters. The argument itself demands attention, not its circumstances, nor those of its author.

Quick Check

A   Match each numbered example below with the appropriate comments from this list: "no argument" (N); "argument basically OK" (OK); "argument inadequate" (I); "authority appeal" (A); "ad hominem" (H); "backhanded authority argument (BH)."

1   "Watch Those Fruit Drinks! Dr. Emilio Pacheco, professor of oral health at Tulare University School of Medicine, warns that fruit drinks are loaded with sugar and little else. 'Two glasses a day,' says Dr. Pacheco, 'and your teeth rot away for a full hour.' "

2   "You miserable, lazy, lying swindler! You snake! You dirty, smelly, cheating, rotten gob of filth!"

3   "This candidate should not be given a high-level security clearance. Her educational credentials are first-rate, true, and she's bright enough and personable. But her lifelong mental instability and flip-flopping from one extreme of the political spectrum to the other means that we should play safe."

4   "People all over America looked at the five leading big screen color TVs. They voted Silver Screen the best picture by more than 2 to 1."

5   " 'Doctors have always known exercise done while lying on the back virtually eliminates strains. Yours is the best exerciser on the market.' Richard Taylor, D.C."

6   "Must Be Right. By a 2 to 1 vote Californians have chosen to permit construction and operation of nuclear plants, making all the more forceful the many arguments that with proper control nuclear energy is safe."

7   "Dominic Pearl, USDA economist, warns that forcing oil company divestiture 'would adversely impact not only at the farm level but all through the economy.' Naturally. That's the USDA talking. If big oil itches, USDA scratches."

8   "Eight out of ten owners of new homes have gas heat."

9   "Of *course* divestiture's a good thing. Look who's against it—Rockefeller, Big Business, all those fat cat politicians from oil states. . . . "

10   "A baby goes through enough trauma just being born. So 1694 hospitals use Piper's Diapers. Shouldn't you?"

Suggested Answers

(1) A, I, or OK; (2) N; (3) OK; (4) A, I; (5) A, I; (6) A, I; (7) H; (8) A, I; (9) BH, H; (10) A, I.

STATISTICS

While not themselves authorities, statistics do resemble authorities in being frequently quoted as gospel, in adding a transfixing air of knowledgeability—and in being misused. If ability to make and handle appeals to authority is important, equally important is ability to do the same with appeals to statistics—"as necessary for efficient citizenship," H. G. Wells once re-

marked, "as the ability to read and write." Whenever making or confronting an appeal of the "statistics show that . . ." sort, good thinkers will be
prepared to ask a number of related questions: "Does it reflect reality?" "Is
it complete?" "Could they have found that out?" "What method did they
use?" "Does it compare the comparable?" "Is it appropriately precise?"
"Are the standards uniform?" "When were the measurements made?" We
will examine these questions in turn, and then consider the arguer's use of
averages and of pictorial devices.

Does It Reflect Reality?   "According to information compiled recently by the U.S. Department of Commerce, more than 7000 Americans have
been killed by lightning in the past 35 years, more than were killed by
floods, tornadoes, and hurricanes." That statistic tells us something worth
knowing. It supplies yardsticks for relating the statistic to other important
facts (floods, tornadoes, hurricanes). It makes a difference. Ways in which
seemingly significant statistics can make *no* difference (or, by misleading,
make a negative difference) almost defy classification. A commercial reports that a product contains 67 percent more PCY-40 than its nearest
competitor, while neglecting to add that PCY-40 does nothing. A flyer lists
a sale item as reduced to a seemingly drastic 60 percent of list price, while
neglecting to add that the store regularly sells the item for 70 percent of list
price. A school district appears officially as 100 percent desegregated, but
because of private schools, redlining, gerrymandering, and prejudicial testing is *de facto* segregated. A country's rate of exchange on its currency, or
its rate on the price of gold, may be quoted to an impressive number of
decimal places, yet the quotation may be nothing more than ceremonial, all
real transactions taking place not at the official rate but at a free-market
rate. Similarly, a country may seem to have a very progressive income tax
structure, with citizens with high incomes being taxed at astronomical rates.
The rates often get quoted (for ye have the rich always with you), but not
the fact that because of loopholes nobody ever pays those astronomical
rates.

Is It Complete?   Most statistics achieve meaninglessness by being incomplete. The information that drivers in their twenties have more accidents than drivers in any other decade-age-group tells us nothing. Even
properly understood, the statistic makes no difference. We cannot tell
whether drivers in their twenties are a safe or an unsafe group until we
know how many drivers there are in that and the other age groups. Half the
truth is zero truth. Always demand completeness.

Most statistics are comparisons. Comparisons have two or more parts.
Demand all parts. Always look for the *base* from which a claim for a difference is made. Statistics like "30 percent more effective," "reduced 60 percent," "down 100 points," "1½ percent interest," and so forth, should trig-

ger an automatic "30 percent more effective *than what*?" "reduced 60 percent *from what*?" "down 100 points *over what time span*?" "1½ percent interest *per what*?" and the like.

Statistics in terms of percentages, rates, or proportions should usually indicate not only the base against which a difference is claimed, they should supply absolute numbers. Informed that "five out of six (or 83.3 percent) of those surveyed said they preferred new whatever-it-is," we would like to be told among other things just how many were surveyed—for all we know it could have been only six. (As one 1930s comic remarked, "Four out of five have pyorrhea, and nine out of ten believe it.") Compare the statistics in the first paragraph of this wire story with those in the following two paragraphs.

Death Rate Dips. Washington (PNS) Information from the National Center for Health Statistics shows that the leading cause of death—heart disease—dropped 4.5 percent from 757,075 deaths in 1973 to 722,550 in 1975.

Of the 15 leading causes of death only three have increased in the same period: the suicide rate increased 5 percent and the murder rate increased 4.1 percent.

Even though the nation's population is growing older, the death rate dipped to 8.9 deaths for every 1000 Americans last year, down from 9.1 the year before and 9.7 in 1968.

The heart statistics are given in both percentages and in absolute numbers. With the addendum that during the period under consideration the population increased about 1 percent, those statistics as reported seem unobjectionable. The statistics in the story's second paragraph are otherwise. If absolute numbers could be supplied before, they should be supplied later too. The incidence of suicide, just to take one example, is many times lower than that of heart disease. So whereas a change of 4.5 percent over two years in the number of heart disease deaths means a difference of 35,000 deaths, a similar percentage change in suicides may be a change of—just guessing—only 1000 deaths. Given transforming religious attitudes and other factors, a change of 1000 suicides nationwide over two years would be insignificant. On the other side of the coin, imagine one of the other afflictions to have an incidence several times that of heart disease. This would increase the absolute number of deaths from the affliction by over 100,000, a national epidemic, even though the percentage increase was about the same as for heart disease. Moral: If you don't include absolute numbers at least include the incidence.

One often sees a related form of incompleteness which does seem to supply absolute numbers as well as percentages. A study may seem newsworthy which compares 10,000 men who used one birth control method for

365 days, with another 10,000 men who used another method over the same time span, the partners of the second group experiencing 50 percent fewer pregnancies than those of the first group. Here we have percentages *and* impressive absolute numbers. But again something vital has been left out. Incidence of pregnancy per year being pretty low, and most modern birth control methods being over 99 percent effective, the score, for all we know, could be: First group, two pregnancies; second group one pregnancy. Such a "difference" could easily be chalked up to chance or experimental error, not to any difference in the two methods: we need to be given the pregnancy figures in absolute numbers.

Could They Have Found That Out?   When confronting any statistic, questions about how the result could have been achieved ought automatically spring to mind. Recently it was authoritatively reported that more than half the money spent on birth control worldwide goes for abortions. That's the kind of statistic likely to stick in people's minds and influence important decisions—which would be a shame. Given the widespread taboos about birth control and abortion, and the very different economics of socialist and third-world societies, the figure can have been no more than only the wildest guess. It should have been presented as a guess.

The unknowable need not be global. An advice-to-the-lovelorn columnist once confessed that the proportion of letters received which were put-ons "runs very consistently about 1 in 4." But is the columnist, an educated, sophisticated city person, never part of the set of advice-to-the-lovelorn letter writers, that reliable a judge of put-ons? The real proportion could easily have been double, or half, the columnist's estimate. Similarly, a statistic like "Only 80 of an estimated 800 rape cases occurring in Sacramento County last year were reported" should arouse immediate suspicion, since the discovering of an unreported rape by the police would be rather exceptional.

On the other hand, one mustn't be too hasty. There may exist ways—good or not—of estimating unreported rapes. Ways sometimes exist of arriving at statistics which might at first seem impossible to obtain. In his lively book *Practical Statistics Simply Explained* (Dover, New York, 1971) Dr. Russell Langley illustrates the point with the statistic that there are 3300 fish in a certain lake. Short of draining the lake, is the statistic impossible to obtain? No; catch, tag, and throw back 100 fish. Return later, catch another hundred, three of which, let's say, turn out to be tagged. So 100 fish are 3 percent of the total (3300). (Comment: In form this is the common estimating technique called double, or sequence, sampling. But isn't its use in Langley's example questionable if the fish population varies significantly in propensity to get caught [which would make the estimate too low] or if the act of tagging the first sample caused those fish to become frightenable or to soon die [which would make the estimate too high]?)

What Method Did They Use?   That chain store which boasted of its less than 1 percent profits staked its plausibility on our forgetting that there is more than one way to arrive at a statistic. Good statistical reporting sketches methodology. It takes little space and leaves strengths and weaknesses open for all to see. The rape estimate, for example, was probably arrived at by plugging last year's reported rapes into a ratio formula. But it would be nice to be told that, and to be filled in a bit on how the formula was obtained. The formula probably came from a study based on personal interviews with a cross section of the general population—with such a traumatic, touchy subject as rape, a most unreliable technique. Ratios based on interviews could underestimate rape incidence severalfold. They might conceivably even overestimate the incidence. Let's face it, the statistic is only a wild guess.

In sketching methodology the following news report goes in the right direction, but not far enough.

> Throwaways Waste Energy. Kansas City (PNS) A study released by the Midwest Research Institute here this week revealed that every time you drink a six-pack of beer you're helping to waste energy equivalent to 1½ pints of gasoline. To get a throwaway container to you takes about 4200 more Btu (a standard measure of energy) than is required for a container which is reused ten times. If the energy equivalent of a gallon of gas is 125,000 Btu, then every one-way container wastes the equivalent of over 4 ounces of gas.

The report sketches where the "1½ pints" comes from, and makes clear for challenge, if necessary, the assumption as to the energy content of gasoline. Unfortunately, it fails to do likewise for "4200 Btu." How did Midwest Research come up with *that*? Does the reporter mean aluminum cans, milk cartons, aspirin bottles, or what? Are the many marginal costs of two-way containers being taken into account? (For example, a trip to a suburban supermarket just to dump off last week's milk, juice, booze, and pop bottles must "chug-a-lug" a good portion of any two-way energy savings.) The thing is, the comparison is *tremendously* complex. Until we have some idea how it was arrived at, any conclusions we base on it must be tentative.

Sketching methodology can answer the question, "How could they have found that out?" Frequently they couldn't have found it out because a method attempts to quantify the unquantifiable. Suppose that we are told that "three out of four surveyed thought that new whatever-it-is gives 50 percent cleaner-smelling wash." Even with absolute numbers specified and a comparison wash supplied, we would need to know much more about methods in order to make sense of the test. Was that wash, as seems probable, evaluated according to the respondents' subjective reactions? If so, it was ridiculous to ask them to estimate a percentage. No olfactory concept, let alone such a vague one as "clean-smelling-ness" can stand a percentage breakdown. Could a nonsubjective olfactory concept be *made* expressible in percentage, somewhat as sound in decibels has been made expressible in percentage? Maybe, just maybe, it could. But in any event just how an osmoscope, an odorometer, would measure "clean-smelling-ness," let alone measure it in percentage, I am not sure. Even if it could, we would then have yet another meaningless, because useless, statistic. For if market research is correct—advertising has indeed made people want their washes to "smell clean." But "smelling clean" is something *people sense* about their washes, not something which some needle does on a machine.

Here is one more example, too silly to resist.

> Sex and Brains. Heidelberg (PNS) Does a correlation exist between a woman's attitude toward sex and her intelligence quotient? M. J. Wunderlos, a physician who has studied more than 400 women, claims that sex is five times more important to intelligent women than to comparable women who are not very intelligent.

Whether or not the silliness is Wunderlos's fault, or the reporter's, the report is clearly nonsense. How could "*five times* more important" be meaningfully measured? And what counts as "sex" (let alone that questionable relation between intelligence quotient and intelligence)?

In addition to sketching methods, reports of statistics ought to identify the source. (The two news stories above are good in this respect.) When it matters, we can then follow a statistic up, checking the document which is its source. And the credentials and reputation of the giver can be evaluated along lines sketched for evaluating authority. (Does Dr. Wunderlos's being a physician seem to place him in a position to make his claims?)

Does It Compare the Comparable?   A statistic which compares the yearly income earned by typical California workers with that earned by their New York State counterparts is probably useful. Although there are differences in cost of living and life-style between New York and California, there are also enough similarities that differences can be taken into account. Compare that comparison, though, with another which one sees every so often, which compares the yearly income earned by typical American workers with the many thousands of dollars less earned by their Russian counterparts, the usual conclusion being that everything's much rosier in the West. Probably it is rosier, but the statistic doesn't show it. Very little of what makes life rosy would be reflected in the paycheck of a worker in a socialist country. For example, do American workers get an apartment for $16 a month, free health care, stable prices, efficient public transportation, cheap football tickets, or freedom from financial worry about old age? In comparing totally different situations the statistic obscures more than it reveals. Even a vast improvement, a statistic reporting not incomes but the relative standards of living of the American and Soviet worker would give only the beginnings of a meaningful comparison. The idea of a standard of living, an index of material consumption, was something cooked up in the West. Socialist countries have different ideals from capitalist countries. Members of socialist societies are supposed to be satisfied if they and their comrades have enough. Therefore, if Russian workers' standards of living turn out to be much lower than those of their American counterparts, one cannot automatically conclude that things are rosier in the West. They may be rosy or not rosy in either place. For instance, is it necessarily better to have two toilets than one? Is it better to have six washers that last five years each, or one that lasts thirty? (Or laundromats in parks, with beer gardens and playgrounds?) Is it better to have two cars in the garage, or no cars in the garage but cheap, efficient public transportation? It depends on so many factors that comparisons still boggle the brain. For example, what is the point of extensive travel if things are rosy around home? Escaping the monotony of one's polluted, unvaried environment may require an $8000 camper, but if the environment close to home is pleasant already, why go any further than the sports complex or greenbelt?

Many statistics report changes. If rises or falls in a statistic are to mean much, the standards before the change and after it must be uniform. The commercial which has the actor frying bread in a quart of such-and-such oil, with the oil after the frying measuring only a tablespoon less, should make us wonder. Did the actor compare room-temperature oil (before) with warm oil (after), which would have expanded? Bearing in mind that a quart of hot oil takes over an hour to cool back to room temperature, let us put cynicism aside and hope that he did not. Before being impressed with a statistic reporting a change, it is good to ask, "Could the change have been due to changed conditions." The "soaring crime rate," to use the cliché, probably is cause for concern. The FBI uniform crime statistics mount steadily. But what proportion of the increase is due to increased crime? Changes in methods of police department funding now give departments incentive to report as much crime as possible. Moreover, the great increase in the number of insurance claims, the trend toward professionalism in local police departments, and other factors have turned the compilation of crime statistics, formerly a casual affair in many places, into something more rigorous. Result: Up go the statistics.

Another example: Alarm about the drop in College Board, Scholastic Aptitude, and other college entrance test scores nationwide has sent parents off blaming teachers, television, or the disintegration of our moral fiber. Before jumping to any such conclusion, however, let us ask, "Are things the same as before?" Assuming that they have really dropped, do the scores really reflect changes in educational quality? Before a responsible positive answer can be given, a number of questions ought to be answered. First, "Might there have been changes in the test instrument?" If the tests have been made harder, or very different, then it becomes risky to compare this year's scores with those of past years. Second, "Are there differences in who is taking the tests?" Social changes could be firing the college ambitions of various groups. If a different segment or a greater proportion of high school graduating classes is taking the tests, the results could be lowered. Third, "Are the graduating classes the same?" There have been fewer high school dropouts recently, which might lower graduating class quality. Fourth, "Has education changed, but not necessarily for the worse?" The drop in scores could reflect the tests being behind the times. If Johnny and Janie can do fewer equations, or can't speak French, or read Shakespeare, maybe they can design a better rocket, or prepare a banquet, or bargain in Swahili. And probably there exist further questions.

Sometimes a change in a statistic reflects only a change in the base from which it is measured. Many indexes, such as that of inflation, are measured from a base year. When things start getting unmanageable (one hesitates to say embarrassing), agencies sometimes change the bases. On this principle, a kind of semantic deflation, the dollar used to be worth a mere 32 cents. Now it's worth much more. (Ain't statistics wonderful?) Another way in which changing bases can shift on the unwary involves the adding and subtracting of percentages. If my earning power goes down 50 percent one year and then up 50 percent the year after, am I back where I was? Then there are the pitfalls of comparing changes from radically different bases. If Zaire, let us say, has a 10 percent annual growth rate and the U.S. maintains a 3 percent growth rate, is the United States being outstripped? Hardly, since in Zaire a new mine and a rail line would probably have a major impact on the economy. In dollar amounts, the United States would be widening the economic gap between the two countries by many billions.

When Were the Measurements Made?   There is no excuse, when they are easily available, for not using the latest figures. At one point during the long Vietnam conflict the Gallup poll showed that those claiming that they desired a total U.S. withdrawal climbed to an astounding 73 percent. Many of those sharing this majority view deceptively continued to use the 73 percent figure even as the country's political climate altered and the peak dropped. Or consider this bit of "news":

> Food Stamps Spur Business. Washington (PNS) A Department of Agriculture study released today reveals that every dollar in food stamps produces $6.22 in new business activity. But Dr. Eldon Lancaster, Department of Agriculture economist, said he did not regard precise figures as of primary importance. "The report compares the situation with a stamp program and without one. Food stamps spur 5 to 6 percent more activity than the same amount of aid given as cash," said Lancaster. The study estimated the "multiplier" effect of food stamps and other aid by using an "input-output study" produced by the Commerce Department in 1967. On that basis, economists calculated the $2.7 billion in 1974 food stamp aid produced $16.8 billion in business activity.

The story seems to broach hot new information. Notice the present tense, and the terms "related today," and "reveals." Actually, no new study was done, unless you want to count as a study the simple plugging of the 1974 budget into that 1967 formula. And that formula's applicability to today's very different economy is surely a matter for conjecture. Similarly, that statistic on unreported rapes last year in Sacramento County was probably achieved by plugging last year's data into a ratio formula developed years ago in a different social climate. Do we have new information? The answer is, "yes and no"; the "no" portion should be recorded along with the "yes."

Besides a "when" question, "where?" may sometimes be appropriate. For example, rape data for Sacramento County obviously would have been gathered in Sacramento County, but where would the ratio formula data have been gathered? If Sacramento County differs from wherever that data came from, the difference could affect the statistic.

Is It Appropriately Precise?   "Precise," we noticed in the last chapter, is one of those words which usually, but not necessarily, commends. Although large numbers of digits or decimal places and fractions of percentage points tend to add authority to statistics, this authority may be nothing but illusion. Compare these sentences, which appear back-to-back in the *Guinness Book of World Records* (Sterling, New York, 1972):

> There were an estimated 1,678,815 Smiths in the United States in 1964. There are, however, estimated to be 1,600,000 persons in Britain with M', Mc, or Mac (Gaelic "son of") as part of their surnames.

Are U.S. census takers superior to Britain's? That is not likely. The second statistic but not the first tells it "like it is." No mortal endeavor could possibly count to the last member of anything half as scattered, elusive, and fluctuating as a group of 1,600,000 human beings. Since it may be off by thousands, the "Smiths" estimate would be better expressed as "an estimated 1,679,000," "an estimated 1,680,000," or "over a million and a half."

("Over" would be legitimate here, though frequently it is used merely to make us react more strongly, as in "over 90 percent popularity" where the actual figure was 90.3 percent—that .3 percent expressing a tolerance too fine for the method to measure.)

Think of the adverse conditions under which data get collected: on battlefields from exhausted, partisan personnel under fire; in barrios where experience has taught a distrust of outsiders; at the frontiers of perception from subjects unused to reporting such experiences; from documents submitted by respondents with everything to gain by one result and everything to lose by another. If data are crude, then the statistics which rest on that data must be crude. Otherwise, ignorance will have been dressed up as knowledge. Some of the data processing profession's saner members employ a phrase which expresses a fact which those who use computer data, or any statistic, ought to etch on their consciousness: "Garbage in, garbage out!"

Mark Twain once solemnly reported the Mississippi River to be something like one hundred million and three years old. It turned out that three years previous Twain had learned the river to be a hundred million years old, proving that any fool can add. Twain's report was, of course, tongue in cheek. Unemployment statistics (just to take an example of a type) are never given tongue in cheek. A stock market surge, headlines like "Unemployment Down," and all sorts of political credit taking typically follow as small a drop as 10,000 or .2 percent in the unemployment rate. Yet people familiar with the way employment statistics are collected and computed agree that changes of at least hundreds of thousands, let alone a mere 10,000, are even in doubt. For one thing, those percentages result from samples—very large samples, yes, but on statistical grounds alone even large samples yield data falling within a plus-or-minus range. (More about this in the next chapter.) For another, the statistic never claimed to reflect those actually out of work (a value which would be hard to measure), but only to reflect those actively seeking work and failing to get it. Just sample the uncertainties. Hard times can depress unknown masses of people into not looking for work. (Result: unemployment would go "down"!) At the same time hard times can stimulate new job-seeking segments of those unknown tens of millions outside the many occupations not reflected in employment statistics—small farming, homemaking, jack-of-all-trades, being self-employed, etc. (Result: Unemployment would go "up.") Almost all indexes are good for showing long-term trends but are not worth much over the short haul. Watch that "typical market basket of groceries" which the network said went up 2 percent last month. Is the cost of groceries up 2 percent? Maybe, but watching the way that basket gets filled ought to make you wonder. Here it is September, let's say, and because they bought fresh peaches last month, they buy fresh peaches this month. Because they bought no turkey last month, they buy no turkey this month, even though turkey is on sale. No wise shopper would shop out of season or pass up a good special. But to get continuity from month to month the network must. Result: Valuable data, but data which cannot really stand tolerances of a couple of percentage points.

Significant Figures   The physical sciences employ a system which other disciplines would do well to adapt, the system of *significant figures*. In that system any expression of a measurement also states the degree of precision with which the measurement was made. The number of significant figures in an expression is determined by its number of digits or zeroes, not counting zeroes not preceded by a digit. Thus "7.25 grams" and ".00725 kilograms," each containing three significant figures, would be identically precise. Imagine measuring the edge thickness at point p of an iron plate under standard conditions using a micrometer caliper. Although the caliper is calibrated to read thousandths of a centimeter, the measurement turns out, let's say, to be exactly three centimeters. Now since this sort of micrometer has been determined to be accurate to the nearest .001 centimeter, we know the measurement to be between 2.9995 and 3.0005 centimeters. We would express it not as "3cm," not as "3.000000 cm," but as "3.000 cm"—not as one, or seven, but four significant figures. The thickness of the same plate measured with a meter stick, accurate to the nearest tenth of a centimeter, would be "3.0 cm," that is, between 2.95 and 3.05 cm, two significant figures. We report no more, and no less, than we know.

When scientists join measured data with constants, they preserve the proper accuracy and avoid useless computation by making the item of data containing the fewest significant figures the index of the number of significant figures in the result. What is the volume of a cylinder with an .80 cm radius which is 14.2 cm high? Since our least accurate measurement is to two significant figures, there would be no point in using the 3.1416 value of pi in computing the volume; 3.14 will do fine (one extra digit being retained in order to avoid magnifying an otherwise insignificant error). So we have $3.14 \times 0.80 \times 0.80 \times 14.2$. But we do *not* get "28.53632 cc," we get "28.5 cc."

When computations and measurements are speculative and rough, use of precision ought to be rough too. Those who think that digits add dignity would do well to consider this snippet of thinking-out-loud which occurred during a conversation with a renowned nuclear physicist:

> Let's see, it's easier to move something short than something long, so let's try a 5½-inch projectile. Pi r squared times the length times 2.54 times 19 is about 10 to the fourth. 10 to the fourth divided by 60 times 13.3 is 12½. The square root of 12½ is 3½. Yeah! Pretty nifty, a gun-type fission bomb.

Readers with training in the physical sciences will recognize the procedure to be entirely typical. The physicist has not bogged himself down in useless, meaningless detail but has extracted the essence of each figure.

Averages   An American family's income, the annual date of the last frost in Walla Walla, the price of consumer goods this month, the air quality in Sheboygan, high tide at Malibu, a conglomerate's profits—all such data are likely to be found as averages. Like all classes of statistics, averages have their uses and abuses. Knowing very little about the opponent's upcoming batting order we would probably go with our fastballing relief pitcher with the best earned run average. On the other hand, knowing that two of the next three batters can't do much with breaking stuff, we would be wise to disregard earned run averages and to go with our reliever who has a higher earned run average but who possesses a deadly curve. When we need to emphasize similarity or speak generally, when we want to lump together or sum up, or when we don't know details, averages provide valuable tools. However, when we need to get at details, point up differences, map distribution, or emphasize extremes, the average can prove more hindrance than help.

Many people think that averages are arrived at in only one way: take the measured value of a number of items and divide by the number of items. Thus, if the total personal income of the 111,000 citizens of the Republic of Bananonia last year was $400 million, divide $400 million by 111,000 to get an average income of just over $3600 a year. Such an average is called the *arithmetical mean*. Now given Bananonia's low cost of living, for $3600 one could live royally. The mean makes Bananonian economic conditions look pretty good. But instead of an average, a lumping statistic, let us consider a more *distributing* statistic, the following breakdown:

Republic of Bananonia, 1976 Personal Incomes

Income, dollars	Number of individuals	Total dollars
100–200	100,000	15,000,000
200–1000	10,000	6,000,000
1000–10,000	0	0
10,000–100,000	0	0
Over 100,000	1000	379,000,000
Total	111,000	400,000,000

Compared to the mean, the breakdown tells much more. When given information only in terms of an arithmetical mean, automatically ask, "What is the spread around the mean?" If there is much of a spread, as with Bananonian personal income, the mean usually proves to be of little value. Yet suppose that we do want to comment on the lot of the average wage earner in Bananonia? Besides the arithmetical mean there are at least a half-dozen other widely used ways to calculate averages, each with its own strengths and weaknesses. Since our spread around the mean is so great, and since so many Bananonians earn less than $200 a year, a *mode* income in this case would express what we want. The mode is simply the most frequently occurring value or range of values. We could say, therefore, using the mode, that the average Bananonian wage earner makes only $100 to $200 a year. (Or we might take the mean of the mode category, using its $15,000,000 total, and say that he or she makes around $150 a year.) Another good expression of the average here would be the *median*, that figure falling between an equal number of higher and lower figures. If we had a breakdown of every Bananonian's income we would choose that income with about 55,000 incomes above and an equal number below. Given Bananonia's medieval economy, the median and the mode are going to be pretty close. Were there a somewhat more progressive spread, the median would fall somewhat above the mode. To make himself look good, Bananonia's generalissimo would probably express the country's personal income picture in terms of the mean, while Bananonia's revolutionaries would undoubtedly seize on the mode and the distribution—or at least its upper and lower extremes.

Our generalizing tendency inclines us to assume that values are going to distribute evenly and closely around the mean. This tendency needs to be resisted. To sweeten the case for buying one of the popular makes of automobile more than one firm has tried quoting, for example, the statistic that nine out of ten cars of this make registered in the United States in the last eleven years are still on the road. If this sounds impressive it shouldn't. Given the sales records of these makes, with most vehicles having been sold in the most recent several years, it was probably also true that something like nine out of ten cars of these makes registered in the United States in the last eleven *thousand* years were still on the road. The median age was about two years. In other words, as regards durability, the statistic is virtually meaningless.

Pictured Statistics   Without graphs and charts we would be worse off. Not only do well-constructed pictorial statistics accomplish visually what written or spoken statistics accomplish verbally, for tricky masses of data they accomplish if better. Just imagine your favorite television news anchorman rattling off last month's closing stock averages. A thousand words could not begin to equal the picture we get simply from glancing for a few seconds at a saw-toothed graph.

Like verbal statistics, pictured statistics should tell the whole truth— not only in what they actually state but also in the impression they leave. If the casual hearer or viewer comes away angry, or relieved, or saying "Wow," then the facts which the statistics present should have merited those reactions. And if verbal statistics are tricky, pictured ones are more so: a misleading picture may be worth 10,000 misleading words.

Perhaps the commonest pictorial statistic is the familiar two-axis graph, consisting of a vertically ascending linear scale and a rightward-extending horizontal linear scale. The velocity of a rocket, a dieter's weight loss, last year's traffic fatality picture—such data plot nicely against time on such a graph. Science students can actually *see* the equation by which velocity increases. Dieters can understand why next month's pound-shedding will be smaller. Legislators can appreciate the effects of their mandating three-day summer weekends.

The evolution of any viable species, however, inevitably fosters the evolution of parasites. If a graph looks "flat" because the trail of values marked across it does not rise or fall rapidly enough, the sensationalizing chartist simply compresses the horizontal axis, and *voilà*, what looked flat now looks steep, even though the graph reports precisely the same data. The same "miracle" may be performed not by compressing the horizontal axis but by expanding the vertical axis. And compressing the one while expanding the other phenomenalizes the lackluster even more. Of course, not all data are lackluster. Some of it may be embarrassingly spectacular, and to minimize its impact, graphing gremlins would not hesitate to "flatten" the data by applying the above techniques in reverse. Now although no person who has cultivated the habit of reading graph axes carefully and learning to ignore angles of slopes is going to be influenced one whit, enough people may be sufficiently impressed to make a difference. Moral: Cultivate those habits.

If one does not read its axes, one is better off not looking at a graph at all. Another practice is to amputate the vertical scale at top, or bottom, or both, surgery which when fairly performed focuses attention on change, but which when unfairly performed sensationalizes by magnifying rises and falls. A graph on an edition of the evening news presented the recent employment picture by means of a scale on which the fluctuation occupied nearly half of the graph's vertical dimension. A close look at the vertical scale revealed that entire scale was cropped at both top and bottom to express a range of only four percentage points.

Sometimes graph scales are not linear but logarithmic. On the most frequently encountered sort of logarithmic chart, doubling the height squares the value—twice as high as 5 is 25, twice as high as 10 is 100, and so forth. On the linear chart the velocity of that science student's rocket will show up as an ascending curve. This could be misinterpreted as an improving rate of performance. Actually, the rocket's rate of change of velocity, its acceleration, will probably be constant. A logarithmic scale will express this as an ascending straight line. And, since that rate of change is not changing, as the hastily read linear scale might lead us to believe, the logarithmic scale expresses it better. Logarithmic scales are also good for comparing rates which fluctuate from very different absolute bases. Suppose that we want to compare enrollment fluctuation of a tiny liberal arts college with that of hundred-times larger Michigan State University. Any chart on which Michigan State's absolute numbers appeared would make the small college's fluctuations microscopic, yet the rates of growth or decline for the small college may equal or exceed those for the larger school. Logarithmic scales accommodate such vast differences. Again, there is no substitute for reading chart axes, and, with logarithmic charts, for also demanding further statistics expressed in absolute numbers.

Graphic distortion is really a form of equivocating, usually on relative terms. Bases of comparison, whether deliberately or not, get shifted. Not all graphic equivocations, however, are on relative terms. The pictograph, the device which presents data by means of little pictures, can be simply ambiguous. Imagine a device which attempts to document the steady rise in American yearly per capita liquor consumption since Prohibition by depicting a series of increasingly large bottles, one at each regular interval along a horizontal axis. The ambiguity should be apparent: Are we to compare the bottles' relative heights, their relative areas, or their relative volumes? Our tendency to underestimate increases in area resulting from increases in height and width, compounded by our tendency to underestimate volume increases resulting from increases in area, causes the "bigger bottle" technique used here psychologically to underplay the rise in consumption. If the bottles' gallonage were labeled, we could interpret the graph correctly, but in such a case what, then, except confusion, does expressing the data pictographically really add?

Constructing nonmisleading pictographs is not easy. Contrast the "bigger bottle" device with a device which depicts the liquor consumption data by means of one of the familiar five-gallon water cooler jugs placed at each interval along the time axis, with the 1934 jug being one-tenth full to represent the half-gallon consumption for that year, and with the more recent jugs showing a progressively increasing consumption to the nearly half-full level of the present. Although this device improves on the "bigger bottle" technique, it will still mislead many people. Since water bottles, not liquor bottles were pictured, some people will come away unclear that liquor consumption has been represented. Still others, not without a certain logic, will have noticed the bottles' empty portions and concluded that people are drinking less! Pictographs, in other words, must accommodate the world's optimists *and* its pessimists. If one insists on a pictograph for our liquor statistics, probably the best technique would be increasing numbers of little fifth-of-a-gallon liquor bottles at each station along the graph's horizontal axis together with, of course, a verbal experssion of the gallonage for that year.

Quick Check

A   In a short phrase or sentence, say what, if anything, would improve each of the following statistics. For instance, "OK as is," "Give absolute numbers," "Express less precisely," "Needs a base," "Sketch method," or "Change the comparison" can be used.

1   "Nine percent of all dental students are now women, double the percentage of two years ago."
2   "This whiskey is seven years old."
3   "Recent figures on bank concentration show that a 47.95 percent of the country's total bank deposits are in only five states."
4   "Last year the political liberties of 743.2 million persons worldwide declined."
5   "In France it takes from fifteen months to five years to get a new phone installed."
6   "Following Mr. Mintoff's order to British troops to leave Malta, unemployment among the island's population of 320,000 rose by 800 percent, figures showed today."
7   "Two of every three heroin users eventually resort to a violent crime."
8   "Eighty percent of all new homes selling for under $20,000 in 1976 were mobile, the government revealed Saturday."
9   "Sales of vodka have surged by more than 320 percent in the last fifteen years, while bourbon sales have climbed less than 25 percent during the same period."
10   "Yes, ma'm, I'll give you a *real deal* on this new hatchback—$300 off the sticker price."

Suggested Answers

(1) Give absolute numbers; (2) State how measured, state relation (if any) of age to quality; (3) Express "47.95 percent" less precisely e.g., "nearly half"; (4) Define "political liberties," express as guess, or better, nonstatistically; (5) OK as is, though specifying average time would help; (6) Supply absolute numbers and time span; (7) Unknowable—if not, sketch methodology; (8) OK as is; (9) Show absolute numbers; (10) Return the statistic to reality by adding that less than 10 percent of new cars sell for sticker price.

Examples and Comments

A   Explain the strengths and deficiencies of the following arguments and appeals.
1   The mystery, however, has, it seems, been explained. Dr. Dirk Beuningen, author of the best-selling *Visitors* has evidence that the discrepancies were caused by visitors from outer space. A colonel in the Royal Air Force, Dr. Dr. Beuningen, 57, has written over a dozen books, which have been translated into seventeen languages, has lectured widely, and last year was

invited to give the presidential address at the Society of Extraterrestrial Intelligence at the Waldorf Astoria Hotel in New York."

Comment This citation typifies the mistaking of renown for expertise and the acceptance of questionable authority in place of more direct evidence. So concerned is the writer of this piece with Beuningen's questionable credentials, each of which adds nothing to the last, that no space is left for Beuningen's evidence. Being a flyer, popular author, and lecturer is lovely, but since anyone with modest storytelling talent can coast to undeserved prominence on the strength of a potboiler or two, only the testimony of recognized experts in this somewhat eccentric-filled field counts for anything.

2 "Mr. Gregory's arguments against birth control for blacks are fallacious. The reason Mr. Gregory hides behind the 'natural way' is that he is too selfish to care about his children's future and too unsure of his manhood to give his wife any relief from being a baby machine."

Comment This is a typical ad hominem. What never gets discussed is "Mr. Gregory's arguments," which stand or fall on their own merits, and not because Mr. Gregory hides, if he does, behind the "natural way," or isn't sure, if he isn't, of his own manhood (whatever *that* is). Instead of engaging in name-calling, the author of this piece could use the space to assess Gregory's case and to *show* how Gregory's attitude imperils children's future and harms women.

3 "What do doctors recommend for patients in pain? Each year, doctors give over 50 million Med-a-cin tablets to their patients in pain. If doctors think enough about Med-a-cin to dispense all these tablets, what better recommendation can you ask? Med-a-cin for pain."

Comment By repeating the word "doctor" this pitch attempts to exploit the shamanistic awe in which we hold the medical profession. Even if we assume that the dispensers of those millions of tablets are M.D.s, the pitch falls short of providing reasons for using Med-a-cin. First, although 50 million may seem impressive, don't forget that that's only the number of tablets dispensed, not the number of dispensers, which could be only a small fraction of doctors, the rest preferring something else or nothing.

Second, although widespread physician recommendation may indicate that Med-a-cin is not harmful in some cases, it by no means indicates that Med-a-cin is not harmful in *your* case. That elderly arthritis sufferers, say, got 50 million Med-a-cins does not mean that a sufferer of recurrent gastrointestinal pain or of chronic headaches should be taking Med-a-cins. They may be downright harmful, and in this respect the ad seems particularly blameworthy.

Third, and closest to the topic of authority, we have here a phenomenon encountered occasionally—the citing of something as showing expertise which does not really test that expertise. Their handing out those pills does not really test the M.D.s' authority. The two billion pills annually distributed gratis to the medical profession are given away by doctors because that *type* is indicated, and drug firms have insured that their specific brand happens to be at hand. If Med-a-cin, which costs double what aspirin costs, is available as a free sample, why not give it out rather than aspirin? Unfortunately such a practice usually leaves the false impression that the specific brand has been recommended.

4   "My advice, Mrs. Sanchez, is, see that your son becomes a good carpenter or mechanic—one of the trades. And they pay very well. You may think he's smart, and he is a nice boy, we all agree, but his ETS and IQ scores show that he's not really cut out for college."

Comment   About the chances of young Sanchez's succeeding in college, this counselor may well be right. IQ and ETS scores do correlate, though not overwhelmingly, with success or failure in college. This should not be surprising, since the class which designs the tests, the white middle class, also staffs the colleges. It is wrong, however, to accept such test results as gospel, and especially wrong in a case like the present one. Young Sanchez, I am imagining, is not of the white middle class. If he comes from a Spanish-speaking family, or has gone to slum schools, his test results may be low even though his intelligence and abilities are high. Young Sanchez may still have trouble in college overcoming cultural "handicaps," but if he's reasonably bright there is no inherent reason why he should not succeed. The ridiculous awe in which test results are held should not prevent society from giving him every chance.

5   "Liberty Declines. Freedom House, an institution founded in honor of the late Wendell Wilkie, reports that only 19.8 percent of the world's population now lives in freedom. About 35.3 percent are partly free and 44.9 percent not free, the report said. Ranking countries on a 1 to 7 freedom scale, it rated the United States, Britain, France, and West Germany as 1. Sweden and Israel were rated as 2, South Korea as 5, Egypt as 6, and the U.S.S.R. and Korea as 7."

6   "The criticism, however, cuts deeper than that: it alleges that Toynbee's method is fundamentally analogical, and his analogies are fundamentally unsound, because they cannot be put to the test. To this, of course, Toynbee does not plead guilty, for he cannot, without repudiating the work of a lifetime." (D. H. Fischer, *Historians' Fallacies: Toward a Logic of Historical Thought*, Harper & Row, New York, 1970, p. 255.)

7   "What the experts say: 'Doctors have always known, exercise done while lying on the back virtually eliminates strains while slimming and reshaping the body. Yours is the finest Reducing Exerciser program on the market.' Richard Taylor, B.D., D.C." (Advertisement.)

8   "Can a machine take a tender look at your finances? You bet it can. Just give your Cosmopolitan agent a few up-to-date facts. Then he feeds these to

Cosmopolitan's giant computer, housed at our headquarters in Connecticut. The computer, with its vast store of information, calculates the best insurance program to fit your budget and goals."

9 "Silver Screen Draws Record Crowds. New York (PNS) More Americans have become moviegoers than ever before, according to *Variety*. The paper reported that U.S. box office receipts were in the range of $1.8 billion to $1.9 billion—up 7½ percent from the take the year before."

10 "The new Deauville. Sunbelt Airlines senior vice president for maintenance operations, Dwayne Kniffel, thinks its engineering integrity makes it the best luxury car he has ever driven. 'My life is devoted to reliability in aircraft, and I want the same thing in a car. Deauville delivers.' "

11 "Greek Tourism Up. Athens (PNS) Greece earned $383 million in receipts from tourism during the first eight months of last year, the National Tourist Organization reported. This figure marked an increase of 23.2 percent in earnings from tourism over the previous year."

12 "Safety Features Work. Since the safety hoopla started by Ralph Nader in the 1960s began being translated into concrete safety features by Detroit, the rate of highway death has dropped from 5.3 per 100 million vehicle miles to 3.4 per 100 million vehicle miles. So says Vernon Ford, head of Citizens for Safety Action. Part of the decrease, said Ford, is due to the lower speed limit. The rest is due to safer automobiles."

B Comment on the following statistics, taking the approach most likeley to unmask deficiencies.

1 "The mercury content of the hair of Shoichi Yokoi has increased fourfold since he returned to Japan from Guam last February."

Comment It is difficult to say whether Yokoi has gotten polluted with mercury or not, since the base in relation to which the increase occurred is not reported—four times an insignificant amount is still likely to be insignificant. For all we know, Yokoi could have become mercury *deficient* in Guam. Absolute amounts need to be given. We need to know something about the normal mercury content and its normal fluctuation.

2 "PKW's expertly engineered engine is up to 28 percent quieter."

Comment Incomplete. Quieter than what, a Mack truck? Not only does the comparison need to be anchored, "quieter" needs explanation. How is "quieter" measured: inside the passenger compartment, under the hood, by noticed noise, by decibels, or what? And especially, don't neglect that "up to."

3 "Boasting a diameter of 3.36 meters, the crater measures 10.5504 meters in circumference, the largest ever recorded for a meteorite of this type."

Comment Obviously the result of multiplying 3.36 by 3.14, the 10.5504 figure is ridiculously expressed. Even 3.36 is suspicious, a meteor crater being most irregular in dimensions. Even a mean diameter would be difficult to calculate. "About 3.3 meters" probably would tell us all we need to know.

4 "Cases of sickle-cell anemia have doubled in the last decade."

Comment Doubled from what base? The total number of cases, or the number of cases per thousand population, needs to be known in order to estimate whether the increase is significant. What makes the statistic less than useful is the disease's recent rise in public attention. Formerly little known or studied because of racism, sickle-cell anemia has only recently leapt to prominence. Increased awareness, increased presentation, increased diagnosis: up go the statistics.

5 "Some people think trucks are unsafe. But did you know that only 12 percent of the trucks on the road have ever been involved in an accident?"

Comment 12 percent is low!? Since "safe" here is a conclusion we are supposed to draw about the whole industry, we need to know, especially about not only the trucks *on* the road but also those *off* the road—those which have been totaled. Also, it might be worth following up "involved in an accident." "Safe" implies more. Do trucks block vision, create blinding sheets of water, kick up gravel, etc.?

6 "Accentrin reduces pain up to 40 percent."

7 "An estimated 66.7 percent of all heroin users eventually resort to a violent crime in order to support their habit."

8 "Thoughtful citizens, the Philipses have managed to cut household energy consumption in the past eighteen months by over 30 percent."

9 "The census is least efficient at counting male unmarried, young urban blacks. 'At least 20 percent elude our census takers,' said Edwards."

10 "Doctors prefer the Tristan formula 5 to 1."

11 "And if you are unable to pay by the end of the month, sir, no worry. You will be charged only a low 1½ percent interest on the unpaid balance."

12 "You are 16 times safer here than at home." (Sign, oil refinery.)

13 "Today there are 9,001,112 people who speak Hungarian"

14 "Despite the efforts at pollution control, lung cancer is still on the rise—up 1.5 percent over last year."

15 "83.3 percent of those tested prefer Twisties."

16 "The average 'one-pound' loaf we tested weighed only .997 pounds."

17 "We are in the fortunate position of being able to account for virtually all of Egypt's Old Kingdom architectural monuments, and . . ."

18 "Still a Bargain. Before inflation a twelve-course meal in Italy cost $5. Now it's up to $6. Come where your dollar now buys more. Come to Italy." (Advertisement.)

Applications

A By using your experience or doing research, state what backs the following labels or endorsements. (Here, as elsewhere, a pooling approach makes sense. Divide up the job, sharing the information and sources with others.)

"Grade AA"	"Member, Better Business Bureau"
"Made in USA"	"Appellation Beaujolais Supérieur Controlée"
"USDA Choice"	"Class A Cigarettes"
"Top Grain Cowhide"	"Selected Pecans"
"V.S.O.P."	"Recommended, Mobil Travel Guide"
"PG"	"Academy Award Winner"

B List a half dozen or a dozen similar labels. (If short on ideas try your pantry, closets, garage, furniture, etc.) Research what backs the labels.

C Research what one or more of the following mean, how and by whom they are measured, and what controversy or doubt, if any, attends them.

The gross national product
The consumer price index
The Brookings Institution "Riot Index"
The unemployment rate
The EPA mileage ratings
The wholesale price index
The Dow-Jones industrial average

D Collect a number of authority appeals, apparent ad hominems, and statistics from various media sources. Comment on their appropriateness and quality.

E Discuss the following. Are the criteria fair, establishment-entrenching, narrow, well-conceived, or what?

Proponents of unproven methods of cancer management range from ignorant, uneducated, misguided persons to highly educated scientists with advanced degrees who are out of their area of competency. Some proponents hold Ph.D. or M.D. degrees. . . . Certain common features are noted among those with some scientific background or degrees:

They tend to be isolated from established scientific facilities or associates.

They do not use regular channels of communication for reporting scientific information. . . .

They claim that prejudice of organized medicine hinders their efforts.

They are prone to challenge established theories and attack prominent scientists with bitter criticism.

They are quick to cite examples of physicians and scientists of the past who were forced to fight the rigid dogma of their day.

They are often inclined to use complex jargon and unusual phraseology to embellish their writing.

Their records are scanty or nonexistent. . . .

They may use proven drugs or other methods of treatment as adjuvants to the unproven therapy, and if a favorable effect on cancer is shown, claim that it is the result of their unproven remedy.

They may have multiple unusual degrees such as N.D. (Doctor of Naturopathy), Ph.N. (Philosopher of Naturopathy), or Ms.D. (Doctor of Metaphysics). These degrees may have been received from correspondence schools.

Their chief supporters tend to be prominent statesmen, actors, writers, lawyers, even members of state or national legislatures—persons not trained or experienced in the natural history of cancer, the care of patients with cancer, or in scientific methodology. [The American Cancer Society, *Unproven Methods of Cancer Management*, 1976 (quoted in *Harper's*, June 1976, p. 59).]

Generality

This chapter and the following two, "Comparison" and "Cause," bear strong points of contact. This chapter discusses among other things arguments for generalizations. But some generalizations are causal, some are arrived at by analogy, and some arguments which are technically analogical (weather forecasts, market predictions) methodologically resemble causal and generalizing arguments. The three chapters thus form a group, though in addition each handles topics which would be out of place in the others.

A number of blind men, the fable goes, confronted an elephant. One man grabbed the trunk. "Oh, it's a kind of snake." "Not at all," cried a second, who had hold of a leg, "it's rather like a tree." "Nonsense," a third chimed in from behind, "it's like a rope." A fourth maintained that it was like a mountain. These blind men, in *generalizing*, abuse a most useful and familiar instrument. "I eat there every night; it's a very uneven restaurant." "Poll Finds Ford, Carter Neck and Neck." "L.A. is a cultural desert; I've been there." "It's cold," complains a customer after one bite of pizza. "That's the trouble with the niggers," says the bigot, switching channels, "they want to be just like us!" These bits of reasoning claim for *all* something believed known about *some*. In each there is a conclusion ("like a rope," "cultural desert," "cold," etc.) and a basis for it (grabbing the tail, a three-day visit, one bite, etc.). The conclusions are all general statements, not themselves pieces of reasoning but rather the results of reasoning. Before discussing generalizing, this chapter's major topic, let us examine in some detail a topic of equal importance: general statements themselves.

THE LOGIC OF GENERAL STATEMENTS

Traditionally, general statements have been characterized by their outward form, by their containing certain terms in certain slots. As this characterization has advantages it will partly be retained. Principally, however, the classification principle used here is not form but meaning. Not intended to be exhaustive, mutually exclusive, or to carry weight of themselves, the following categories all embody logical points which cause trouble when ignored.

Generalizations   Generalizations are about "all," "no," or the equivalent. ("No" is "all" turned on its head: "All of the residents voted" equals "No resident did not vote." "Jay exhausted every possibility" equals "Jay left no stone unturned.") Generalizations can be either true or false. They are called generalizations even though someone making statements of such forms may not be generalizing. One may be summarizing the results of a head count ("Hyena Patrol all present and accounted for, sir") or elaborating the consequences of a definition ("the sum of the interior angles of any polygon is always 360°").

Generalizations can be factual or definitional. Normally, one generalizes to factual, not to definitional, generalizations. "Abalone are gastropods" and "No U.S. senator's official age is under 25" are not arrived at by counting abalone or caucusing senators, for *part of being* an abalone, or senator, is to be gastropod, or over 25. Both generalizations would be definitional. On the other hand, "Morro Bay abalone today exhibit higher mercury concentration than those tested twenty years ago" and "No U.S. senator has a reported net income of less than $50,000" would be arrived at not by knowing the definitional criteria for being an abalone or a senator, but by sampling abalone or raiding IRS files. Both these generalizations would thus be factual. Like most distinctions, that between factual and definitional generalizations works over only a certain range. Borderline cases abound (sharp readers may have spotted a problem in the head count example), and undoubtedly there exists subject matter in which it is best to throw out the distinction altogether. Nevertheless, awareness of the difference can be useful. (That academy report on poverty mentioned in Chapter 3 actually contained the sentence, "One fact remains clear: the poor do not have enough money.")

Hard Generalizations For convenience let us give the name "hard generalization" to generalizations about each and every, or not one single, member or part of a group or whole. A hard generalization is falsified by one or more counter instances. Thus, someone who maintains that Mary Cassatt never worked in watercolor will have to take back and qualify the generalization if confronted with one or more Cassatt watercolors. Suppose the watercolors all turn out to be early work. The generalizer might then qualify the original remark: "The *mature* Mary Cassatt . . ." Thus qualified, the generalization would still be hard, though with narrowed scope. One late Cassatt watercolor would be enough to upset it. Although by no means infrequent, hard generalizations consitute a smaller proportion of general statements than has sometimes been supposed. Many generalizations outwardly similar to hard generalizations, even couched in the same words, turn out to be less venturesome than a quick examination of their outward form might suggest. Since they are cushioned against one-instance rebuttals, let us call them "soft."

Soft Generalizations In arguing about the public mood Maynard reminds his friend, "Don't forget, Shirley, people today still remember Watergate." Now although Maynard's statement is about individual Americans, it would be irrelevant here for Shirley to object, "But wait, Esther Jones, for one, does not remember." It would also be irrelevant for Shirley to proceed to multiply Esther Joneses unless she could show that they were everywhere. And it would be wrong to conclude from Maynard's statement that every person remembers Watergate. Maynard is talking about the majority of people, about the typical person, not about every single one. This hedge is built into the statement's content and general context. A hyperbolic version—for example, "Don't forget, Shirley, everyone out there still remembers Watergate"—means the same thing. Let me repeat the point in different form. Consider two outwardly identical statements which in differing contexts are not identical at all. Consider the remark, "But wood floats." First, imagine it made in defense of choosing a wooden instead of a cement sailboat. Second, imagine the same remark made in disputing a charge that logging operations wreak havoc on lake-bottom ecology. The context of each remark gives "wood" a different scope. The reply, "But wait, water-saturated wood doesn't float" would fail to rebut the remark about the sailboat. The remark is *not about* water-saturated wood. Nor is it about ironwood or any wood except those varieties out of which sailboats are primarily built. However, the reply *does* rebut the remark about logging operations. In that remark water-saturated logs fall within the scope of "wood"—which there obviously means wood which is the object of operations using lakes for logging ponds. (So ironwood would be irrelevant there too.)

Much everyday reasoning depends on the hardness of hard generalizations. If a guide assures us that all the food in the cache is fit to eat, we conclude that the jerky in the cache is fit to eat. We stake our health on the guide's generalization being unexceptionable. That many generalizations are unexceptionable, however, scarcely means that all are. Mistaking a soft generalization, or any general statement, for a hard generalization, and drawing from it a conclusion warranted by only a hard generalization, would be an oversimplification. When a general statement is improperly *objected to* on the basis of a so-called "exception," which it never was intended to cover, we have the fallacy known as *secundum quid* (or, the whole mouthful, *a dicto secundum quid ad dictum simpliciter*, which can be freely translated as "from a qualified statement to an unqualified one"). If anyone were to think the truth, "Wood floats," false because of ironwood or water-saturated wood, that person would have fallen victim to *secundum quid*. The mistake's mirror image, the improper *application* of a general statement as a hard generalization, would be *a dicto simpliciter ad dictum secundum quid*. This explains one of its usual titles, *dicto simpliciter*. Maynard's concluding that Esther Jones must remember Watergate would thus be a *dicto simpliciter*. For reasons not worth going into, *dicto simpliciter* is sometimes called "the fallacy of accident" and *secundum quid* called "the converse fallacy of accident." But in any case, since there exists no substitute for explaining in plain English, let us not linger over titles, or be tempted to indulge in high-class name-calling, but rather go on to notice further sorts of general statements which sometimes get mistaken for hard generalizations.

Moral Principles   "But that's private property," one man says to another who has asked him to rifle a vending machine. Implicit in this admonishment is the principle that private property is to be respected. How does the principle arise? Certainly not from *generalizing over* instances. If moral principles and their derivatives should be considered as generalizations at all, they are not factual generalizations. If not the result of generalizing, then are they definitional? That category is at least closer. Moral behavior is introduced *together with* moral language and moral principles. The three are inseparable. Learning to wait one's turn in line, for example, is introduced with the idea of waiting one's turn, and vice versa. Children learn the expression "take turns," *and* learn to form lines, *and* learn the value of forming lines all at the same time. So, when adults reprimand someone who has butted in line, complaining, "Considerate persons wait their turn," they in effect *remind* the person: Someone who did not know that considerate persons wait their turn would have less than a complete grasp of what it is to be considerate. In this way moral principles are integral with the whole social fabric. When moral principles get separated from that fabric, they get reduced to formulas. Following formulas blindly and acting morally differ considerably.

To invoke a formula in justifying action which is outside the framework of morality from which the formula is derived would thus be a *dicto simpliciter*. A satirical but definitive example of such pseudo-morality occurs in the movie *Dr. Strangelove*. American bombers have been sent to destroy Russia, but it's all a mistake. Only the President can recall the bombers, by sending them a code word. The one man who knows the code word cannot telephone it to the President for lack of a dime to work the pay phone. After explaining his predicament to a nearby military officer, the man asks the officer to shoot the lock off a vending machine in order to get change. The officer refuses: "I can't do that; that's private property!" This formula (a version of the principle, "Never take what belongs to others") expresses an idea integral to a whole way of life. With understanding the formula goes understanding the *point* of the formula, which has to do with people's welfare and feelings, with avoiding strife, injury, death, and the like. The officer knows the formula but neglects the point of the formula, neglects the principle. His is sheer idiocy, yes, but only because it is so extreme. His refusal bears striking points of contact with the shallowness not infrequently found in those in responsible positions, and with the moral lapses of us all.

Less extreme action making a similar point occurs in Book I of Plato's *Republic*, in which Cephalus, comfortable and conventional, everybody's picture of a nice, old, rich grandfather, gets put on the spot by Socrates, who asks him exactly what he thinks justice is. Cephalus can do no better than repeat the childhood slogan that justice is "to speak the truth and pay your debts." Maybe this is not a bad reply to so devilish a question; after all, what would *you* answer? In any case, Socrates will have none of Cephalus's reply: what, he retorts, if someone lent you a weapon when in his right mind and later in a fit of rage asked for it back? All those present agree that it would not be right to return it then. And so it is agreed that justice cannot be defined as to speak the truth and pay your debts. (Might Socrates himself be guilty here of *secundum quid*?) The exchange does bring out one thing: that formulas fail as a basis for moral action unless they are accompanied by a deeper understanding, an understanding which someone like Cephalus, gentle and good though he may be, supposedly lacks. (Unfortunately, Socrates thinks the sign of understanding is being able to construct a spotless, essentialist definition, something which itself would seem to be in quite the same danger of becoming a slogan. Well, this is not an ethics book.)

Physical Laws   The subject of the logical status of scientific laws, if one may judge from the controversy, is rather difficult, and will receive here only minimal comment. Philosophers of science have sometimes taken the laws of the physical sciences to be factual generalizations. Such laws are, of course, factual, but they differ from factual generalizations. To establish a factual generalization is to recognize that members of a certain class of item (for example, Navajo rugs) have a certain property (for example, wool weft). By sampling the items one then arrives at the conclusion that all, or probably all, or a percentage, of such items also have that property. From the beginning one has a grasp on what counts as a member of the class, and on what counts as the property. One then puts item and property together into a generalization. Arriving at physical laws has not gone this way. With the introduction of basic laws has come a whole conceptual realignment. Rather than, "Look!, all x's are y," we get instead, "*If* you define x this way and y this way and z this way, *then* look at all the data which fall into place!" Rather than a new fact built on old facts, we have a completely new scheme, a new pattern on which to construe facts.

There are further reasons for preferring the "pattern" to the "generalization" reading. Unlike generalizations, scientific laws, once established, are not falsified. Not easily so, at least. Much more sophisticated than the sorts of assertions which can be either simply true or false, scientific laws get evaluated by other criteria—by their range of applicability, by their felicity with other theory, and by the accuracy of the deductions which can be made based upon them. Typically, scientific laws allow great clusters of exceptions, requiring tables of corrections and "fudge" factors. Unlike generalizations, scientific laws do not become falsified by exceptions, or even by pervasive clusters of exceptions, in certain areas of their supposed application. So if physical laws are generalizations at all, they must in their own ways be very "soft" indeed. Like other general statements which are not hard generalizations, scientific laws, too, can be subject to oversimplification and hence to *dicto simpliciter* and its opposite.

Collective Statements   Hard and soft generalizations apply to individual members of the subjects in question. In logical jargon generalizations *distribute*—they apply *distributively*. "No Elks are blacks" applies to each Elk. "All paint produced 1/4/78 passed control" applies to every batch or can. Some general statements, on the other hand, do not distribute, as exemplified by the old joke about the people next door, "your average family," having 2.3 children. What holds for a warehouse of prunes, or the medical profession, or the white race, does not necessarily hold for the individual things of which those classes are composed. No prune weighs 700 tons, no physician is over 2000 years old, and no white person is scattered over the face of the globe.

It is easy to slide into thinking that what holds for the parts of the class must hold for the class as a whole, and vice versa, a slide which needs to be resisted. To argue from a characteristic of the parts of a group to a characteristic of the whole, the group itself, is to commit the fallacy of *composition*.

To argue from a characteristic of a whole, or group, to a characteristic of the parts, or members, commits the fallacy of *division*. (You might find either error referred to as "the fallacy of aggregates.") Each mistake can usually also be seen as a subspecies of equivocation. In composition the term equivocated upon appears in the premises in a distributive sense and in the conclusion in a collective sense. In division a term appearing collectively in the premises appears distributively in the conclusion. Even though candidate A and candidate B may be their party's two strongest candidates it by no means follows automatically that A and B would make the party's strongest ticket. (For example, candidates might uncontrollably hate each other, or the ticket might not balance.) To argue thus would be distributive-collective equivocation on "strongest," or composition. Conversely, even though a state's delegation to a national political convention may be un-committed, this does not mean that the members of the delegation are individually uncommitted. (Which was just what an advertisement did im-ply in an attempt to rebut charges that the front-runner had the nomination sewed up.) This would be collective-distributive equivocation on "uncom-mitted," or division.

Much good reasoning does proceed from parts to whole, and vice ver-sa. From a remark in a book that a certain ship was planked with wood it is obviously right to infer that the ship was a wooden ship. From knowing that a green bathroom wall is composed of large tiles of a certain color, there would be no arguing with the inference that the wall is composed of green tiles. Such inferences, however, are underwritten by additional knowl-edge. We know that ships are classified by the material of their shells. (But notice that a wood-frame house re-sided with aluminum doesn't become an aluminum house.) We know that with the size and optical conditions of a typical bathroom, large surfaces of color x can't be a radically different color than their 16 in^2 components. (They can appear darker, however, or give an entirely different effect than one might imagine when buying the tiles.) And the inference that A and B make the strongest ticket might be perfectly logical—if underwritten by the fact that the candidates cooperate well and that the ticket would balance beautifully. Plenty of reasoning along very similar lines would be faulty. For example, that a ship is riveted entirely with iron implies nothing about the ship being an iron ship. That a bathroom wall in a Sunday supplement layout or pointillist painting is green does not tell us about the colors that make up that wall which, after all, may be of blue and yellow dots. The point is, the *principle* is faulty. And it is when arguing in areas where we lack that specific knowledge to under-write the inference—where we cannot say, "For this subject matter we know that what holds for parts holds for whole," or vice versa—where we are "flying blind"—that we rest on the principle. There we do argue falla-ciously. A Roman historian of philosophy reported the following exchange.

Zeno asked Protagoras, "Tell me, does a single millet seed, or the thousandth part of a seed, make a noise when it falls?" When Protagoras said no, Zeno continued, "Well, does the bushel then make a noise when *it* falls?" When Protagoras said it did, Zeno said: "But then must not the noises stand to one another in the same ratios? For as the sounding bodies are to one another, so must be the sounds they make. Therefore, if the bushel of millet makes a noise, then the single millet seed must also make a noise, and so must the thousandth part of a millet seed."

As this Zeno performs or cites no experiment, his argument rests squarely on the whole-to-parts principle. The argument's fallaciousness should be apparent: what holds for bushel-sized bodies by no means must hold for seed-sized bodies. And we have no knowledge that what holds for seed-sized bodies must hold for thousandth-seed-sized bodies. We do know, of course, that a millet seed will make a noise when it hits, a fact on which the convincingness of the argument relies. ("Noise," don't forget, was always defined then, as it is only sometimes today, by what people hear.) But even here Zeno is flying blind in concluding that the noise it makes will be in proportion to its percentage of the bushel.

One small warning. What looks like composition or division may not be. One should be clear that a distributive-collective or a collective-distributive shift has been made. Compare two brief arguments, equally famous. The first is from Adam Smith's *Wealth of Nations* in support of a free market.

> Each individual will further his own interest to the best of his ability. The result is that all individuals together—the society as a whole—thereby achieve maximum economic advance.

The second argument is from John Stuart Mill's *Utilitarianism* in support of legislating according to the principle of the greatest good for the greatest number.

> Each person's happiness is a good to that person, and the general happiness, therefore, a good to the aggregate of all persons.

Despite the arguments' outward similarity, isn't Smith's argument flawed by composition, but not Mill's? Mill's argument avoids making the distributive-collective move, for what is a happy society ("the aggregate of all persons") but a society consisting of happy individuals? One could not say here, "The society is happy, but its citizens are not." Mill's move is distributive-distributive. In Smith's argument, on the other hand, the distributive-collective move is made. Greater internal activity in a "free" economy may, but does not necessarily, mean "maximum possible economic advancement." To simplify, imagine a three-unit economy, consisting of Number One, Number Two, and Number Three. "Furthering one's own interest" let us call "trying harder." Now in an unregulated economy, trying harder commonly takes the form of attempting to climb over competitors. In trying harder, Number Two may waste resources by trying to wrest economic goodies from Number One and Number Three, who waste resources trying to wrest economic goodies from the others, and so on. The result can be needless duplication, waste, and stifling economic strife. More likely, Number One and Number Two, say, will combine to gang up on Number Three and any potential Number Four. The result would be monopoly, just the opposite of free competition. In fairness to Smith, we should hasten to add that in his time—the first flowering of the Industrial Revolution—when resources and markets awaited exploitation and exploiters were relatively few, his argument would have been more cogent. Nevertheless, as part of a generally applicable economic theory, Smith's reasoning leaves something to be desired.

Statistical Generalizations   A statistical generalization applies a percentage or proportion to a class. From the composition of a college lecture audience of 48 men and 42 women, a campus visitor might generalize that 47 percent of the student body is women. If careful, the visitor might say that the student body "is over half men," or that it "is fairly evenly divided as to sex." Any of these would be statistical generalizations. The projections of public opinion polls are statistical generalizations from percentages found for carefully selected samples.

Unlike hard generalizations, not very many statistical generalizations are distributive. A 60 percent twinning rate in a breed of sheep does not mean that this ewe or that, or this flock or that, has a 60 percent twinning rate. To distribute the twinning rate to the individual flocks or ewes would be division. As probabilities, however, statistical generalizations to some extent do distribute. If the twinning rate is 60 percent then this ewe, or this flock, chosen at random, has a 60 percent *chance* of twinning or of continuing the percentage.

Quick Check

A   Where possible, identify the following as definitional, factual, hard, soft, collective, or statistical.
1   Over 50,000 Vietnam veterans have committed suicide.
2   No apples are left.
3   In 1976, eleven out of thirteen southern states went for Carter.
4   Surprisingly, fully 25 percent of the Whistler prints sold that day went for under $1000.
5   Doctors have known about it for 2500 years.
6   Doctors don't want to make house calls these days.
7   The three-toed sloth actually has five toes.
8   Arsenic is 100 percent effective.

9 Arsenates are salts.

10 Congress has voted itself a pay cut once before.

B Where the following are arguments, label them appropriately, or better, in a phrase or so, pinpoint the trouble, if any.

1 Yes, Johnson'll be tops. He's Princeton '77 and Princeton's tops.

2 More than four of five adult French do not attend mass regularly. But in the village of St. Pierre, fully 80 percent attend mass regularly.

3 Fernand-Vergelesses chronometers are constructed of the finest precision Swiss parts. Fernand-Vergelesses, Switzerland's finest.

4 Look, son, it may be a real gun and it may be loaded, but it's Marie's not yours. Never take what doesn't belong to you, even from a 7-year-old. You march right back out there and give it back!

5 Come down and pick it up. I'm sure it's done. We finished every job in the place.

6 Svenska II has the least frequency-of-repair record of any car in its price range. It's always a bet, of course, but if you shell out the bucks for one, you'll probably find yourself in the shop less often than with a comparable car.

Answers

A (1) not a general statement; (2) factual, hard; (3) statistical; (4) statistical; (5) collective; (6) factual, soft; (7) definitional, a little soft ; (8) hard, factual; (9) hard, definitional; (10) collective.

B (1) division; (2) no argument; (3) composition; (4) *dicto simpliciter*; (5) valid (distributes a hard generalization); (6) valid (randomly distributes a probability).

Having discussed general statements and certain errors which arise from misunderstanding them, let us proceed to the question, "What sorts of *arguments* can be given for them?"

GENERALIZING

To generalize is to be an idiot, said Blake, generalizing. Blake's inconsistency should remind us that generalizing cannot really be avoided. What counts is to generalize intelligently, not idiotically, and to be articulate in assessing the generalizing of others.

In their simplest forms, arguments for generalizations are these:
Head count:

A_1 is b.

.   .   .

.   .   .

.   .   .

A_n is b.

All the A's are A_1 through A_n.

Therefore, all A's are b.

Simple projection:

A_1 is b.

.   .   .

.   .   .

.   .   .

A_n is b.

No A's have been found not-b.

Therefore, all A's are b.

Statistical projection:

A_1 is b.

.   .   .

.   .   .

.   .   .

A_n is not b.

x proportion of A_1 through A_n is b.

Therefore, x proportion of all A's is b.

The subscripted A's represent the items counted and the b's what is found in the items. (The three-dot vertical elipses mean "serially through," and "n" is the last member of a series of whatever length.) Thus, (using a "head count" example), if Supreme Court members (A's) vote "aye" (b) unanimously, the decision will have been recorded by the clerk as "Blackman, 'aye'" (A_1 is b); "Marshall, 'aye'" (A_2 is b) and so forth, clear through to the ninth justice (A_9 is b). And since there are no members other than the nine counted, the decision will be recorded in the generalization, "All A's are b" or "Unanimous."

Unlike the head count, simple and statistical projections *project*, from a number of A's known to be not, or not known to be, all of the A's. In order to avoid an expensive and perhaps dangerous delousing of a half-million refugees, a clinician would be wise to examine a small number of refugees first, fifty A's, let us say, deciding since they all are louse-free (b), that the rest of the refugees are likewise. This would be simple projection. It is unlikely that all such refugees examined would be louse-free. Uniformity of result being relatively uncommon, statistical induction in practice proves the more useful. Were the clinician to discover lice in, say, six of fifty, by projecting the 12 percent figure to the whole refugee population the clinician might then be able to decide that a delousing was or was not warranted.

Are simple and statistical projections adequate? The question is misleading. When compared against the head count, they look unconvincing. We think of all those unexamined A's. Reckoning projections a poor second to the head count, however, would be no more fair than reckoning a radar image of an oil tanker a poor second to a full daylight view. Admittedly, constructing ships from blips is in form and detail a poor second, yet form and detail at night or in fog are hardly the point. Like radar, simple and statistical projections frequently provide exact and powerful—and the only—tools for getting the job done. This point deserves elaboration.

The Power of Projection   Although it is sometimes maintained that only the head count is truly accurate, in many cases a head count or high-proportion enumeration may involve a much bigger "leap of faith" than a good projection. Methods which project may be superior. Sometimes the group in question will be in such flux that head-counting would be fruitless. By the time the enumeration was "complete," members would have been added to the group while others would have ceased to exist. In other cases, as with large populations of wildlife, to get the items to hold still long enough to count, or to distinguish among them, may prove impossible. Methods which project, on the other hand, can assess such groups quickly. Furthermore, several quick projections taken in the interval it would have taken for a head count (assuming one is possible at all) can reveal the rate and character of change, something which a single head count cannot do.

There exist other ways in which projections can be superior to complete or high-proportion enumerations. Frequently the counting process itself interferes with the group counted, so as to make complete or high-proportion counting futile, as when the testing process ruins or alters a product. (Think of shotgun shells, cans of tuna, photographic film, etc.) Related to this difficulty is that in which the counting would call attention to itself in such a way as to affect its own results. A poll of 1500 American voters which consists of simple questions on current events typically uncovers considerable ignorance. A sample of *all* American voters, or half of them, on the same topic would prove nothing more about how informed the American voter is than would a well-chosen sample of 1500. It would prove less. The very act of contacting millions of voters would necessarily call such attention to itself, and take so long, that the group being surveyed would change. Knowing that they were going to be asked, an unknown number of voters would begin paying an unknown amount of attention to current events. In similar fashion, overly large surveys would interfere with their own results by scaring off portions of populations (think of bird-banding, or the census) or by attracting atypical samples. (Think of surveys consisting of paid interviews or free groceries, or which involve counting techniques that attract the curious or the thrillseeker.) Furthermore, insisting on a head count would quite destroy the point of conducting any preliminary estimate. To forecast the tonnage of a finished product before processing may be important, but not if the procedure involves processing all the product. One could not speak of an estimate or a forecast here at all.

Therefore, to the point is not the question, "Is induction any good?" but the question, "When is and when isn't induction any good?" The art of induction, of making intelligent projections, is called *sampling*.

SAMPLING SAMPLING

The goal of sampling is to obtain a *representative* sample, one which contains proportionally all relevant characteristics of the class projected to. An unrepresentative sample is said to be *biased*. The class projected to (and, we hope, sampled from) is called the *universe, parent group*, or *population*. The sections which follow discuss phases of the topic of obtaining representative samples, a trickier business than it might at first appear to be.

Randomizing   Sometimes a representative sample can be obtained by making a *simple random* or *probability sample*, one in which each member of the parent group has an equal chance of being selected. "Random" here means something quite other than arbitrary or haphazard. Randomizing is one art in which intuition and common sense have been trick players. What seems random may not be so at all. To choose a student to answer a classroom question I closed my eyes and whirled round and round, my finger stuck out as pointer. The student on whom the pointer fell was asked, "Was that procedure random?" The student said yes. The class agreed. They were wrong. In order that the whirler's pointing ends up somewhere in the class and not in the direction of the blackboard opposite it, the whirler aims for the middle of the class. And we have no way of knowing whether whirler miscalculation would distribute evenly throughout the class. The whirler might consistently over- or undershoot, or hit the middle every time. Furthermore, this whirling technique produces bias in favor of students in the front row, who not only block their fellow students behind but loom large in the foreground.

Where bias comes from sometimes surprises even the experienced. Despite the infinite care which went into contructing the draft lottery used in the early 1970s, statistical experts were able to criticize the procedure. For although the samplers stirred the lots lots, apparently they did not stir them enough to distribute the various birth dates evenly. In order to avoid bias the statistically sophisticated rely on mindless means—coin-flipping, card-drawing, or more professionally, published tables of random numbers. Such tables, some of which fill multiple volumes, are derived and tested by computer. A typical simple random selection might proceed as follows: Imagine that a rancher wants to determine the tonnage of his almond crop. Having numbered consecutively his 9600 trees, he could employ a table of random numbers, a randomly chosen fragment which looks like this.[1]

---

[1] Des Raja, *The Design of Sample Surveys*, McGraw-Hill, New York, 1972, p. 364.

13	70	43	69	38	81	87	42	12	20	41	15	76	96	85
26	99	82	78	99	05	22	99	52	32	80	91	38	51	09
72	53	95	81	07	98	14	74	52	58	73	10	40	91	90
22	08	08	68	37	16	36	62	20	02	35	98	44	53	23
21	61	90	53	85	72	86	94	87	18	50	11	31	25	22
47	38	55	66	50	96	96	78	34	45	52	78	34	35	20
96	68	13	07	31	29	70	09	16	66	81	09	36	12	17
45	92	93	44	87	72	26	75	82	31	72	69	25	51	40
51	99	50	88	62	54	90	51	01	39	18	70	17	20	75
32	31	32	26	03	55	74	15	28	81	04	55	20	72	79
67	62	30	02	88	17	37	25	42	86	00	32	75	57	37
03	08	89	77	12	41	15	25	52	30	93	11	12	47	35
45	10	04	66	94	70	33	74	97	23	40	97	73	67	55
62	48	46	97	04	36	31	27	29	84	85	35	16	02	29
59	59	33	63	53	43	60	30	15	81	67	59	48	98	13

The sampler would select, say, twenty multiples of four digits by proceeding in any direction from a randomly selected point and discarding any multiples over 9600 and also any repeated multiples. (This would be sampling without replacement.) The sampler might start by dropping a pencil casually on the table. Let us say the pencil just happened to fall with its tip pointing a bit up from and to the left of the 09 in the next-to-top pair of digits in the table's right column. The sample could proceed according to this scheme: "Read from right to left, going to the line above when having come to the end of a row, and going to the lower right of the preceding page of the table when having exhausted all rows. The rancher would thus choose trees number 9015, 8319, 0823 and so forth. (The pencil ritual insures, among other things, that one is not beginning from a favorite number.) The trees bearing these twenty numbers could then be harvested, their crop weighed, and this result multiplied by 480.

"Random," like "large," or "washes whiter," is relative. As the question, "Washes whiter than what?" should hop immediately to mind, so should the question, "Random with respect to what parent group?" In the almond example the parent group might be different than a parent group used on the same ranch to make irrigation or spraying checks. The subject being the almond crop, the question should be, "Are all 9600 trees all the producers of the crop?" There exist all sorts of ways a sample may turn out to be not part of its parent group. At one university the same freshman English final exam was to be given to several thousand students. To test the exam it was given a week early to a small, random number of students, each pledged to secrecy. One result was that the exam seemed too difficult, and only the objections of absolutist professors kept it from being made easier. When given to the parent group, however, the exam produced normal results. Apparently, the sample students had not had enough warning. Indeed, given the study habits of the average freshman, the extra week of study time could easily account for the improvement: the sample (with x weeks of study time) was not part of the parent group (with $x+1$ weeks). Election pollsters face an analogous difficulty. The parent group from which they would like to sample (those who actually cast ballots) is an unknown quantity. Those polled of course say that they have registered and intend to vote, but it is by no means certain which of them really do vote. Pollsters also confront time difficulties similar to those faced by the almond-crop and examination samplers, in that changes can occur in the parent group between the sampling time and the time of the event projected to—yet another argument for small, manageable samples which can be taken as near to the event as possible.

As noticed above, one source of sampling bias can be sampling itself. The rancher who selected numbers for the trees from which to estimate the total crop was prepared to discard repeated numbers. Such a procedure, called sampling *without replacement*. In some circumstances sampling without replacement significantly affects the parent group. A jack being drawn from an ordinary deck of cards and not replaced obviously decreases the odds of drawing another jack. Replacing the jack in the deck for each draw obviously makes the chances of drawing a jack on the second draw identical to those of the first. Techniques in which the selected items are thrown back into the pot for possible reselection is called sampling *with replacement*.

Failure to distinguish between sampling with and sampling without replacement may account for the psychological trick called the "gambler's," or "Monte Carlo," fallacy, in which the victim imagines that each successive loss increases the chances of a win on the next round. The gambler probably proceeds by a kind of vague analogy. He or she subconsciously imagines that because in cards and similar games where loss and nonreplacement increase the odds in favor of the bettor on the next round, so in games *with* replacement, a loss will likewise increase the odds.

Stratifying   In the almond case the simple random sample of twenty trees might be sufficiently precise only if the trees did not vary greatly in yield. A disproportionate number of very low-yielding or very high-yielding trees in the sample could throw the results off considerably. To minimize such a possibility one could *stratify* the sample. A stratified random sample can be taken wherever variations in the parent group are familiar and known to affect the result. Suppose of that rancher's 9600 trees that 1000 are young trees, 600 more are in an area with poor drainage, another 1800 are recovering from a blight, and the rest are relatively uniform in age, condition, and past productivity. Since the basis of each grouping is known to affect production, each grouping provides a stratum from which to draw a random sample. The four samples might be made equal in size for each stratum and then weighted to reflect their stratum's percentage of the parent group, or the samples might be made to differ in size according to such a percentage. Some public opinion polls are stratified samples. Pollsters sample so many urbanites, so many senior citizens, so many farmers, so many men and women, and so on since samples with many strata lower the odds that large variations will occur.

Other Varying Techniques   There exist numerous other methods for varying the instances, each suited to its own subject matter and to the degree of precision desired. Only a few can be discussed here. *Systematic sampling*, for which a better name would be *interval sampling*, selects every third, or three-hundreth item, beginning at a randomly selected starting point. Used intelligently, interval sampling is a valid technique. But consider this ad: "Quality comes from quality control. Our bottlers pull bottles of Colacola off the line at regular intervals and put them through at least five tests . . ." Fine, only let us hope that the bottlers did not sample systematically ("at regular intervals" may be the advertising copywriter's ignorance showing). Since factory bottle-cappers consist of capping gadgets arranged like daisy petals, regular-interval sampling might never uncover a defect. Imagine ten "petals." To sample every 300th, or every 10th, or even every other bottle, would be foolish, for if one of the capping gadgets were defective there would be a 9 in 10 chance with the first two proportions, and even odds with the third proportion, that the defect would never show up. In order to avoid cyclical bias in cases like this, one random-samples within each interval of 300 or 10 or whatever.

Another varying method, *cluster* sampling, yields, in general, samples less precise than simple or stratified random samples of the same size. However, since cluster samples can usually be taken faster and at much less expense than other kinds they do provide a useful tool in the generalizer's repertoire. As the name implies, cluster sampling is taking the sample in clusters as the clusters occur in the parent group. Clusters can be chosen intelligently or not. Attitude-surveying GIs in thousands of military installations throughout the world, except for the Pentagon, would be formidable, out of the question. It would be much simpler to interview GIs at selected bases, clusters. But which? Drawing the sample from close to home—New York City, Heidelberg, or wherever—could introduce bias. In such cases it would be normal to combine random and cluster sampling. First make a random sample of clusters (bases), stratified or not, then sample at random from within each cluster.

In polling, *quota* sampling, which is something like cluster sampling, is sometimes used. In quota sampling the investigator selects so many instances in each stratum of a stratified sample, not at random but as they may be found. Directions for obtaining a quota sample might read, in effect, "Go out and ask these questions to twenty women over 40, thirty women between 25 and 40, ten women between 18 and 24," and so forth. Where to find the instances is left by the organization somewhat to the discretion of the pollster. Like any sampling technique, quota sampling may be conducted intelligently or not. It would be foolish, for instance, in surveying physicians' attitudes on public health, to fill one's quota from among the strata represented in a large group-practice clinic. Instances would not be properly varied.

Sampling techniques can get complicated. To illustrate let us notice in detail how the Gallup organization gets its national election sample.

The Gallup Poll has designed its sample by choosing at random not individuals . . . but small districts or election precincts. Since there are about 200,000 election districts or precincts in the nation, a random selection of these small geographical areas provides a good starting point for building a national sample.

The process is started by selecting an interval that will yield approximately 300 sampling points throughout the United States. Districts are chosen exactly as names would be selected if a master file existed. Since all districts are not the same in population, the selection process must, of course, take account of this.

As the reader can see, this process is essentially the same as the selection of every 13,500th name from an alphabetical list of persons of voting age in the nation. The difference, as noted, is that one procedure selects an individual, the other a geographical unit, say the third precinct in Ward 3, Scranton, Pennsylvania.

Once having selected the geographical unit, the task then is to carry on the process of selection by choosing at random a given number of individuals residing within this geographical or election unit.

This is done in the following manner. After the third precinct, Ward 3, appears on the list of the 300 units selected, using street maps and block statistics for this ward in Scranton, an assistant in the Princeton office chooses a random starting point within the ward or district.

The interviewer is instructed exactly where to begin his work. The interviewer, following instructions, counts off the number of dwelling units—it may be every third or every fifth or every twelfth dwelling unit—and then proceeds to make calls at these designated households.

In this system of random selection, the choice of the dwelling is taken out of the hands of the interviewer. As a reminder to the reader, it should be pointed out that the area or district has been selected by random procedures; next, the dwelling within the district has been chosen at random. All that now remains is to select, at random, the individual to be interviewed within the household.

This can be done in several ways. A list can be compiled by the interviewer of all persons of voting age residing within each home selected in a given block. He can then select individuals to be interviewed by a random method. Ingenious methods can be employed to accomplish this end. One survey organization in Europe, for example, instructs the interviewer to talk to the person in the household whose birthday falls on the nearest date.[2]

The sample, notice, is a random sample of unequal clusters (precincts or districts) weighted by interval-sampling 300 of them. Then interval sampling selects the dwelling unit, with the individual interviewees being chosen at random.

Sample Size   Besides varying the instances, the responsible generalizer should get enough instances. But how many is enough? Let us begin with the negative. Whatever "enough" is, it is not likely to be millions or even many thousands. Although very large samples may add impressiveness to projections, this impressiveness is largely illusion. In themselves very large samples indicate nothing, the classic case in point being the 2,300,000 monster sample from which in 1936 the *Literary Digest* projected that Alfred Landon would be elected President over FDR. (That sample consisted of responses to a mail questionnaire sent to the *Digest*'s readers and to the nation's ten million telephone subscribers.)

Samples which represent high percentages of their parent group also look impressive but in themselves add nothing. That no percentage alone guarantees reliability can be driven home if we recall the old story about how the Chinese measured the height of their emperor, whom none had ever seen, by computing the arithmetical average of the heights which each of his hundreds of millions of subjects guessed him to be: even a 100 percent enumeration of ignorance is still ignorance. Recently one university public relations office got the local newspaper and its wire service to carry the results of a marijuana survey which had been taken during registration. An extra computer punch card was included in the packet of cards with which the students registered. The survey was voluntary, its respondents anonymous, and according to a response of 83 percent of just over 12,000 total students (with about 100 "prank" responses weeded out), a surprisingly low percentage of this university's students had ever tried marijuana, and only a fraction of that percentage were regular users. These low percentages, however, mean nothing. Given the intimidating atmosphere which surrounds registration at a large university, given the real or imagined presence of "Big Brother," given that punch cards can be traced, and given that marijuana penalties were at the time severe, would *you* have filled out such a card or filled it out truthfully?

[2] George Gallup, *The Sophisticated Poll Watcher's Guide*, Princeton Opinion Press, Princeton, N.J., 1972, pp. 50-52.

The topic of proper sample size becomes technical very quickly. Nevertheless, given misunderstandings frequently expressed by the general public, including the educated, certain points easily understandable to lay persons need emphasis.

Proper sample size depends on the desired precision of the results, on the number of instances in the sample, on the variation within the sample, and on the size of the parent group. Perhaps surprisingly, the size of the parent group is usually the least important factor in the list. A sample of 500 seems infinitesimal compared to a parent group of, say, 200 million. We focus on that 200 million. This is psychological illusion, which can perhaps be dispelled by considering our sample of almond trees. Bias, if any, would come from *within* that sample if the sample contained a disproportionately large number of high-bearing or low-bearing trees—a sample of 20 out of, say, 96 million trees. George Gallup in the work just quoted explains:

> Suppose that a hotel cook has two kinds of soup on the stove—one in a very large pot, another in a small pot. After thoroughly stirring the soup in both pots, the cook need not take a greater number of spoonsful from the large pot or fewer spoonsful from the small pot to taste the quality of the soup.

Two important elements in answering the question, "How many is enough?" are the margin of error which can be tolerated and the desired degree of confidence that the result will be within that margin. The degree of precision in any sample is called its *sampling error*, an index of the mathematical probability of a sample of that size falling within a certain percentage range. The sampling error is not an actual error, then, but a statement of a theoretical margin of error. Imagine a random sample of 750 out of a very large number of x's and y's, which turns up 55 percent x's, and 45 percent y's. According to the laws of probability, a sample of such size and proportion could be expected to fall between 51 percent and 59 percent x's, and between 41 percent and 49 percent y's, in 95 cases out of 100: the sampling error is 4 percent at a 95 percent confidence level. Double the sample and the sampling error would drop to about 3 percent; halve the sample and the error would increase to about 6 percent. (Other things being equal, the precision of a sample increases with the square root of the sample size—which partly explains why large samples don't accomplish that much.) Although the 95 percent confidence level is standard, in many kinds of sampling a higher level—99 percent—is sometimes used. At the higher level the sampling error for a sample of a given size would obviously be greater.

The sampling error is an integral part of any projection. Unawareness of this can cause over-reliance on projected figures. If a projection has a sampling error of 1 percent, then it would be wrong to rely heavily on changes in the projection of .1 percent or .2 percent. Yet exactly this is done repeatedly with government figures, such as monthly unemployment percentages or the cost-of-living index, statistics which measure only long-term trends, not anything like the monthly or quarterly "changes" which many politicians and media people seem to think significant. Based on samples, the projections, on mathematical grounds alone (not to speak of all the uncertainties in data gathering), simply will not stand such forcing. Similar overreliance occurs when anyone stresses the significance of poll-based percentages which are less than the sampling error. Surveys using samples of 1500 carry sampling errors of about 3 percent; those using samples of, say, 350 carry sampling errors of about 5 percent. Anyone who bet heavily on a candidate who had polled two percentage points better than the nearest rival on the basis of either of such samples could be in for a statistical shock.

POLLS AND SURVEYS

Of all the kinds of generalizing arguments, public opinion polls have probably generated the largest amount of misunderstanding. There is so much temptation to abuse them. Polls get glowingly cited when they support, bad-mouthed when they don't. Opponent-damaging parts of secret polls get leaked at wrong moments. Both sides in a race say that the polls favor them, the spread between the percentages claimed sometimes being in the dozens. And everybody remembers the failures. Harry Truman had a picture on his desk of himself being carried while victoriously holding aloft a newspaper proclaiming in end-of-world type the poll-based finding that Thomas E. Dewey has been elected President. Everybody who has seen the picture remembers it, just as they recollect the polling faux pas surrounding the 1970 election of Edward Heath as British Prime Minister over Harold Wilson. What *other* polling results do they remember?

Polling and Policy   Before venturing into the topic of quality, let us reflect briefly on the whole institution of public opinion sampling. Are polls and surveys good for us, or ought they be discouraged?

On the negative side one must note the use of sampling to trade on human weakness. In general, the truth may set us free, but those truths about us which commercial and political opinion surveyors know how to extract can be used not to free but to exploit. Having revealed to surveyors our guilt feelings about indulging in sweets, a can of beer, meals at a fast-food-chain, and the like, we open ourselves to new exploitative efficiencies in the form of hundreds of "*you deserve* such-and-such" gimmicks, very few of which appeal to reason. Having revealed to pollsters our collective irrational bugbears and heart's desires, we open ourselves as voters not to *education* in ideas and programs, but to political pandering to those bugbears and desires. As Garry Wills explains:

Each candidate [and, we may add, elected official] tries to hold a basic consti-
tuency, while wooing the vast muddle of independent or undetermined voters,
using roughly the same platitudes, cleared by similar pollsters: "Tell me what
you want to be told, so I can tell it to you." The candidates scroonch together
in the middle and mill there, left-right, right-left, dos-à-dos.[3]

But if polls and surveys can lead to lowering the quality of what the
public gets, it has opposite effects too. Polls and surveys have shown people
to be wise as well as foolish. They have revealed public receptiveness to
smaller, more efficient automobiles. They have spotlighted its last-straw
exasperation with its share of the tax burden, its desire for more wholesome
food, and its opposition to several unwise military ventures. Furthermore,
polls go a long way toward counteracting the isolation which high office
imposes. When speakers for special interests give high officials distorted
views about the "public mood," about popular support or opposition to
programs, or about public receptivity to a new idea, high officials have
access to the public's real feelings. And polls not only counteract the isolation of high officials, they counteract "pack journalism," that temptation to
learn about the world not by experiencing the world but by fraternizing
with one's journalistic colleagues and reading their copy.

Like most tools for gaining knowledge, therefore, polls and surveys are
best seen as morally neutral—tools which can be used for good ends or for
bad. The real task, then, is to understand them so that their use, and the
extent of their use, will be beneficial.

Survey Quality Thousands of organizations exist which undertake
polls and surveys. Most of their business the public never sees, being in the
form of commercial surveys: Whom does the public blame for high oil
prices? What qualities do people associate with various textile materials?
Are they ready for open advertising of prophylactics? Commercially speaking, what is the public's *mood* this quarter? Does potential candidate *J.* have
hidden strengths or weaknesses which she has as yet failed to exploit or
suppress?

Common sense should warn us that of the thousands of firms and the
many others who engage in polling research, some are bound to be more
competent than others, some more inclined than others to self-serve by
dishing up what the client wants to hear, and some downright crooked,
even though the overwhelming proportion may be both competent and of
high integrity. The moral of all this is simply that one ought not to take
polls at face value, any more than one ought to take any other authority at
face value. Since professional polling contains few trade secrets, any poll
worth considering ought to display its methodology. Unfortunately, when

[3] Garry Wills, "Carter on His Own," *New York Review*, Nov. 25, 1976, p. 30.

polls are reported in the media, completeness and even sense too often fall victim to brevity. In the electronic media even what is obviously essential is frequently omitted. A CBS poll on American attitudes about the Martin Luther King assassination can be taken as typical. CBS News reported to the nearest percentage point only the results, saying nothing about how the poll was conducted. Now although CBS would not conduct a second-rate poll, their report is objectionable nevertheless. For one thing the poll as reported is quite indistinguishable from a second-rate poll. And in a sensitive area where everyone's motives are suspect, nothing untestable ought to count for much. For another, considering how little time or space it would take to fill out the details, responsible journalism owes the public not just information but also a bit of education as well.

Now what makes for completeness? Besides the result, opinion survey reports ought to state at least the following: (1) The sponsor's and surveyor's name; (2) the sample size (and perhaps the sampling error); (3) the date of contact; (4) exactly what population is being sampled and the method of contact (phone, personal interview, mail, etc.); (5) the degree of non-response; (6) the exact questions asked. While not sufficient to enable the audience to judge for itself, the foregoing facts at least allow it to distinguish worthless surveys from those which seem reliable. Now why are all these facts important?

Sponsor's and Surveyor's Name Only surveyors and sponsors not willing to lay their reputations on the line would want to remain anonymous. And although it would be arguing *ad hominem* to discount a well-done, fully-reported survey because its sponsor had an interest in the result, still it is not irrelevant to know that interest, since many surveys are not well done and most are not fully reported. (Obviously, the sponsor's name should be withheld from the respondents until they have answered. A well-dressed gentleman not long ago asked another shopper if a certain brand of frozen pizza was a good kind. Taking him to be making a hidden-camera commercial, the shipper proceded to sing that brand's praises. The gentleman, however, was buying pizza and really did want to know. Moral: Keep it anonymous.)

Date of Contact Obviously crucial. In general, the more recent the date of contact the better. Events can make even yesterday's results obsolete. A politician's foot-in-mouth blunder, an international atrocity, a revelation, can cause percentages to plummet or skyrocket overnight. Further, some polling dates are more valuable than others. In the 1976 Presidential race that "spectacular" thirty-percentage-point lead which the media kept implying President Ford was overcoming (or challenger Carter was blowing) was not that spectacular, and would not have seemed spectacular had the media reminded us whenever they quoted it that the thirty-point spread was based on polls taken after Carter's nomination but before Ford's. While Carter was riding the groundswell of new victory and benefiting from hours of nationwide publicity, Ford and Ronald Reagan were still slugging it out for their party's nomination. "No one even remotely familiar with American politics," Tom Wicker wrote in the *New York Times* shortly after the election, "could have believed that Carter ever had such a lead."

What Population Sampled? Method of Contact The *Literary Digest* poll mentioned above was a mail survey with a typical percentage of response, less than 1 in 4. Even legislators polling their constituents by means of easily completed punchcards scarcely do better. No poll with such a small percentage of response can be worth much, for there is no reason to believe that those actually responding typify the parent group. People who return mail ballots either have plenty of time on their hands (senior citizens, the underemployed, those with labor-saving appliances or servants) or strongly favor one particular result. A scheme of resolicitation, or call-backs, can be useful in decreasing the percentage of nonresponse and in estimating bias, and responsible surveyors always incorporate such schemes. The results of mail surveys ought to be tentative at least.

Another objection to the *Literary Digest*'s survey technique has wide-ranging implications. The sample, chiefly telephone subscribers, was not a sample of the parent group. In 1936, those who had telephones scarcely constituted a cross section of the electorate, large blocs of phoneless voters, particularly in the South, being omitted. Today, with nine out of ten households having phones, the bias would be less acute (though phone surveys still generate about a 5 percent Republican bias). Surveying by telephone has its own advantages and problems. Cheap and fast, for certain purposes, especially commercial ones, the telephone survey cannot be beat. But it generates considerable nonresponse, although several call-backs still cost less than one attempt at reinterview. Further, the telephone survey generates a sample biased in favor of those who are home who answer the phone. But if those are close to being your parent group (as they may be if you are attempting to project how many people just watched such-and-such a soap opera), then there may be little such bias. And experience is supposed to have shown the telephone survey to be inferior to the personal interview at getting at the truth, for which there is nothing like a persistent questioner with a friendly face. Then there is the problem of unlisted numbers (in New York now up to 1 in 5), a bias which can only partly be solved by randomizing phone numbers. People who have paid for unlisted numbers are not likely to enjoy telling some interviewer what deodorant they use.

Sample Size The importance of this is obvious. In addition, as in all cases where there is one, the sampling error—the margin of error and level of confidence—ought to be mentioned in order to counter the transfixing effect of numbers.

Questions All the statistical expertise in the world cannot counteract bias built into a faulty sample. And when a sample consists of human being, the sources of potential bias multiply logarithmically. Human beings are notorious for saying one thing and doing another. They tend to ego-boost, to self-serve, or to react first and, if at all, think second. Sometimes they aim to please at truth's expense, to follow the herd, or to fear the questioner or tax collector. The careful survey will attempt to take into account, and where possible avoid or lessen, such sources of bias.

Responsible surveys consisting of people's responses to questions must be designed in order to eliminate the charge that the questions themselves color the results. Questions undergo scrutiny by experienced critics in order to uncover poor wording. Then they are tested on samples of respondents. The questions are asked, then followed up with questioning designed to bring out respondents' comprehension and true feelings. Alternative formulations may be given to split samples in order to detect differences between formulations.

Questions must be easy to understand. Anything which confuses respondents may generate percentages of "no opinion" responses higher than the percentages of those who actually do have no opinion on the subject. Good questions should be short and cover only one subject. Complex queries should be split into more understandable components. It has been noticed, for instance, that when a question is posed about such-and-such a means to a generally desirable goal, some respondents will answer positively in terms of the goal, and from their answers seem to favor the means. Further questioning, however, revels that they do not really favor the means at all. They have confused the means in the question with the goal. To remedy such inaccuracy, the question should be divided, one question for the goal, the other for the means.

Questions must be worded so as to avoid coloring the responses. Anything which blocks a considered answer is likely to mask a respondent's feelings. The question, "Are you a racist?" would likely evoke close to 100 percent negative replies, the term "racist" having come to connote someone on the order of a Judas or a Hitler. Racist feelings would never surface. To probe for racial attitudes should involve less unsubtle questioning, on such topics as quota hiring, bilingual schooling, mixed marriages, busing, and the like. Even these topics' names tend to be trigger words, terms to be avoided in the formulation of neutral, nonprovocative questions.

A related source of potential question-generated bias lies in people's tendency to project what they imagine to be a favorable self-image—to think of themselves as churchgoing, industrious, open-minded, or "with it." Their actions often belie their words, as many a sponsor of market-researched yet failed attempts to produce "good" popular commercial television will attest. Questions like, "Are you in favor of keeping Civic Ballet going?" elicit a high proportion of affirmative replies, yet what do the replies mean? Questions like, "Would you pay $8.50 a seat to see the Civic Ballet?" or, "Would you sign this $10 pledge form to insure continuation of

Civic Ballet?" typically indicate something quite different. Obviously, any serious action should be built on replies to questions like the latter two, and not on replies to questions like the former. Sometimes deciding where true feelings lie is difficult. At one time George Wallace's national strength was difficult to estimate because among a large segment of voters Wallace's politics were not considered quite respectable. Wallace claimed to have greater strength than the polls showed, a claim hard to dispute until election day.

Those species of higher mammals which must rely on occasional bursts of ferocity in order to survive have been endowed by evolution with other behavior patterns which keep members of the species from each other's throats. Humans seem to be one of those species. When greeted we typically smile, become friendly: we aim to please. In this behavior can lie yet another source of sampling bias. People are inclined to say what they think others, or the pollster, want to hear, and not what they in fact think. One polling organization once surveyed a randomly selected split sample of white voters. The topic was race and politics. Half the sample was asked their questions by clean-cut white pollsters and half was asked theirs by clean-cut blacks. Results were as might be expected: answers given to the white pollsters differed significantly from those given to the blacks. Forewarned, forearmed. Reports of surveys dealing with women's issues, for example, should not neglect to mention the sex of the interviewers as well as that of the respondents (well over 90 percent of all interviewers are women).

Examples and Comments

A Using concepts and techniques discussed in this chapter, as well as common sense, explain to someone inclined to accept the following items at face value just what is, or may be, wrong. Or, if an item appears logical, defend it against misunderstanding.

1 "Med-a-cin is a combination of medically tested, proved ingredients. Take Med-a-cin and be sure."

Comment An exaggerated version of exactly the argument by which the Pharmaceutical Manufacturers Association attempted to convince the FDA not to ban unproved combinations of proved components. The argument commits composition. Obviously, combinations may interact to produce unknown, possibly harmful, new combinations, or reduce effectiveness. A combination of, say, penicillin (which kills microbes in the act of cell division) and tetracycline (which works by inhibiting cell division) would be valueless.

2 "Swinging Seventies Not So Swinging. Sacramento (PNS) The so-called sexual revolution may need revising in the light of a survey taken last Tuesday. A scientifically designed sample of 500 people who had been married more than five years was given a series of questions about sexual behavior including the question, "Have you ever committed adultery?" Surprisingly, only 8 percent of the men and 5 percent of the women responded in the affirmative."

Comment The evidence reported warrants no conclusion at all, let alone that wildly general headline. Besides being incomplete the report contains two glaring errors. First, adultery being a touchy subject, fraught with social and legal sanctions, an unknown, possibly large, number would be inclined to clam up about their involvements. The question is ridiculous. Second, the researchers probably biased the result further by asking only those who had been married five years, thus omitting younger respondents, those whom the so-called sexual revolution is supposed primarily to be about. The sample is not of the parent group. (And if the sample excludes divorced individuals it is doubly ridiculous.) Moreover, although a "scientifically designed sample of 500" would probably be adequate at the level of precision and confidence the material demands, the argument's other inadequacies cast serious doubt that its design is indeed scientific. Further, we need to know how and where the poll was taken. (By phone, mail, personal interview? Was it taken only in Sacramento? The conclusion demands a national sample.)

3 "I don't care, Jethro, cancer is cancer and the truth is the truth. If Grandpa asks, you've just got to tell him. It simply isn't right to tell a lie."

Comment Truth-telling is right because normally there is some point in telling it. But in the present example, there seems to be not only no point in telling the truth, there is quite a case *against* telling it. So whatever is right in this case, it is incorrect to argue that Grandpa ought to be told simply because lying is wrong. Of course, one might argue that Grandpa ought to be told because a person needs a chance to put his life in order, or a chance to save his immortal soul. Fine. Grounds such as these would be relevant (not necessarily sufficient)—quite different from those of the original argument. (The argument is a *dicto simpliciter*.)

4 "With personal incomes 78 percent higher than those of the Israelis, Kuwait's citizens are obviously able to afford those manufactured goods their Japanese partners are willing to supply."

Comment Division. "Incomes" apparently means *per capita* income, an arithmetical mean, collective, which the argument proceeds to distribute to the bulk of Israelis and Kuwaitis. We need here to know not just the average, the mean, we need to know the *spread* around the mean. To this end knowing the median or mode incomes, or statistics on income distribution, would tell us more. Perhaps more important, this argument compares the incomparable. Israel is modern and socialist; Kuwait is just emerging from feudalism. Life in either country being 180° different, even a rounding-off hedge like "double" (let alone that bogusly precise "78 percent") really means little.

5 "Surely we must admit," said Socrates, "that the same elements and characters that appear in the State must exist in its citizens. It would be absurd to imagine that among peoples with a reputation for a high-spirited character the states have not derived that character from their individual members." (Plato, *The Republic*.)

Comment This reasoning is very tricky. The argument could be a candidate for both composition and division were the collective-distributive and distributive-collective moves made. But as with Mill's reasoning discussed earlier, Socrates' reasoning could be argued to make no such moves. For what it means for a state to be high-spirited is about the same as what it means for its citizens to be high-spirited. If we maintain that Lebanon, say, is a violent country, we mean that Lebanese as *individuals* are prone to violence, and imply nothing about Lebanon as a whole being violent, war-like. On the other hand, Socrates does argue here for a general principle— that "the same elements and characters that appear in the state must exist in its citizens." And although Socrates may be basically right, his argument ought to be regarded as suspicious. A strong connection does exist between the character of the citizens and the character of the state. But that there is a strong connection does not mean that the characters of the two are identical. A state could be aggressive in foreign affairs yet placid in internal relations.

6 "Raising tuition at State University by $800 a year, as my opponent has suggested, would not, I repeat, not, provide the tax relief she claims. The net to the state, about $50 million, may sound impressive. Don't let that figure fool you. It works out to less than $5 per man, woman, and child."

7 "Last Tuesday, Polling Associates telephoned the final number on each white page of the Georgetown phone book and, with call-backs, were able to contact 74 percent. Of that 74 percent, 75 percent were registered voters who said they intended to vote in next Tuesday's school board election. When we asked them which of the four candidates, Jefferson, Kamanaka, Martinez, or O'Brien, they intended to vote for, the results were as follows: Jefferson 23 percent, Kamanaka 11 percent, Martinez 21 percent, O'Brien 27 percent, undecided 18 percent. So it looks as though the incumbent, O'Brien, will squeak by for yet another term."

8 "Students Rate Profs Highest From Whom They Learn Least. A study conducted by Dr. John Harrigan at Galt State University has yielded surprising results. Harrigan had the students in Galt State's eighteen Math 1 class sections rate their professors overall on a five point scale from excellent to poor. These end-of-semester ratings were then compared with the students' scores on the standardized final exam. The class of the professor with the highest rating had the lowest exam average. A comparative inverse correlation between professor rating and exam score held for the other classes also. "The correlation," said Harrigan, "was good enough to be stated as a principle: If you want to learn something, take the guy you'll hate."

9 "Since a check revealed that every tenth orange coming off the conveyor belt was stamped, there's essentially no chance that every orange didn't get stamped."

10 "With 4 percent of the precincts reporting we have a winner. Brown is the next governor of California."

11 "Busing Unpopular in the East. A survey of a random sample of 500 parents of school-age children in the greater Boston area reveals widespread resentment of crosstown busing in order to achieve racial balance. Over half the parents surveyed indicated that they would put their children in parochial or private schools rather than have them bused."

12 "U.S. Wastes Food Worth Millions. Washington (PNS) Americans in the economic middle waste more food than their rich and poor counterparts, according to a study published Saturday. Carried out in Tucson, Arizona, by University of Arizona students under the direction of Dr. William L. Rathje, the study analyzed 600 bags of garbage each week for three years from lower-, middle-, and upper-income neighborhoods. They found that city residents throw out around 10 percent of the food they brought home—about 9500 tons of food each year. The figure amounts to $9 to $11 million worth of food. Most of the waste occurred in middle-class neighborhoods. Both the poor and the wealthy were significantly more frugal."

13 "America's TV Likes. Pollsters phoned 5000 statistically selected viewers around the country and asked them to name a favorite in each category—variety, comedy, favorite actor, favorite actress, etc. Then they used the top vote-getters as finalists in a follow-up preference poll of another 2000 viewers. The sample was taken from a possible 59 million households with phones, 90 percent of the total number of which had television sets. Results are as follows. Favorite TV comedy show: "All in the Family" (followed by "Good Times" and "Sanford & Sons," in that order). Favorite TV actor: Alan Alda and Telly Savalas (tie, leaving Peter Falk third)."

14 "Certainly the authorities are agreed that it is medically impossible for this patient to regain any sensation at all, that neural impairment is too far advanced for her to remain anything but a vegetable. But such facts miss the real point. This is a human being we are dealing with. We must preserve human life wherever possible, and hence every means of keeping her alive must not be denied this patient. It would be wrong to 'pull the plug.' "

15 "Being a general practitioner in a rural area has tremendous drawbacks—being on virtually 24-hour call 365 days a year; patients without financial means or insurance; low fees in the first place; inadequate facilities and assistance. Nevertheless, America's small town G.P.s seem fairly content with their lot. According to a survey taken by *Country Doctor*, fully 50 percent wrote back that they 'basically like being a rural G.P.' Only 1 in

15 regretted that he or she had not specialized. Only 2 out of 20 rural general practitioners would trade places with their urban counterparts, given the chance. And only 1 in 30 would "choose some other line of work altogether."

Applications

A   Analyze one or more media reports of generalizing arguments. Given reasonable space limitations, have critical details been omitted? Where the analysis uncovers particularly strong points, or deficiencies, highlight these, and, where appropriate, suggest remedies.

B   In the form of a brief report, share your experience of applications of sampling—for example, in your academic field, in the military, in accounting, in a job you have held.

C   In the form of a report or essay, speculate further on the pros and cons of opinion polling, market research, governmental indexes, or a similar institution. Should citizens help such projects or not?

D   Design a sample of items in a supermarket, students at a college, blocks in a city, or on a topic which interests you. Defend the sample's representativeness.

E   How are election-night projections accomplished, with only "one percent of the precincts reporting"?

F   Under a title such as "Systems and Components," "A State and its Citizens," or "A Painting and its Elements," explore the relationships, or supposed relationships, between the whole and its parts.

G   Deepen, counter, or deepen and counter this chapter's sketches of scientific laws, moral principles, or generalizations.

H   Using material from the chapters covered so far, construct, administer, score, and defend a "Quick Check," or "Examples and Comments" section.

Comparison

When we place two or more things or classes of things together in order to measure them against each other, we make a comparison. When a similarity, a likeness, seems to be found, we have to that degree an *analogy*; when a dissimilarity, a difference, seems to be found we have to that degree a *disanalogy*. Analogies go by various names: "simile," "fable," "precedent," "model," "mock-up," "metaphor," "caricature," *"roman à clef,"* "extrapolation," and so on. The ease with which that list could be doubled, and doubled again, hints how basic and pervasive analogy is: "Man," writes W. H. Auden, "is an analogy-drawing animal; that is his great good fortune."

Does Auden exaggerate? Comparisons underlie the acquisition and practice of language, morality, the simplest technology, and the most abstract science—in fact, everything distinctly human. Analogical inference is everywhere. Engineers reason from the simulated conditions of wind tunnels, miniature lagoons, and aircraft in free fall. Politicians, commentators, and voters look to the past to analyze and guide policy. Judges apply legal precedent to new cases; other people criticize its application. Researchers experiment with fruit flies, monkeys, prison inmates, or college sophomores, applying the results to less available or less tractable groups. Moralists, prophets, cartoonists teach and admonish by fable and parable.

In spotlighting what might otherwise go unnoticed, analogies sometimes succeed like nothing else. Comparing a falling apple to a circling planet, the human psyche to a city, a reptile's foreleg to a bird's wing, language to a game, an individual's religious life to a love affair, or a painting to an event (comparisons which when first made seemed far-fetched), has suggested undreamed of direction for new investigation. Analogies, moreover, frequently prove to be just the instruments to crack thick skulls. They can pop things into perspective. "It looks like a cage for crickets," Michelangelo is said to have remarked of the just-begun cornice for the dome of the Florence cathedral. The cornice was never finished.

Like anything which can lead, analogies can also *mis*lead. The wiseacre who spotted that Governor Thomas E. Dewey "looks like the little man on a wedding cake" may have cost Dewey the Presidency for no reason at all. After naming man an analogy-drawing animal, Auden observes that "his danger is of treating analogies as identities." If this is so, however, it need not be so. "Once analogy-bitten, twice analogy-shy" might make a good proverb. But to disparage analogical procedures or to avoid them, as some would try, seems misconceived.

Not only are comparisons valuable, they are indispensable. And to suppress them when they are afoot makes difficult the task of getting at reasoning processes in order to be convinced or to spot error. It is best to wear one's analogies, and all thinking processes, on one's sleeve. The real skill, then, is not to avoid comparisons but to use them creatively, and to see both likeness *and* contrast.

Analogies and Analogical Arguments   There is some difference between simply stating a resemblance between two things and *drawing a conclusion* from a resemblance. Whereas the former is simply an analogy—a statement—the latter is an *analogical argument*. Whoever uses it argues *by* or *from* analogy. Someone may reject a blue nylon swimsuit because the last one faded badly. Someone may rest easier with determinism upon hearing the operation of the human brain likened to that of a computer (which is solely a function of circuitry and input). Or someone may defend a proposal to spend $5 on a movie director's latest effort, citing the director's uniformly good previous work. Analogical arguments fit the following scheme.

A_1 is b and c.

$$\cdot \quad \cdot \quad \cdot \quad \cdot \quad \cdot$$

$$\cdot \quad \cdot \quad \cdot \quad \cdot$$

$$\cdot \quad \cdot \quad \cdot \quad \cdot$$

A_n is b.

So, A_n is c.

A_1 through A_n are two or more items or classes; b and c are what can be said of them. That is, two or more things or classes of things (A_1 and A_n are found similar in some respect or set of respects (b). Further, each thing or class, except one, is known to exhibit an additional characteristic or set of characteristics (c). Thereupon the inference is drawn that the remaining item or class resembles the other(s) in that additional characteristic or set (A_n is c). Arguing this way we do not generalize about instances, we do not argue for a generalization, but instead draw a conclusion about a single instance. Thus, to take two examples:

	(A)	(b)	(c)
A_1	old suit	blue, nylon	fade
A_2	prospective suit	blue, nylon	
So,	prospective suit		fade

	(A)	(b)	(c)
A_1	"Hulot's Holiday"	by & featuring Tati	good movie
A_2	"My Uncle"	by & featuring Tati	good movie
A_3	"Playtime"	by & featuring Tati	good movie
A_4	"Traffic"	by & featuring Tati	
So,	"Traffic"		good movie

The conclusions rest, then, on the analogy (b) between the subject of the argument (A_n) and the items or classes to which it has been compared (the other A's).

Differences—at least as important as similarities, which are flashier—never seem to get their due. Symmetry, if not good sense, suggests that argument from *dis*analogy should claim at least a small niche alongside its positive counterpart, from which it does not differ greatly. Arguments from disanalogy would look like this:

A_1 through A_n are b, c, and d.
A_{n+1} is b but not c.

So A_{n+1} is not d.

That is, two or more items or classes are in some sense comparable (b). (If they were in no sense comparable, we could gauge neither similarity nor difference.) Comparing A's reveals not similarity but difference (c); whereupon the conclusion is drawn that A_{n+1} will differ in an unexamined respect $(A_n + _1$ is not $d)$. A parent deduces that because one child is in a happy, generous mood today (d) the other child will be in a grouchy, cantankerous mood (not d). A cryptologist concludes that because the word patterns in a letter fail to match those of five specimens of its author's freely-written letters, a sixth letter was dictated under duress. A motorcycle gang tribunal decides that because two violators of a club rule differ in both the degree and the circumstances of their violations, the lesser violator should not get the punishment prescribed for the greater violator.

So much for form. What of the question of adequacy?

MASTERING ANALOGICAL REASONING

When somebody argues, say, that since it would be silly for patients to tell their doctors how to cure them, it would likewise be silly for students to have a meaningful say in university decisions, we should not be swept along by the comparison. Is it apt? Or when someone compares the marvelous system of systems, which, from the mightiest to the most minute, is known collectively as the universe—when the person compares the structure and workings of this system to the structure and workings of a well-made watch and concludes that since from observing the watch we must infer an intelligence responsible for the watch, so from observing the system of the universe we must likewise infer an intelligence responsible for the universe, namely God, we must likewise ask, "Is *this* comparison apt?"

To handle analogical reasoning ably one would do well to have certain techniques at one's fingertips. The following points seem to be taken into account by the thoughtful and articulate (at least some of the time!). Any assessment begins with a sizing-up. The thoughtful person will be clear as to (1) exactly what is at issue; (2) exactly what is being compared. Especially, the thoughtful person will be clear as to (3) exactly what are the real similarities and differences. Sizing-up is preliminary to action. Next, one should be able either to (4) attack half of the comparison; (5) attack or defend the analogy; (6) change it; (7) extend it; or (8) attack the pivot.

Exactly What Is at Issue?   Being clear exactly as to what the issue is is obviously important and is too often neglected. In our academic-medical example, is the topic grading policy? Is it hiring and firing faculty? Is it general university administration? (Using an analogical argument to support a point not at issue would be to argue irrelevantly.) Of course, in a given case what is at issue may not be clear. Seeing this is progress, for one is then in a position to point that fact out, and to proceed in defining the issue.

Exactly What Is Being Compared?   Failure to be clear, and to specify, exactly what both halves of the comparison are mars many an argument. It may mar the medical analogy. In that argument the point may hold for the professor-to-student relationship (this is itself arguable) but not for the relationship which holds between university and student. Possible imprecision here may lead both arguer and audience astray. Note that points 1 and 2 are really just preliminaries for 3.

What Are the Relevant Similarities and Differences? To master analogical inference one must become skillful at spotting similarities and differences. One will be misled by not seeing important differences when they are there. Likewise, failing to heed a fair analogy—if the shoe fits and one does not wear it—is to be equally misled. When considering a difficult and important analogical argument, one may try to achieve perspective by listing similarities and differences.

Students sometimes proceed as if just anything could be a similarity or difference. They forget to use common sense. What makes a supposed similarity or difference relevant? One must observe its bearing on the issue at hand. In the question concerning the swimsuit, the immediate issue is color fastness. The general issue would be the sorts of interests to be satisfied by purchasing a swimsuit. Therefore, that the suit one formerly owned and the suit one now contemplates purchasing are both nylon (similarity) would be relevant, since colors are known to be more fugitive in some fibers than in others. And that the last suit was bought eight years ago (difference) would be relevant because of possible advances in dye technology, detergents, swimming pool antiseptics, and the like. (In a technologically more static civilization the time difference would be less relevant.) That both suits have a pocket would be irrelevant (at least in the absence of evidence to the contrary) because we know that such matters do not affect color fastness. Nor would difference in sizes matter, unless the previous suit was a child's size. (Manufacturers have been known to slight quality in soon-to-be-out-grown children's clothing.)

The first three points have to do with analyzing arguments from analogy. The remaining five concern acting upon the analysis.

Attack Half of the Comparison Surprisingly often, facts about what is being compared are misrepresented or ill-understood. And since analogies typically convey more psychological force than logical force, any chance to nip a misleading analogy in the bud should not be missed. If possible, attack a premise. For example, one often sees the argument that as it is foolish for a household to live beyond its income (there are debts plus interest), so it is foolish for governments to live beyond income, to deficit-spend. Although the comparison carries considerable force, the force is more psychological than logical. The first half of the comparison is false. It is *not* always foolish for a household to live beyond income. Consumerized as we are, we are inclined to think of spending as dispersal. We shoot our paycheck on another TV, go into hock for a camper or a shag carpet, or blow a grand on a vacation. But not all spending is dispersal. It may be wise to go into debt to buy a house, even at inflated interest rates, if real estate values are soaring. Money borrowed for education typically returns many-fold. Even consumer items—vehicles, insulation, tools, certain appliances—can more than repay the costs and risks of debt. What is foolish is not debt, but foolish debt. The false premise being exposed, the implications with regard to governments, thanks to the analogy, fairly interpreted, may turn out to be a good deal clearer.

Attack or Defend the Analogy   Analogies frequently prove to be poorly thought out. Thinking them out (see "relevant similarities and differences," above) supplies ammunition for debunking poor ones and for defending good ones. Point out the *dis*analogies. And for good arguments show that presumed dissimilarities have little or no bearing on the issue. "You bought that swimsuit eight years ago," the clerk might reply, "Nylon doesn't fade as it used to."

To the watch-universe comparison one could perhaps reply by attempting to undermine the childlike wonder which leads the argument's adherents to embrace the analogy. We have considered the lilies of the fields; in fairness let us also consider the stinging flies which infest those stinking bogs where lilies grow. Disease, floods, wars, earthquakes, tempests, famines—all the furniture of Voltaire's *Candide*—could be paraded. And yes, it may be true that only God can make a tree. That line suffers inspirationally, however, when its object is changed from trees to tapeworms, or poison ivy. And what of that impression of celestial clockwork? No astronomical body keeps time as well as a reasonably well-constructed timepiece—if Kepler had had accurate instruments he might never have formulated his laws. The laws of nature all require fudge factors and lists of exceptions in order to fit the phenomena. Rather sloppy workmanship for a universe-maker, it would seem. In David Hume's *Dialogues Concerning Natural Religion,* the character Philo does a rather thorough job of exhibiting such differences. None of the differences touch the question of God's existence; of course, that is not Philo's intent, but they do throw into profound doubt the attempt to use nature's marvels to demonstrate a Supreme Being.

Change the Analogy   Discovering the original comparison to be deficient may suggest a better-fitting variation, one which leads in another direction, In our academic-medical example the doctor-to-patient relationship has been linked to that of university-to-student. But a university is a large institution and is in this respect nothing like one's doctor. A large institution, such as a hospital, could be substituted in order to produce a closer parallel, perhaps along the following lines:

It may or may not be true that "doctor knows best," but does *hospital* know best?" Whoever has spent time in hospitals will have answers which could provide constructive advice to hospital administration. Hospital directors might do well to listen more to patients. Now if patients get neglected, bullied, treated like inanimate objects, overcharged, and poorly fed, so do university students. Hospitals are at least beginning to get consumer representatives on their boards of directors; might not a similar move improve universities?

Occasionally, instead of a closer analogy, a *counter* analogy is useful in restoring balance to a situation that has been systematically unbalanced by one of those bad analogies which, like crabgrass, stubbornly persist. In discussing art, many writers rely on what might be called a "hydraulic" picture of creativity, as in this passage from G. K. Chesterton:

> The artistic temperament is a disease that afflicts amateurs. It is a disease which arises from a man not having sufficient power of expression to utter the art within him; it is essential to every sane man to get rid of the art within him at all costs. Artists of a large and wholesome vitality get rid of their art easily, as they breathe easily, or perspire easily. But in artists of less force, the thing becomes a pressure, and produces a definite pain, which is called the artistic temperament. Thus, very great artists are able to be ordinary men—men like Shakespeare or Browning. . . . Whistler could produce art; and in so far he was a great man. But he could not forget art; and in so far he was only a man with the artistic temperament. There can be no stronger manifestation of the man who is a really great artist than the fact that he can dismiss the subject of art; that he can, upon due occasion, wish art at the bottom of the sea.[1]

The hydraulic part of such reasoning as Chesterton's is widely shared and readily accepted. Even the language of creativity—as when we speak of "*ex-press*-ion"—reinforces it. Its hold is misleading, not easily broken, and unlike the medical analogy, does not seem amenable to an obviously better (different) analogy. Therefore, a counter analogy may help. For example:

> According to Mr. Chesterton, it is "healthful" for the artist to "get rid" of harmful "pressure." This language could almost lead one to believe that one is listening to a laxative commercial. If creation really is release of pressure, then we should find artists the healthiest of us all, when in fact artists are, if anything, less healthy than the average human being. Now although Shakespeare and Browning did lead ordinary lives, Mr. Chesterton neglects those legions of prolific, indisputably great artists who led tormented, unordinary lives—Michelangelo, Tolstoy, Rembrandt, Beethoven, and Van Gogh come first to

---

[1] G. K. Chesterton, "On the Wit of Whistler," *Heretics,* John Lane Co., New York, 1906, pp. 242–243.

mind. No, creation is not a release of something bad. (Is art bad?) Rather it is an *act of nourishment*. Like Saturn feeding on his children, artists *feed* on creation. This explains why creative bursts leave their subjects artistically stronger, not artistically spent, as Mr. Chesterton's view implies, and why such bursts beget increased, not decreased, activity. And it explains what Mr. Chesterton may be excused for not seeing in Whistler, his prolific contemporary—that Whistler was a very great artist.

This counter analogy, no better than Chesterton's, must not be pushed further than to break the hold of the hydraulic picture. Otherwise we will have done no more than substitute one headache for another.

Extend the Analogy As noted above, many analogies convey more psychological than logical force. Instead of wasting words in trying to break an argument's spell, one can sometimes make use of this spell. One can turn the magic against its perpetrator by extending the analogy. Thus elaborated, the analogy may actually support a thesis contrary to the one claimed for it, or lead to ridiculous consequences. (The latter result would be a *reductio ad absurdum.*) In Book I of Plato's *Republic,* Socrates maintains that the proper function of the ruler of a state is to look after the welfare of its citizens. He argues that as the true calling of the physician is to be a healer of the sick, and as a ship captain's basic responsibility is the safety of those on board, and as horsemanship considers the interests of the horse and sheep-herding the well-being of the flocks, so the true calling of the ruler of a state is to care for its citizens. Although Socrates's conclusion may or may not be true, does his argument show it? A reply to this argument might take a form along lines begun by Socrates's opponent, Tharasymachus:

> Yes, physicians do indeed heal the sick, but physicians do this primarily for their own benefit—in order to collect fees and build a practice. Dead patients don't pay. And horsemanship: the horseman considers the interests of the horse, naturally, but primarily to reach destinations, or sell horses—that is, for profit. Don't forget, horses with broken legs are shot. And the sheep-herder: the sheep-herder tends the flocks not out of affection for his or her charges but for the sake of the meat and wool they provide. So according to this analogy, if it is any good, the rulers of states will also "fleece" their charges.

Against the design argument of God, Hume's Philo (*Dialogues Concerning Natural Religion.* part V) replies not only by attacking the watch analogy but by extending it *ad absurdum:*

> In a word, Cleanthes, a man who follows your hypothesis is . . . left afterwards to fix every point of his theology by the utmost licence of fancy and hypothe-

sis. This world, for aught he knows, is very faulty and imperfect, compared to a superior standard; and was only the first rude essay of some infant deity, who afterwards abandoned it, ashamed of his lame performace; it is the work of some dependent, inferior deity; and is the object of derision to his superiors; it is the production of old age and dotage in some superannuated deity; and ever since his death, has run on at adventures, from the first impulse and active force, which it received from him.

Attack the Pivot An analogical argument can be thought of as "pivot-ing" on an implied generalization (a more plausible reading in some cases than in others). The rejection of the blue nylon swimsuit rests on the gener-alization that "blue nylon fades," and the defense of spending too much on the latest Tati rests on the assumption that any Tati movie will be good. The pivot generalization, if true, underwrites the argument and, if false, weakens or ruins it. The following example illustrates. A philosophy class was discussing a case which involved Johnny Appleseed, when a student's face darkened.

> Wait a minute! We shouldn't be talking about planting trees, because you *can't* plant trees. I mean, to plant a tree you've got to have a tree to plant, right? Putting seeds in the ground, that's planting *seeds,* not planting trees. Of course, you can *trans*plant trees, but not plant them.

Instincts which shout "Equivocation!" here are essentially correct. The in-ference is linguistic and analogical. The student's "can't" in "you can't plant a tree" is about what does or does not make sense—as in "A batter can't bat 2.000." (The fact may be brought out by trying retorts such as, "Do you mean that you can't do it even if you were to have unlimited bionic assistance?") To counter the student's conclusion helpfully is not easy; an "*Of course* you can plant trees!" will just cement the conclusion in his mind. It may be more helpful to show that the student's inference pivots on a false generalization. That it does may be seen in the remark, "to plant a tree you've got to have a tree to plant." This remark is an instance of the generalization, "to f an x you have got to have an x to f." That generaliza-tion is false. Granted, to eat a hamburger, you've got to have a hamburger there to eat; to plant a bomb, you've got to have a bomb to plant. The student seems to have in mind facts such as these. But such facts do not justify the *general* formula about having to have an x there to f. To invent a better mousetrap, need the mousetrap have been there *first*? In fact, to want a dime, to seek the summit, to write a symphony, to disprove a theo-rem, to refuse a change of venue, and hundreds of similar constructions, fairly require the *non*existence or *non*presence of the x. Upon the false generalization the student pivots from (presumably) true premises to false conclusion.

Now by no means is it being claimed that there are exactly three steps in sizing up analogical arguments and only five ways to handle them. But perhaps the foregoing furnish a basis for the reader to formulate a personally tailored checklist.

Quick Check

A   Where the following are analogical arguments, state the conclusion and the pivot, without worrying about evaluation.

1   "Since no person has seen reason except in a human figure, the gods have a human figure." (Epicurus.)

2   Attendance was perfect the first three class meetings. Therefore, attendance will be good all semester.

3   An FDA study shows that heavy, continued use of hexachlorophene soap produces toxic blood levels in humans equivalent to those which cause brain damage in rats. If the study was carefully done, it seems certain that such use produces brain damage in humans too.

4   "The bees have only one king, the flocks only one head, the herds only one leader. Can you believe that in heaven the supreme power is divided, and that the entire majesty of that true, divine Authority is broken up?" (Prudentius.)

5   "Sheer torture." That's how race car driver John Dildarian describes the boulder-strewn, zigzag roads of Mexico's Sierra Madre, the baking, chuckhole-filled tracks through the Sonoran desert. "But my Perry steel-belted radials came through great." A thousand miles of sheer tortue prove that Perry steel-belted radials can stand up to what you dish out. And more. Can you honestly say your car deserves less?

B   Without worrying about their adequacy just now, characterize Lee's comments, below. Does Lee attack the analogy directly, change it, try a *reductio ad absurdum*, attack half the comparison, attack or defend the pivot, or what?

1   Board member Smith: "I make my children pay for their own toys. It works. People appreciate what they pay for. That's why I favor instituting a moderate tuition in this community college district."

    Lee: "Board member Smith seems to think that we all will appreciate relations with a prostitute more than with our spouses. Now, maybe Smith is right, but . . ."

2   Fisher: "Imagine having your fingers crushed and caught in a car door. You suffer and wait. Nobody comes. Horrible? Yes, yet that is exactly how a muskrat or lynx feels when caught in a steel-jaw trap. It's time the thing was outlawed."

    Lee: "I don't want to say you're wrong about outlawing traps, Fish, but your argument is unfair. In a trap or car door the victim is going to be in some shock; pain is secondary. What makes the car door experience so horrible is less the pain than the *dread*, the fear that nobody will come. And since animals don't conceptualize the future, they are spared the dread."

3   Professor Brown: "Most people spend only a fraction of their waking hours in mathematical calculation, in reading politics, literature, or history, in creating or looking at art. There are hundreds of courses in these subjects at our school, and rightly so. Yet this college has only one course in speech mechanics, even though we all spend many hours a day speaking. Speech mechanics deserves representation along with the rest."

Lee: "Professor Brown implies that we would do well to have courses in *whatever* we spend time doing every day. Surely this is false. We would *not* do well to have courses in breathing, or procrastinating, or coffee-drinking; and I can think of even more intriguing possibilities."

4   Dr. Krebs: "This disease has *got* to have a cause. Measles has a cause, cholera has a cause, yellow fever has a cause. . . . The trouble is, we *can't find* it."

Lee: "Although Dr. Krebs's thinking may not be very informative, I hope that nobody doubts it. All diseases *do* have causes. We know that not from having *discovered* causes for every disease, but, so to speak, by definition. The sentence, 'This disease has no cause' is unfathomable."

5   Leslie: "Testing high school writing programs by standardized multichoice exams is cheap and effective. After all, putting an essay together is not unlike solving a jigsaw puzzle. You put the right piece at the right spot at the right time. And that's just the sort of thing those tests test best."

Lee: "That's if you have the pieces there first and if they fit together only one way. No, writing is more like composing music. You start out with nothing—no materials, no order. If high school writing programs were music, Leslie would be turning out not composers but winners on 'Name That Tune.' "

Answers

A   (1) *Conclusion:* the gods have a human figure; *pivot;* whatever has reason has a human figure; (2) not an analogy argument; (3) *conclusion:* heavy use of hexachlorophene soap produces brain damage in humans; *pivot:* with regards to brain damage from toxins, at least, what holds for rats holds for humans; (4) *conclusion:* divinity is unitary; *pivot:* all leaders are unitary; (5) *conclusion:* you should use Perry steel-belted radials; *pivot:* Perry steel-belted radials come out great under any conditions.

B   (1) tries *reductio ad absurdum;* (2) attacks analogy directly; (3) attacks pivot and hints at a *reductio ad absurdum;* (4) defends pivot; (5) changes the analogy, then tries a *reductio ad absurdum.*

HISTORICAL COMPARISON

Responsible citizenship requires competence in drawing guidance from historical experience and in assessing the alleged lessons of the past. We need to judge policy and criticisms of policy. We need to know where our interests lie—even, perhaps, to the point of saving our own skins.

Historical comparisons differ little from other analogical reasoning. In an argument from historical analogy, one or more historical situations, together with a present or impending situation $(A_1$ through $A_n)$, are found similar *(b)*. The past situation or situations contain an additional characteristic *(c)*. The inference is then drawn that the present or impending situation also exhibits the characteristic $(A_n$ is *c)*. Then an implication for policy is drawn, or left to speak for itself. The following piece of Navy Day rhetoric may be taken as typical of one species of the genre.

> Every country which has achieved international hegemony has had a superior naval force. Not until Athens destroyed the Persian fleet in 400 B.C. did she emerge as a power in the eastern Mediterranean. Rome dominated the entire Mediterranean for centuries only because of maritime power. Britain began her ascension to power only after Alfred the Great built the fleet that stopped Viking plunder of England's coasts and rivers. And after the Hanoverian kings modernized the British Navy, Britain was able to become an imperial power.
>
> If we doubt the lesson in all this we have but to turn to the naval build-up of the Soviet Union. In little more than a half century after a devastating revolution. Russia is able to extend her tentacles of interest throughout the world only because she has become formidable on the seas. Today, Navy Day, the lesson for America is plain. Our well-being, our survival as a great nation, depends on an efficient, strong United States Navy.

The issue here, given the interservice struggle for defense dollars, is how many resources to commit to the Navy. Though it could be more specific, the argument does meet that issue squarely. As strong navies have been a cornerstone of imperial power in the past, so they are today. Hence, if the United States wants to maintain imperial hegemony, she must continue to support a strong navy.

This argument succumbs to the dangers of oversimplification inherent in historical analogy—the temptation to ignore detail in favor of the from-the-ship generalities learned at school. Even on a superficial level this argument is suspicious. Notice the pivot. Is the key to *any* country's international hegemony a strong navy? Conceivably it is now, but it was not so formerly. The pivot is false. Think of imperial China. Think of the Tartars, Incas, Mughals, Macedonians, Arabs, and so forth. More serious than its false pivot, however, is the argument's substitution of inference for observation. Good analogies aid observation, not hinder it. The above analogy, if good, should lead into the whole new state of affairs into which nuclear and electronic technology has thrown modern military strategy. This the analogy does not do. The Vikings or Napoleon could not blow Britain's ships out of the water at will, as can conventional or nuclear missiles today. If today's ships *are* defensible then the subject of antimissile defenses must be discussed, as well as the question of submarines versus surface vessels, and perhaps the whole complex matter of arming for nonnuclear war. Insofar as the analogy diverts attention from such topics—the real issue—it is a red herring.

The argument also attempts to exploit America's rivalry with the Soviet Union. The analogy implicit in the phrase "tentacles of interest" suggests a marine monster intent on engulfing a victim. But that the Russians are building a strong navy scarcely means that the United States should automatically build one too. Let us sow a counter analogy. Suppose that American colonials had argued that because England had been successful with massed marching formations they should adopt massed marching formations too. Such an argument would have been foolish. Massed formations would have denied the colonials the advantages not only of fighting techniques adopted from native Americans and of the little-cleared terrain of the New World but also of the technologically-advanced long-bore rifle—in short, the very advantages which made the recoats sitting ducks. And until the "sitting ducks" matter has been addressed in the naval inference, no argument about past naval superiority will be satisfactory.

That arguments from historical analogy can be weak and diverting, as the naval argument seems to be, does not mean that all such arguments are weak and diverting. The naval argument deals in wide-ranging, vague generalities, as historical analogies short enough to be quoted in logic books frequently do. When such arguments do turn out to fit the facts, it is because of unsupplied detail, the sort of detail which gives richness to the historian's narrative and ultimately makes or breaks a case.

Good brief historical analogies do at least have the virtue of turning our attention to that detail. J. W. Fulbright's August 24, 1970 Senate speech on the Middle East contained the following advice on how Israel might make best use of her position of advantage after the 1967 war, advice which is still interesting since despite the many developments since 1970 the situation remains fundamentally the same.

> After the First World War the French tried to gain security in somewhat the same way that Israel seeks it today. They, too, were confronted with a potentially powerful but momentarily weakened antagonist and they tried to perpetuate that situation by occupying the German Rhineland, temporarily detaching the Saar, and compelling Germany to pay reparations. The effort to make France secure by keeping Germany weak was a failure. Now, twenty-five years after the Second World War, France has nothing to fear from Germany although Germany is still strong and in possession of all the western territories France once wished to detach. France is secure now not because Germany has lost the power to threaten her but because she has lost the wish to do so. The

analogy is imperfect and simplified but it holds: Israel will be secure when and if the Arabs lose the wish to threaten her.[2]

Fulbright's argument does lead us into details. Between the two situations there exist a number of differences, perhaps what Fulbright meant by calling the analogy "imperfect and simplified." For one thing, "the Arabs" consider not just the occupied lands but *all* of Israel rightfully theirs. That Germany rested satisfied does not mean that Israeli surrender of the occupied territories would satisfy Israel's neighbors. This raises the critical question, what *would* the Arabs settle for? Answering that question forces further searching for the sorts of facts which would answer it. Another difference is represented by the Palestinian refugees. No people displaced from German territory were pressuring France to return their homeland. Later in his speech Fulbright did suggest a plan by which the Palestinians could be satisfied, a plan which, if plausible, may save Fulbright's argument from a seemingly fatal disanalogy. The argument raises another interesting parallel unmentioned by the author, that between Jerusalem and Berlin, a parallel which might be useful for extending the analogy in enlightening directions. So although the analogy is only moderately strong, it does turn our attention toward the facts of the case, not away from them. Like good analogies it does not mesmerize; it suggests.

MORAL COMPARISON

To behave justly is close to, or is, being fair. Fairness dictates equal treatment—similar action in similar circumstances. Therefore, much moral argument will be analogical. Defenses usually stress analogy of treatment in analogous situations, or disanalogy of treatment in disanalogous situations. Condemnations and entreaties usually stress disanalogy of treatment in disanalogous situations, or occasionally, analogous treatment in disanalogous situations. The American Cancer Society argued before the Federal Trade Commission along the following lines:

> The public ought to be informed on cigarette packages how much tar and nicotine they are taking into their lungs when they smoke a certain brand of cigarettes. Consumers are given this information concerning the drugs they take, the foods they ingest, and the drinks they imbibe. Why should they not be given similar information concerning the cigarettes they smoke?

If eating, drug taking, drinking, and smoking are alike, and ingredient labeling makes sense for the first three, then it makes sense for smoking too. The

---

[2] J. W. Fulbright, "Old Myths and New Realities: The Middle East," *The Congressional Record*, vol. 116, no. 147, p. 2.

argument highlights dissimilar treatment in similar situations, pleading therefore that a change is justified. The following judgment typifies moral argument from disanalogy.

> The defense has argued that like previous violators, BLASCO should get the minimum penalty. This argument neglects the fact that unlike the previous violators, BLASCO, having the convictions of those violators as precedent, has nevertheless continued to engage in practices identical to those for which the previous violators were convicted. Moreover, the number and extent of the violations have far exceeded those of any previous violator. Therefore, this court orders not the minimum but the maximum penalty.

Because the crime is different, different punishment fits it.

That moral judgments *should* be made on the basis of true perceptions of similarity and dissimilarity does not mean that they are always so made. At one time or another, on one subject or another, moral blindness afflicts everyone. Sometimes effective at restoring moral vision is the moral parable, which is simply an argument from hypothetical analogy, dressed in the trappings of a tale. When King David desired to add the beautiful Bathsheba to his collection of wives, the fact that Bathsheba was married to Uriah the Hittite did not stop David, who ordered Uriah to the front line of battle. There Uriah was abandoned to the enemy, whereupon David married Bathsheba. Shortly thereafter David was conversing with the prophet Nathan. Nathan told this story:

> There were two men in one city, the one rich, the other poor. The rich man had exceeding many sheep and oxen. But the poor man had nothing at all but one little ewe lamb, which he had brought and nourished up, and which had grown up in his house together with his children, eating of his bread, and drinking of his cup, and sleeping in his bosom: and it was unto him as a daughter. And when a certain stranger was come to the rich man, he spared to take of his own sheep and oxen, to make a feast for that stranger, who was come to him, but took the poor man's ewe, and dressed it for the man that was come to him. And David's anger being exceedingly kindled against that man, he said to Nathan: As the Lord liveth, the man that hath done this is a child of death. He shall restore the ewe fourfold because he did this thing and had no pity. And Nathan said to David: Thou art the man.

David sees the justness of the analogy. The shoe fits; he wears it and repents.

Of course, moral parables, and similar devices, such as caricatures and fables, may, like any analogy, be close or not, fair or unfair. When someone alludes to the story of the goose which laid the gold egg, to the incident of the Trojan horse, or to the myth of Sisyphus, or, as Nathan does, invents a story to fit the situation, we must not let the child in us be delighted by the tale. In all crucial aspects does reality exactly fit? Allusions may be quite explicit, their analogical implications being open for all to see, or they may be veiled. Let us consider the latter sort.

IMPLICIT COMPARISONS

In his discussion of Whistler, Chesterton never really says that art is a fluid or even like a fluid, and would probably have chafed at the insinuation that he had said that it is. Similarly, the student who said that one cannot plant a tree probably would have chafed at being told that he thought that planting a tree is like eating a hamburger or planting a bomb. Many analogical arguments are more or less hinted at, or are hidden, even from their authors. They sometimes lurk in seemingly innocent explanatory metaphors and similes. They hide beneath veiled references. They even occur, as in the student's case, cloaked in the grammatical structure or semantics of the terms and constructions by means of which people express themselves.

Implicit comparisons may be innocent or beneficial, either leading nowhere, or nowhere harmful, while helping to explain and to brighten, or beneficial in the way that explicit comparisons are beneficial. But it would be wise not to *assume* them to be harmless or beneficial. For this reason the careful reasoner will have developed facility at making implicit comparisons explicit.

In distinguishing analogies, mere statements, from analogical arguments one can never be entirely successful. Supposing that one were successful, the trick would be more psychological than logical, for when a seemingly nonargumentative analogy is drawn, associations and implications blossom forth which can lead toward conclusions. Apparently innocent explanatory analogies often conceal tremendous persuasive force.

Consider a couple of catchphrases from recent history. In the early 1960s there was a lot of talk about "penetrating into the soft underbelly of China." The phrase seems to have been no more than a vehicle to express the fact that China's most vulnerable frontier was its southeast. Yet at the same time, possible Freudian implications aside, one cannot help suspecting that this vague image, reinforced by the paunchy profile revealed on the map, actually contributed to the thinking of those who couched their analyses in these terms. They seemed unable to focus on geographic realities— impenetrable jungles and determined populations struggling for existence on home territory. The "soft underbelly" people were opposed by those who feared "getting bogged down" in a land war in Asia. That vague image is no less misleading. Although most of Southeast Asia is hilly, and most military objectives stand on high ground, the "bogged down" figure succeeds in evoking the stereotypical swampy jungle of the John Wayne war movie. Not only catchphrases need to be made explicit; many an original, veiled metaphor has concealed, questionable implications. For example, an academic recently disparaged the idea of using student opinion in evaluating professors, calling it "scholarship by Nielsen rating." Here we have not a catchphrase but a deliberate, original metaphor. Does she really mean to suggest that college students in their evaluations would match that reputedly horrible, mindless lack of judgment shown by the general public in its television preferences? Ask her, and she may reply, "Oh, I never meant to suggest *that*." Whether she meant to suggest that or not, however, the effect of the flamboyant phrase approximates that of an explicit, deliberate suggestion. Its innuendo, if wrong and harmful, ought not to go unchallenged. The innuendo ought to be translated into an explicit argument. Whatever one's position on the use of student input in evaluating faculty, to imply that students would proceed in that matter as the public proceeds in determining its television preferences is wild. The personnel is different, the purposes and motivations are different, the stakes are different. One ought here to cry, "Foul!"

When there is question, therefore, as to whether to treat a catchphrase or colorful metaphor as just an analogy or as an analogical inference, it seems better to err on the side of inference. At worst one will be charged with naïveté. The alternative is potentially harmful falsehood. A liberal politician once tried to dissociate himself from radicalism by means of the slogan, "I am not one of those who believe that in order to save this country it becomes necessary to destroy it." In one shot this politican produced a faulty analogical argument, equivocated on "destroy," and knocked down a straw man. That a U.S. officer's notorious epitaph for the village of Ben Tre ("In order to save the village it became necessary to destroy it") symbolized the madness which the politician's constituents saw in the Vietnam war mentality enabled the politician to use the epitaph's negative connotations to his own ends. But even the most violent radical would not have wanted to destroy this country as Ben Tre was destroyed. Again, a cry of "Foul!" seems called for.

Quick Check

Where the following pieces make less than explicit comparisons (some of which may be moral or historical), make the comparison explicit, not worrying just now about evaluating it. A good dictionary should explain unfamiliar references.

1 "If the child has a tantrum, above all do not punish the child. Tantrums offer a healthy release of pent up emotions. He or she will merely bottle up the anxiety and hostility."

2 "What is tragic about the Palestinian Diaspora, as about any exodus, is that the displaced are unwelcome wherever they go."

3 "Israel's drive for lebensraum created millions of refugees, and forced those Palestinians left behind in Israel to say (as Garibaldi said) 'I am a foreigner in the place of my birth.' "

4 "Not confined to any social, economic, or ethnic group, child abuse can strike

anywhere. Its symptoms are well-known not only to social workers from Harlem to rural Nebraska but to physicians and psychiatrists from Park Avenue to Beverly Hills. The child abuse syndrome does respond to treatment, but only for those who seek it. If you know a parent or parents who suffer from this sickness, help to stem the epidemic. Urge them to call. . . ."

5   "Obviously, the way to control metastatic spread [of cancer] and alter its frequency of secondary colonization is to block one of the important steps in the metastatic process. One of our approaches has been to discover how tumor cells in the circulation can recognize when they are traveling within certain organs, and once this recognition occurs, what means they use to implant on the surfaces of the epithelial cells lining the circulatory vessels." (Garth L. Nicolson, "The Anti-social Cell," *Harpers,* June 1976, p. 44. Copyright 1976 by Harper's Magazine. All rights reserved.)

6   "Under this administration, education efficiency has improved markedly. I think the balance sheet speaks for itself. The student-to-faculty ratio increased from 18 in 1974 to just over 22 today. The output per dollar, as measured by degrees awarded, has increased over 10 percent and the cost per degree in real dollars has risen only slightly during the period."

Answers

1   Likens hostility or anxiety to a harmful gas or liquid "bottle-up," "release," "pent up").

2   Likens the Palestinians' leaving of their homeland to the ancient Jews' leaving of Palestine ("exodus") and to the Jews' dispersal ("Diaspora") among the Gentiles after the Babylonia captivity. Pleads that homeless Palestinians ought to be treated as homeless Jews were treated.

3   "Lebensraum" likens alleged Israeli need for territory to a Nazi German doctrine known by that term. (The Garibaldi quotation likens Israel's claiming or holding of the occupied territories, and perhaps Palestine itself, to France's absorption of and claim to Nice.) The piece attempts to set up a moral parallel: As refugees from German occupation (or Italians under French suzerainty) claim our sympathies, so Palestinian refugees and Israeli non-Jews have analogous claims.

4   Likens child abuse to, or identifies it with, an illness ("symptoms," "treatment," "epidemic," etc.).

5   Likens the actions of cancer cells to the actions of humans or perhaps other sentient creatures ("discover how cells can recognize," "discover what means they use").

6   By the idioms chosen, education seems to be thought of here as an industrial commodity, and its producer, the university, though of as, and likened to, a corporation.

Examples and Comments

1   "If this were oil coming down from Alaska they would be saying, 'Let's not lose it. Let's put up the money to bring up the pipe. Let's do this and that.' But when it is talent, when it is people, when it is art, and, possibly, when it is black, then there is not the same kind of excitement and there is

not the same kind of support. For the lack of that sort of tapping, or building ways out and putting those pipes in, there is going to be in the ghetto talent wasted—just pouring off like oil into the ground. . . ." (Budd Schulberg, "Can the Disadvantaged in the Inner City Learn to Communicate," in Edmund M. Midura (ed.), *Blacks and Whites,* Acropolis, Washington, D.C.)

Comment   By likening the waste of ghetto talent to the waste of an obviously valuable resource, the author effectively underscores the former's value. Like Nathan rebuking David, Schulberg reminds us of the inconsistency of our actions; we behave dissimilarly in similar situations.

One may ask here, however, do artistic resources really rank as high as petroleum resources? Are the situations indeed similar? Schulberg's vivid analogy does not release him from the responsibility of arguing that they are similar.

2   "If you ask me, 'Why should not the people make their own laws?' I need only ask you, 'Why should not the people write their own plays?' They cannot. It is much easier to write a good play than to make a good law. And there are not a hundred men in the world who can write a play good enough to stand the daily wear and tear as long as a law must." (G. B. Shaw.)

Comment   Exactly what does Shaw mean by "make their own laws"? Exactly what is being compared? Is Shaw comparing with playwriting the actual wording of laws and setting up of legal machinery? Or is he comparing with playwriting the ability to call for and object to laws? If the former, which seems likely, the comparison is apt. Like playwriting, law making requires talent at estimating the product's effects on its recipients, and it requires expertise at mastering numberless factual and technical details. Shaw is correct; the people can't write good laws. On the other hand, if Shaw is arguing against the democratic process, then his comparison is less apt. Since the people continually experience the lack of good laws and the burden of bad ones, they are in an excellent judgmental position. In this way (to change the analogy) they more resemble regular playgoers. They can be expert play *judgers* even though, like most playgoers, they would be unable to *write* good plays.

3   "Nuclear apologists admit that any war, once started, can get out of hand. Therefore, they claim, the object of preparing for war is to avoid it. But in no other activity is this true. No one builds a house in order not to inhabit it; no one buys a car not to drive it; no one orders roast beef to leave it on the plate untouched. But the great virtue of nuclear weapons is supposed to be that they will never be used. The argument quite transcends the boundaries of sense."

Comment   This author should abandon his analogy. The pivot, that all reasonable production aims to consume the product, is false. Both his examples concern consumption. He has neglected the whole area of *preven-*

tion, which is precisely what nuclear weapons advocates base their claims on. It may be sensible to conspicuously arm maximum security prison guards, and sensible to maintain a national defense capability, both of which may serve to deter. What is needed here, if it is possible, is to show that the fact that such deterrents are sensible, if they are, does not mean that *nuclear* deterrents are sensible.

4 "The only proof capable of being given that an object is visible is that people actually see it. The only proof that a sound is audible is that people actually hear it. And so on of the other sources of our experience. In a like manner, I apprehend, the sole evidence it is possible to produce that anything is desirable is that people actually desire it." (John Stuart Mill, *Utilitarianism.*)

Comment What Mill concludes about "desirable" on the basis of what holds for "visible," "audible," and so on, is highly questionable. The surface similarities of "visible," and the others, to "desirable" mask significant disanalogies. Although someone may know a fact "because I saw it," no one knows a fact "because I *want* it," and in this sense desire is not a "source of experience." Further, the test of whether "is visible" and the others apply is what people do experience. "An audible frequency which nobody hears" is self-contradictory. But the test of whether "desirable" applies is not what people do desire. "A desirable law which nobody wants" is not self-contradictory. Although these matters may be too tricky, really, for summary treatment, at least this much is clear: Mill ought to argue his contentions about "desirable" directly instead of from surface similarities between words.

5 "If we consider the food question it will not occur to anyone to affirm that the importance of food consists in the pleasure we receive in eating it. Everybody understands that the satisfaction of our taste cannot serve as a basis for our definition of the merits of food, and that we have therefore no right to presuppose that dinners with cayenne papper, Limburg cheese, alcohol, and so on . . . to which we are accustomed and which please us, form the very best human food. In the same way beauty, or that which pleases us, can in no way serve as a basis for the definition of art." (Leo Tolstoy, "What Is Art?")

Comment This is difficult. To the extent that Tolstoy's comparison suggests perhaps novel possibilities it could be useful. But to speak of *the* function of anything so fundamental as eating is oversimple. Who is to say that with food, pleasure cannot be foremost? In what way, for example, is the advice, "I eat what I like and let nutrition take care of itself" clearly inferior to the advice, "Super new Plankton Bars may taste awful, but they're the most nutritious food known"? (This approach attacks the argument by attacking the premise.) Another approach might be to accept the premise but show it to lead in another direction. For example, "Yes, perhaps nutrition may be the function of eating, but that sheds no more light on the food question than reproduction being the function of sex sheds light on how to conduct our sex lives. Whatever art's function may have been evolutionarily, it is not sufficient to convince us to abide by it today." (Might this counter analogy backfire?)

Yet a third approach might be to attack or defend the analogy directly. Are food and art here that close? Personally, I think here that they are. Does food but not art involve basic human traits? Both seem fundamental. Is art more diverse? The activities surrounding nutrition seem equally diverse.

6 "Are interior decorators really necessary? Yes. But not for the accepted reasons. Since one cannot set one's own broken leg one relies on a doctor. Without a formidable knowledge of legal intricacies one depends on a barrister. Likewise, unless the individual is well versed in the home furnishing field the services of an interior decorator are a distinct advantage." (Helen-Janet Bonellie, *The Status Merchants: The Trade of Interior Decoration,* Barnes, Cranbury, N.J., 1972.)

7 "I do not believe Honeywell would produce torture instruments like the rack and screw, even if the Pentagon asked them to. And I call upon Honeywell to stop producing atrocity hardware." (Edmund C. Berkeley at the 25th Anniversary Meeting of the Association for Computing Machinery.)

8 "One of the dreams that lulls us into this hopeful make-believe is the theory of the so-called atomic standoff. This is the argument that, when both we and the Communists have plenty of atomic weapons, neither of us will use them. To gamble on such a miracle is like betting that two men armed with loaded pistols will merely wrestle until one of them is thrown to the ground and kicked to death." (Stuart Symington, in the Senate.)

9 "It is a crime for an individual to relieve himself or herself in a river, it is not a crime for a corporation to relieve itself in a river." (Ralph Nader.)

10 "Prof Knocks Cyclamate Tests. Ripon (PNS) If cauliflower or lima beans were tested like cyclamates and red dye no. 2, they would have been banned from the market, a CU professor says. Dr. Winifred Dray, member of the CU department of food science, denounced the 'childish emotionalism' which she says surrounds the subject of food additives. 'The rats in the tests which led to the ban were a special strain developed for *susceptibility* to tumors. The amounts of cyclamates those rats got equalled our drinking 800 bottles of soda a day. Sure, eating 20 pounds of cauliflower a day would give you goiter from a chemical called thiocynate. And 20 pounds of lima beans a day and you die from hydrogen cyanide poisoning, the chemical used in gas chambers. To me this doesn't make a good deal of sense. But that's the way additives are tested.' "

11 "The number of automobile fatalities per passenger mile is over forty times the number of airline fatalities per passenger mile. That strict licensing standards and regular medical checkups make good sense for airline pilots nobody will deny. Yet drivers of automobiles are subject to lenient or virtually nonexistent standards. This makes no sense at all. Licensing standards, including regular checkups and frequent renewal, ought to be required for automobile drivers too."

12 "Gin drinking was a serious menace while it was cheap. Tax was levied so that gin drinking ceased to be something done by many people much of the time and became a luxury indulged in occasionally. Hip flasks went out. An announcement that the tax on twenty cigarettes would be increased a shilling a year until the cost £1 a packet would help many to reduce their smoking to one after meals and a few at a party." (Christopher Wood, "How to Stop," in Fletcher et al, *Common Sense about Smoking,* Penguin Books, Harmondsworth, Middlesex, 1965.)

13 "One ought to be able to hold in one's head simultaneously the two facts that Dali is a good draughtsman and a disgusting human being. The one does not invalidate or, in a sense, affect the other. The first thing that we demand of a wall is that it shall stand up. If it stands up, it is a good wall, and the question of what purpose it serves is separable from that. And yet even the best wall in the world deserves to be pulled down if it surrounds a concentration camp. In the same way it should be possible to say, 'This is a good book or a good picture, and it ought to be burned by the public hangman.'" (George Orwell, "Benefit of Clergy," *The Collected Essays, Journalism and Letters of George Orwell,* vol. III, Harcourt Brace, New York, 1971.)

14 "Self-consciousness is the source of all our knowledge of mental things. It is obvious that it is only what goes on in our own minds that can be known immediately. What goes on in the minds of others is known to us through our perceptions of their bodies, that is, through the sense-data in us which are associated with their bodies. But for our acquaintance with the contents of our own minds, we should be unable to imagine the minds of others, and therefore we could never arrive at the knowledge that they have minds." (Bertrand Russell, *The Problems of Philosophy,* Oxford Univ. Press, New York, Chap. 5.)

15 Detox Double Standard. "EDITOR: When the county opened its alcohol detoxification center in 1975 its purpose was to decriminalize what is really an illness and to get the public inebriate and the criminal justice system off of each other's backs. Instead, a two-faced system has evolved. This November, a typical month, there were more than 1200 arrests for public drunkenness but only 460 could be handled at the center; the rest were jailed.

"The unlucky ones face charges of public intoxication, which carries a $500 bail tab that few alcoholics can raise. This is an injustice that the county should act immediately to correct."

Applications

A Collect a number of analogies and analogical arguments, both implicit and explicit, from various sources. Organize them into an "Examples and Comments" section, either commenting yourself, or using the material to quiz others.

B Comment on the five arguments in Quick Check section A, p. 147.

C Evaluate Lee's evaluations, in Quick Check section B, p. 147–148.

D Making use of your study of history, or by doing some research, discuss the analogy contained in one of the following sentences. In the historical half of the comparison, exactly what did take place? Is the implication for policy plausible?

1 "Outlawing tobacco would be Prohibition all over again."

2 "There is fear that Portugal may become another Chile."

3 "Like Rome our society may collapse if we allow the luxurious soft living afforded by the consumer mentality to sap our moral strength."

4 "At SALT we should stand firm, be tough. As the Cuban missile crisis made abundantly clear, firmness pays off in dividends."

5 "We must not abandon our commitment to the captive peoples of Eastern Europe and their aspirations for freedom from Soviet domination. One Munich is enough for any century."

6 "Although there is good reason to study and act on the problems of overpopulation and hunger, and pollution, there are no grounds for panic. The sky is not falling. Humanity has always come through before—as it undoubtedly will again."

E Using materials that you have assembled in connection with this and other chapters, construct, administer, and evaluate a *cumulative* "Quick Check."

Chapter 7

Cause

"Do 'organic' methods produce bigger, tastier vegetables?" "How much good would a $15 billion tax cut do now?" "Could Lee Harvey Oswald have acted alone?" "What is a safe occupational level for vinyl chloride?" Answering such questions calls for causal argument, reasoning which purports to test whether A caused or causes B.

Although the remoter and more technical aspects of causal argument may not directly concern the average person, this by no means implies that most causal argument is remote and technical. In fact, we must give and handle causal argument constantly. Who has not seen hundreds of commercial messages containing purported laundry, mileage, complexion, and headache tests? Every day the news assaults us with medical, military, economic, and environmental claims and counterclaims. We or those we know expect results from psychoanalysis, the rotary engine, Scientology, chemotherapy, health foods, transcendental meditation, filter cigarettes, natural childbirth, and the Democratic Party. Causal reasoning being inescapably present, we would be foolish not to try to become familiar with and articulate about its more accessible aspects.

Now as generalizing arguments attempt to support generalizations, so causal arguments attempt to support causal statements—those which reduce to the claim that *A* causes *B*. Hence, before getting to causal argument, the major topic, let us assemble reminders about what we mean when we claim that *A* causes *B*—a tricky task no result of which could not avoid some degree of controversy.

THE IDEA OF CAUSE

Causes may be particular—this individual thing caused, is causing, or will cause something—or they may be general—this *type* of thing causes this other type. "Mrs. O'Leary's cow caused the Chicago fire" would be particular; "Beer drinking causes high levels of urinary albumin" would be general. Causes may be affirmative or negative. Whereas the two causal sentences just quoted are affirmative, their denials would be negative. Negative causal statements are still causal. They use the idea of causality, and they rest on the same methods that establish affirmative causal statements.

"Cause" has numerous partial synonyms in which the idea of causation is essential. If *"A caused B"* is causal, then so is *"A cured B."* Curing is causing to recover. Similarly, *"A prevented B"* is causing not to become afflicted. All such statements are causal. The idea of cause figures essentially in the ideas not only of cure and prevention, but in such fundamental notions as burning and extinguishing, siring and killing, sucking and blowing, flowing and blocking flow, condensing and vaporizing—and thousands of others. In its more familiar reaches, at least, the idea of causation is so basic as to be mastered by about middle childhood.

Now just what is meant when we say that something is or is not the cause of something else? To begin unloading this loaded question, consider the following account of malaria offered by the neurophysiologist Robert S. Morrison.

> In ancient and medieval times malaria as its name implied was thought to be due to the bad air of the lowlands. As a result, towns were built on the tops of hills, as one notices in much of Italy today. The disease did not disappear, but its incidence and severity were reduced to a level consistent with productive community life.
>
> At this stage it seemed reasonable enough to regard bad air as the cause of malaria, but soon the introduction of quinine to Europe from South America suggested another approach. Apparently quinine acted on some situation within the patient to relieve and often to cure him completely. Toward the end of the last century the malarial parasite was discovered in the blood of patients suffering from the disease. The effectiveness of quinine was explained by its ability to eliminate this parasite from the blood. The parasite now became *The Cause,* and those who could afford the cost of quinine and were reasonably regular in their habits were enabled to escape the most serious ravages of the

disease. It did not disappear as a public health problem, however; and further study was given to the chain of causality. These studies were shortly rewarded by the discovery that the parasite was transmitted by a certain species of mosquitoes. For practical purposes *The Cause* of epidemic malaria became the Mosquito, and attention was directed to control of its activities.

Entertainingly enough, however, malaria has disappeared from large parts of the world without anyone doing much about it at all. The fens of Boston and other northern cities still produce mosquitoes capable of transmitting the parasite, and people carrying the organism still come to those areas from time to time; but it has been many decades since the last case of the disease occurred locally. Observations such as this point to the probability that epidemic malaria is the result of a nicely balanced set of social and economic, as well as biological, factors, each one of which has to be present at the appropriate level.[1]

Over the years we have the same thing, malaria, but successively four causes. ("Bad air" may be less satisfactory than the others, but adjusting it to "swampy areas" brings it alongside.) At no stage would it have been wrong to have said, "What causes malaria is *x*," where *x* accorded with the state of the art of prevention and treatment.

The passage illustrates the connection between the ideas of cause and control, a connection which some attempts at good causal argument ignore. We have an interest in control, in this case, eradication of malaria. And at one stage we had: swampy land, malaria; no swampy land, no malaria. Hence it made sense to prevent malaria by moving to hilltops. Avoiding malaria, however, is only one interest. We must eat, and moving to hilltops denies populations the fruits of intensive lowland farming—hence chronic famine (not to speak of plague), as in medieval Italy. In this sense the second answer, "The cause of malaria is a blood parasite" is better. It leads to more control. Quinine makes lowland development feasible, as in the Panama Canal projects or in some of Italy's great swamp-draining endeavors. But, of course, quinine and swamp draining do not completely satisfy our interests. Not only do cartel prices make quinine too expensive for much of the world, even quinine-treated malaria is a scourge. And the evils of draining swamps are just now being driven home. Even the spraying of swamps to kill vector misquitoes is hazardous. Hence the "best" cause, if we may speak that way, is the latest account, the combination of factors, which includes the greatest potential for prevention and cure. And undoubtedly, as we learn more about just how the parasite works on the blood, the account will take on yet further dimensions.

So when we say that *A* causes *B*, we imply that the situation is one we have an interest in controlling. Furthermore, what we assign as the cause

[1] Robert S. Morrison, "Gradualness, Gradualness, Gradualness," *American Psychologist,* 1960, vol. 15, pp. 187–197.

will depend where we stand relative to that interest. Where we stand may be seen in the state of the art at the time, or in our interests as individuals. Suppose that at 4:45 P.M. the operator of a stamp press crushes a hand. What is the cause of the injury? In one sense the injury was caused by the top of the press descending on and crushing the hand. This would be the *immediate* cause. Such an attribution of cause, as in a medical report, may be true and complete, and may suggest to surgeons how to proceed. That the attribution is true and complete relative to one set of interests, however, does not mean that other attributions are ruled out. It is also true that what caused the accident was the operator raising a control lever. This would be a *proximate* (as opposed to the immediate) cause of the accident. The worker would not be wrong to cite this as the cause, blaming himself. Yet other interests may look at the matter differently still. Industrial designers, for instance, might be able to show the loss to have been due to that poorly-thought-out control lever, which lowers the press when raised. At the same time labor people might not be wrong to blame the accident on too long working days or on the inhumanity of unvaried routine. It even might not be wrong for someone to cite the decline of craftmanship and the work ethic. Causes are not exclusionary: different interests suggest different avenues of prevention or cure, and hence different causes.

If causation is connected with control and with our varied interests, then it is not surprising to find many sorts of causal concepts. Because the degree of control we can or want to exert in a situation varies, causation accommodates various degrees. Thus, some attributions of cause are *statistical.* Someone who quits smoking "because it causes lung cancer" acts on correct information, even though the person may know that the chances of a lifelong heavy smoker expiring from the disease are only 1 in 14. Statistical causation is something like a make-do approximation of what we would like to understand better. If and when we *really* understand lung cancer, as we really understand, say, combustion, we may be able to state categorically, not statistically, what factors will invariably produce the disease.

Another sort of usually preliminary or "second best" causation is the "could" causal statement. Where we lack the ability or interest to say that A *does* or *did* cause B, we may have the ability and interest to say that A *could* cause or have caused B. It may be important to know whether Miss Woods could have reached the erase button; whether the ancient Egyptians could have navigated the Atlantic in papyrus rafts; whether amino acids could have formed in the earth's "primordial soup"; or whether someone who was exercising reasonable caution could have noticed the warning signs. Unlike "did" and "does" causal statements, which require more proof, "could" causal statements are established simply by getting duplicate results in duplicate conditions.

We deal with causality's "could" aspect perhaps as often as with its "did" and "does" aspects. A true "could" causal statement definitively rebuts a claim that something cannot be or have been done. People wanted to know definitively about Miss Woods and that erase button. And frequently we are not in sleuthful or scientific moods. Then we don't demand belief clinched—we simply want disbelief squelched. To the question, "How could it be?" the reply, "Well, here's one way," may be perfectly satisfactory.

Most causation results not from a single chain of immediate and proximate causes, but from complexes of factors. Think of a subject as complex as the physical deterioration of the artistic heritage of Venice, where air pollution, monkeying with ship channels, industrial exhaustion of underground water, lack of finances, ideological bickering, bureaucracy—and an unstable subsoil in the first place—all contribute. When wishing to emphasize the complexity of a problem people speak of *contributory* causes. No one thing is responsible. Speaking of contributory causes, however, does not exclude speaking of a sole cause for the same thing. Certain Italian Marxists, for example, who quite understand the many causes of the crumbling, flaking, and sinking of Venice's artistic heritage, nevertheless do not hesitate to blame the whole sorry state of affairs on the failure of capitalism. And although their assignment of blame may be open to question, the meaning of their words is not: again, different viewpoints, different causes.

Quick Check

A Cram each statement into as many categories at it fits. *Categories:* not causal; causal: statistical; general; particular.
1 Fidrych threw nine strikeouts.
2 As it lacked a sprinkler system, the old clubhouse went up like a torch.
3 Eight exceeds seven.
4 The gym lacks a sprinkler system.
5 The rhythm method is the only officially sanctioned means of birth control.
6 Rattlesnake bites are usually not fatal.
7 The burglar used a playing card to trip the lock.
8 Brenda will meet us at 7:30.
9 Kuhn rejected the offer.
10 Dogs transmit roundworms to humans.
B Where the following reports suggest a single chain of events, identify the subject and its immediate and (in order) proximate cause(s). Where the report suggests not a single chain but several contributory causes, identify the subject, and the contributory causes. Then think of a viewpoint which explains them by means of a single encompassing cause.
1 The patient died from loss of blood from a ruptured aorta.
2 For want of a nail a shoe was lost,
For want of a shoe a horse was lost,
For want of a horse a battle was lost,
For want of a battle a kingdom was lost.

3   "I don't want to take anything away from Kuzmovich," said Coach Filipepi after the rout. "He was magnificent, and without his hat trick the game might have been closer than it was. But the way Joao kept setting Kuz up . . . and the way everybody was at the right place at the right time, and passes seemed to be right there out of no place. . . . And the defense, what little they had to do, coordinated perfectly with the offense."

4   "This city's in a real mess. Our spendable income moved to the suburbs, and the people who replaced those who moved out don't have jobs. Our commercial tax base has moved to industrial parks." So spoke newly elected Mayor Frieda Eisen, as she contemplated the problems facing her at the beginning of her first term. "This city has a per capita city payroll higher than New York's, and a retirement system that could bankrupt us in five years."

5   "It's the Fed. They circulated too much money, overstimulated the economy, which drove up prices. So, if you want to know why you're short at the end of the month. . . ."

Answers

A   (1) causal, particular; (2) causal, particular; (3) not causal (general); (4) not causal (?); (5) causal, general, statistical; (6) causal, general, statistical; (7) causal, particular; (8) not causal; (9) causal, particular; (10) causal, general, statistical.

B   (1) *Subject:* patient's death; *immediate cause:* blood loss; *proximate cause:* ruptured aorta. (2) *Subject:* lost kingdom; *immediate cause:* lost battle; *proximate causes:* lost horse, lost shoe, lost nail. (3) *Subject:* the rout; *contributory causes:* Kuz's hat trick, Joao's set-ups, perfect positioning, deceptive, accurate passing, defense coordinated with offense; *encompassing cause:* teamwork. (4) *Subject:* the city's real mess; *contributory cause:* income to suburbs, replacements jobless, tax base moved to industrial parks, high city payroll, costly retirement system; *encompassing cause:* poor planning (or perhaps individual selfishness). (5) *Subject:* why you're short at month's end; *immediate cause:* inflation; *proximate causes:* overstimulated economy, too much money circulated, the Fed.

CAUSAL ARGUMENTS

Many of us go through life without performing simple tests which would settle causal matters on which considerable enjoyment, effort, or wealth depend. A couple may argue for years about which of two routes is the faster. It never occurs to them to time the trips under typical conditions. Gardening neighbors may dispute the virtues of double-stalk-training tomatoes, never giving their respective contentions the acid test. Is it desirable to use butter—or anything—to baste a turkey? Buffered aspirin, a gasoline additive, a freezer, the more expensive brand, the imported stuff: in your case does using these make a difference? One should put one's subjective impressions to the test. Many a claim that something made no difference has been shown to be false. And many a perceived "difference" has turned out to be purely psychological. Asked about the difference between his firm's best-selling, heavily advertised, top-of-the-line product, and the firm's 40 percent cheaper, little-advertised counterpart, one liquor marketing executive replied, "Frankly, that's a bit embarrassing. I mean, it's mainly a matter of pricing policy."

Conducting little causal experiments on the details of one's life is, of course, only a small aspect of causal argument, and, of course, one can run one's own life as one chooses. Assessing the causal arguments of others, on the other hand, is frequently an obligation of citizenship. Therefore, it is important to have explicitly in mind what good causal argument looks like, and to be articulate at explaining the strengths and weaknesses of those sorts of causal arguments on which the general welfare depends.

Good causal arguments are twofold. On the one hand they contain a *congruence* aspect. They state a connection between occurrences or phenomena; for example, "A was present and B was present," or, "A and B rise and fall together," or "When A responds to S, A always responds B." On the other hand, good causal arguments also always contain an *exclusion* aspect, a ruling out. For example, "The difference could not have been due to chance," or "All other possible factors have been eliminated," or, "There is no way that the difference could be due to the alleged cause." Let us examine each of these aspects of causal argument in some detail, bearing in mind the impossibility of examining the one in total isolation from the other.

The Congruence Aspect   If we connect two occurrences or phenomena, we have a connection but not yet a causal connection, a fact well illustrated by the following two stabs at a cause on the basis of a single connection. First, Huckleberry Finn:

> I've always reckoned that looking at the new moon over your left shoulder is one of the carelessest and foolishest things a body can do. Old Hank Bunker done it once, and bragged about it; and in less than two years he got drunk and fell off a shot tower and spread himself out so that he was just a kind of layer. . . . But anyway, it all come of looking at the moon that way, like a fool.

Twain's caricature rings true. Huck's failing represents a common enough type of bad reasoning, as does this letter.

> *Editor:* It is hard to understand why the law against selling pornographic literature to youngsters under 18 is not enforced here. Is not our alarming juvenile delinquency enough to open our eyes to the greater danger of obscenity? I wholeheartedly join the protest. . . .

These poor souls seem not to realize that *anything*, not just the simple, single connections they see, could have caused the occurrence they try to explain.

Correlations   The previous two arguments attempt to establish causes on the basis of a single connection. But what of a repeated, regular connection between one phenomenon and another? Such a connection is called a *correlation.* Do correlations establish causes?

First let us say a bit about correlations. A correlation connects one phenomenon with another. The existence of mushrooms on the golf course correlates with the existence of recent warm rains. Correlations may be of degree. The pressure a given volume of air, as in a bicycle tire, correlates with its temperature, the hotter the air the greater the pressure, the cooler the air the less the pressure. Success in college is supposed to be correlated with IQ—the higher, or lower, the one, the higher, or lower, the other. Correlations may be *direct,* as in the previous examples, existence being accompanied by existence, rise being accompanied by rise, fall by fall. Or correlations may be *inverse,* existence being accompanied by nonexistence, and vice versa, rise being accompanied by fall, and vice versa. The existence of mushrooms on the golf course correlates inversely with the existence of recent hard frosts. At a constant temperature, air's volume correlates inversely with its pressure, as when one squeezes a tennis ball. And there is supposed to be an inverse correlation between IQ and failure in college. Correlations may be *perfect,* every single rise or fall being accompanied by a corresponding rise or fall, as in the air examples, or they may be *statistical,* as the IQ correlations presumably are, where only a tendency or probability, not a 1 to 1 relation, is conveyed.

That correlations do not themselves indicate agency may be for various reasons. Some correlations are definitional or quasi-definitional, such as that between the number of lottery tickets sold and the chance that the ticket one bought will win, or that between the percentage of recently divorced males in a population and the percentage of recently divorced females. Other correlations may be due to changed standards in record keeping or to changed interests, and reflect no agency at all. Many correlations are coincidence, such as that which probably exists between a complete cycle of moon phases and a human menstrual cycle. Then again many correlations result not from the action of one variable upon another but from that of yet another variable. Undoubtedly, someone could discover an essentially perfect correlation between the dropping of Vermont maple leaves and advent of Vermont snows, yet it would be absurd to maintain that the dropping of the leaves somehow brings on the snows. Similarly, the price of bread and the price of beer may rise and (hypothetically) fall together, due to neither's effect on the other but to rises and falls in, for example, the price of grain, or of labor, or the general cost of living.

Some correlations, though parts of causal chains, do not count as causal because their point in the chain is not the one at which we can exert control, or is incidental to the point in the chain where we can exert it.

There must be some sort of correlation between smokers lighting matches and smokers getting lung cancer, yet we do not zero in on lighting matches. Lighting matches is incidental to the real culprit, smoking. (Of course, if it could be shown that something breathed from the matches was directly related to lung cancer, that would be another story entirely.)

Correlations often prove to be valuable preliminaries to causal discoveries by directing attention to that third variable, the one responsible for both parts of the correlation. The relationship recently claimed between breast cancer and the unusual type of fingerprint called a composite seems wildly coincidental. Yet there might just be a third variable which explains the correlation, and which then could prove to be fertile ground for investigation of the sources of breast cancer. For example, there is a connection between a mother's having suffered a virus attack during pregnancy and her child's having abnormal fingerprints. Could the virus attack also somehow transmit a susceptibility to breast cancer to the offspring? Or, for example, fingerprints are inherited. Could both composite fingerprints and susceptibility to breast cancer be passed along in the same element of genetic code?

Arguing to a causal conclusion from a single congruence (as Huck Finn did), or from a correlation, makes the mistake known as *post hoc ergo propter hoc* ("after it, therefore because of it"), an error sometimes called "post hoc" for short, and which we will call simply something like "bad causal reasoning."

The Exclusion Aspect   Good causal argument needs not only congruence, it needs exclusion. The exclusion aspect, a complex of interconnected details, will be examined under the headings *Causal Hypotheses, Controls, Controlling, Selecting experimental subjects,* and *Significance.*

Causal Hypotheses   A simple causal argument can be seen as built on an "if-then" premise, the *causal hypothesis.* Take any causal question—for example the question, "Is this fertilizer alkaline?" (in which case it will harm my azaleas). The question will be settled by reasoning such as:

> If this fertilizer is alkaline, then it will turn the paper blue. This fertilizer turns the paper blue. Therefore, this fertilizer is alkaline.

Now compare that argument with the following, which is invalid.

> If it's a platypus, then it's a mammal. It's a mammal. Therefore, it's a platypus.

Unlike the latter argument, the former argument, though outwardly similar, is valid. The "if" in the former argument really means "if and only if." The argument is formulated so that the cause may be pinned down, to the exclusion of everything else.

Usually not the "if" part but the "only if" part of a causal hypothesis proves the more difficult to establish. Consider the following.

What had made those cans of paint burst while three-fourths of the same run showed no signs of pressure at all? A check of records and a chemical analysis of representative burst and unburst samples revealed that ingredients and conditions had been invariable throughout manufacture and storage—with one exception. The run had consisted of four equal batches, and according to the analysis, only three of them contained fungicide. Given that fungus growth causes pressure, and that this kind of paint is a good environment for fungus growth, omission of one vital ingredient—the fungicide—accounts for the burst cans.

The investigators reasoned that *if* the lack of fungicide were responsible, that condition would have burst the cans without fungicide (there's the congruence aspect); and they reasoned that *only* if the lack of fungicide were responsible (there's the exclusion aspect) would the cans with fungicide show no pressure and not burst. Were something else responsible, those cans would also have shown pressure or burst. The investigators were able to exclude every explanation except one. (As long as this example is before us, it is worth noting that the cause here was not exactly a thing or an event, it was a *lack*. As one can sin by doing nothing, so can one cause great events by not paying the least attention—fiddling while Rome burns.)

In the paint argument the element of chance does not directly figure. When chance does figure, chance must be eliminated.

Cody's bellyaching about his colleagues washing the department coffeepot with soap became so annoying that they decided to test his sensitivity. They broke in two new pots, just like the old, washing one pot with soap, washing the other only with pure water. Then Cody was presented successive paper cups of coffee drawn from pot "heads" or pot "tails" according to the flip of a coin. To avoid some kind of tip-off, Herschel, who presented the cups and kept score ("Soap," or "No soap"), didn't know which pot the cups were from. They quit at 4 heads and 4 tails cups since Cody hadn't missed once.

His colleagues have discovered that Cody did distinguish. He is the causal agent. Again the reasoning proceeds hypothetically: *if* Cody can tell, then Cody will not miss; *and only if* he can tell will he not miss. The experiment rules everything else out. Cody can't fudge, consciously or not, to protect his ego; he can't get unconscious cues from Herschel; he can't recognize a "new-pot" versus an "old-pot" taste; he can't discern a pattern in the presentation of cups; and so forth. And Cody will not be succeeding just by chance. In this case we have more than a simple congruence, we have a sustained perfect correlation. There being a 1 in 2 chance of getting any cup right simply by luck, there would be a 1 in 256 chance of getting eight independent cups (2^8) right simply by luck. And additional cups, if anyone cared that much, would render the odds astronomical against a string of lucky guesses.

Let us notice two more things. First, whereas the paint investigators were able to test the causal hypothesis by poring over records and by chemical analysis, Cody's colleagues had to conduct an *experiment*. The difference, however, is small. In the one example details (the "variables," as they say) had to be *manipulated* so that the data would fall into place. Second, since in both examples the causal hypothesis suggested itself readily, the examples may present a misleading picture. In many investigations hypothesis after hypothesis must be tested and rejected before the one which pinpoints the cause finally, if ever, comes to light. Like most simple arguments, simple causal arguments are usually no more than elements in the network of arguments, pro and con, which together form a complex case.

The role of hypothesis in negative causal argument is about the same as in positive, the difference being that the facts rule against the hypothesis. Had both fungicide and non-fungicide cans burst, or had Cody missed on about half the trials or more, the two previous arguments, perhaps with an additional twist or two, would have ruled against the supposed causal agents. The following argument, from St. Augustine's *Confessions,* finds evidence against the hypothesis that the stars detail each person's destiny.

> Firminus had heard from his father that when his mother had been pregnant with him a slave belonging to a friend of his father's was also about to bear. . . . It happened that since the two women had their babies at the same instant, the men were forced to cast exactly the same horoscope for each newborn child down to the last detail, one for his son, the other for the little slave. . . . Yet Firminus, born to wealth in his parents' house had one of the more illustrious careers in life . . . whereas the slave had no alleviation of his life's burden.

This argument rules out a causal hypothesis because of its lack of congruence. If the stars detail each person's destiny (let us call this "hard" astrology), then Firminus and the slave should have similar careers. That they did not tells against the hypothesis. Now although this argument effectively rebuts naïve "hard" astrology, "soft" astrology, the doctrine that the stars influence but don't compel, remains unscathed. So do sophisticated astrologies (about which more later), even "hard" versions.

Controls   What backs that "if and only if" statement, the causal hypothesis? Take the simplest possible case, the television commercial in which the actor returns the oil to the bottle after having fried a chicken, the oil measuring only a tablespoon less than it did to start with. Were the results really due to the oil? With this sort of argument the scoffers will have a field day. Why could the results not have been due to a deft frying technique, or short immersion time? Why not to the chicken itself? Especially, why not to some factor which the investigators have not taken into account? How do we know that *any* oil may not have yielded the same result, or a better one? The answer to all this is simple: *"Try* it." Even television commercials can run fair tests. The sponsors could test several oils against their brand. Then if the comparison produced significant differences, the scoffers would be hard pressed.

Good causal arguments are *twofold* comparisons. Something undergoes a change, or fails to. This is one comparison, "before" to "after." But in order that the change or lack of change be attributed to the cause, or that the cause be ruled out, a standard is needed against which to gauge the change or lack thereof. Such a standard is the *control*. Schematically (and at some risk of oversimplification), controls can be explained as functioning as follows: first, a control is matched to the material being tested; it is made or determined to be like that material in every respect except one, namely, the alleged cause. Then a trial is run. Then, if the test material undergoes change while the control does not (and chance has been ruled out), the change may be attributed to the difference. If both the test material and the control undergo change, or if neither undergoes change, then the cause has yet to be identified.

A simple case will illustrate. Suppose that someone baking bread at home and lacking one ingredient, salt, substitutes sea salt. The bread tastes better than before. Now was the success due to the substitution? It could have been due to new-crop flour, good rising conditions, or any number of things. A control batch will provide the answer. At the next baking session the baker should split the batch, keeping everything identical but making half of the batch according to the old recipe, and half according to the new. Then if the sea salt bread is better the improvement may be attributed to the difference: the sea salt. The control batch enables other factors (flour, rising conditions, etc.) to be ruled out, for were one or more of them responsible the improvement would have appeared in the control batch too.

Using a control here helps as well to eliminate another set of factors which could have explained the original difference, those related to that circumstance-governed faculty, taste. Under one set of conditions almost anything tastes good (camping trips confer instant reputations on novice cooks), while under other conditions (heat, illness, etc.) certain foods displease which otherwise please, and vice versa. The control batch gives the experimenter the chance to try both batches under similar conditions, thus eliminating suspicion that at the time, *any* bread, sea salt or regular, would have tasted especially good.

In the laboratory or kitchen, providing a test item with its twin may be easy compared to what must be settled for under other conditions. Many causal questions cry for answers in areas where good controls cannot be constructed. "Is there a connection between underground nuclear testing and earthquakes?" "What makes him suicidal?" "Given the transportation worldwide epidemics they portend?" "What could have caused this temple complex to have been abandoned?" Yet other questions call for controls which would be impractical or dangerous to construct—questions in certain areas of drug research, for example. (To its everlasting shame, an agency of the U.S. government early in this century actually tested treatments for syphilis by leaving the control subjects untreated! Nowadays potential remedies would be tested not against untreated controls but against the most effective present method.)

In the absence of deliberately constructed controls, naturally occurring parallels—*natural controls*—can sometimes be found which approximate the ideal. The paint cans with the fungicide provided the perfect standard against which to test the hypothesis that lack of fungicide burst those other cans. Systematic recording of details made that possible. Sometimes serendipity will do the same thing. Biologists attempting to test the hypothesis that the pufferfish feeds on the coral-reef-destroying crown-of-thorns starfish, placed a pufferfish and a crown-of-thorns together inside a wire cage. Sure enough, after awhile the puffer did nibble on the crown-of-thorns. As happens so often in research, however, the question arose, "Have we a picture of reality here, or have we instead something created by the testing conditions?" The exclusionary aspect of this causal argument would have been weak had not another pufferfish suddenly appeared and attempted to get at the crown-of-thorns inside the cage. The result was a more fully confirmed hypothesis of tremendous practical importance.

Supposed natural controls need close scrutiny. Rarely is the parallel perfect between test material and control. Violent crime may have fallen off in one state which has abolished the death penalty, while increasing in a similar state which has retained it. Have we a "deterrence" argument for abolishing the death penalty? Not yet. How similar are the states, really? Chances are, the states differ physically, demographically, and historically, which makes formidable the confirmation of any causal hypothesis, let alone such a complex one. A dozen questions spring, or ought to spring, to mind: "Is the death penalty enforced, or seen as enforced, in the state which has retained it?" "What are the *details* of the capital or near-capital offenses in the two states?" "What about other states?" and so forth. Such matters demand not cynicism—their results are too important—but caution.

In research the *retrospective* and the *prospective* studies both make use of natural controls. The retrospective study compares data already collected (usually for another purpose). In medicine (just to take an example from one of many areas), our first strong indication of a connection between a disease and its cause is likely to come from a retrospective study—the poring over of hundreds and thousands of death certificates, say, in the attempt to see whether correlations exist: "Of the records listing liver cancer as immediate cause of death, what percentage of the victims would have been chronically exposed to vinyl choride?" "Is this percentage significantly larger than that of those who appear not to have been so exposed?" "Of those chronically exposed to vinyl chloride, what is the death rate from liver cancer compared with that of those not so exposed?" Although the retrospective study can be valuable in *defining* causal issues and in leading to breakthroughs, it is rarely sufficient to settle causal issues. Retrospective data is typically crude. As with any statistic, that question about changed standards ought to be ready. Th:nk of the potential differences between test and control. Physicians may indicate only the immediate cause of death—pneumonia, heart failure, and the like—while not noting or knowing that the immediate cause is only a complication of something else. After a retrospective study, a *prospective* study may be useful. Observe similar data as they come in, if possible seeing that conditions are controlled to a degree greater than were those in the past.

Even second-best attempts at controls are preferable to no attempt. They highlight deficiencies and data to keep watch for, and suggest direction for new investigation. It is surprising that intelligent, educated people so often rest satisfied with uncontrolled results. In the following segment of an interview, psychologist H. J. Eysenck voices a scepticism which, whether here justified or not, it would be well to hear more often. To a question about psychoanalysis and about therapy for schizophrenics, Eysenck replies:

> If you want to show that a given therapy works you have to compare the percentage of recovery with the percentage of recovery of the group who haven't been treated, or have been treated in some other way which you consider inferior. This of course Laing and Cooper and the others have never done. Until it is done, what can one say? They treat a small number of atypical schizophrenics, some of whom get better and some don't. No accurate statistics are presented. . . . Some of these people would have gotten better if they hadn't been treated at all. Why should I be convinced by statements that they're doing some good to these people when there is no real evidence for it?[2]

Controlling The term "control" denotes not only the standard against which a supposed causal change is measured but also the whole process of monitoring and regulating the many details, which could affect the result. Lack of fungicide could be pinpointed as the cause of those bursting paint cans only because someone had systematically recorded details of manufacture and storage. Control means not only monitoring details, it means heading off trouble by regulating details, variations of which could affect the result. The careful investigator controls the variables. In frying those chick-

---

[2] *Penthouse,* July 1970, p. 21f. Copyright Penthouse International Ltd. and reprinted with the permission of the copyright owner.

ens, for instance, the experimenter would control for oil temperature and quantity, for the fat contributed by the chickens, and for a dozen other details. Frequently some little thing, or what seemed a little thing, or what wasn't noticed at all, makes the difference. And although the controlling of variables may be a skill of detail and experience, its more familiar aspects are available and useful to us all. In many tests a financial venture is in the offing, or could be. Thousands of hours' work may be at stake, or countless lives. Then—and investigators face this constantly—no variable, insofar as is practical, can be left uncontrolled. The following section of deposition illustrates the sort of casualness which has no place in causal investigation.

> **Q** Do you have copies of the reports you sent in?
> **A** No, it was all verbal. . . .
> **Q** When you started giving patients doses did you keep a record of who these patients were?
> **A** Yes.
> **Q** Did you have any means of making any direct observation from the patients. By this I mean this, I know some clinical researchers wrote papers in which they said they would give the drug and every thirty minutes they would look at the patient and make some physical observation on what the patient seemed to be doing.
> **A** No, this was not done. The people took these in their own home.
> **Q** And would report back to you how often?
> **A** When they would come in for a visit, or if they would call, by phone.[3]

When variables must be left uncontrolled everything in a good investigation will be watched closely. Conclusions will be tentative, tempered by the consciousness that, like everyone else, investigators learn best from their mistakes.

Even our bread baker (if we may stretch a point) should be leaving nothing to chance. Who knows what may become of the discovery, or more realistically, what may become of discoveries borne of good habits? The loaf size and rising conditions of the test and control batches should be identical. If total batch size exceeds oven capacity, necessitating two bakings, loaves from each sub-batch should be baked at each baking, their positions varied in the oven, and any variations between bakings or deviations from normal conditions recorded. Those tasting the batches should be neither famished nor sated, neither ill nor pregnant, neither committed to the success nor committed to the failure of one type, nor aware of other tasters' reactions. In order to counter any *placebo effect*—the tendency for "effects" to occur for no other reason than that subjects expect them to occur—the tastes should be presented *blind,* the subjects not knowing which

---

[3] James Ridgeway, "More About Thalidomide," in Sanford, *Hot War on the Consumer,* Pitman/New Republic Book, New York, 1969, p. 99f.

stimulus, which batch, they are sampling. Better yet, the tastes may be presented *double blind* with, in addition, those presenting the samples to the tasters not knowing which batch they are presenting. The Cody experiment was double blind. If there were few tasters and the result mattered, the tasting could be *replicated* (jargon for "repeated").

To avoid a possible *order effect,* half the subjects should be given the test material first, and half given the control first. In this regard the Cody experiment ended fortunately. Had Cody suffered that species of order effect called the "fatigue" effect, in which senses become dulled upon successive stimulation, had Cody started missing after his second or third sample, his missing could not have been attributed to this inherent insensitivity. The test would have had to have been conducted over a longer time span.

Where an order effect is possible, and in many other situations, experimenters add the element of *crossover,* in which test and control are reversed in a later trial. Crossover double-checks the equality of the test and control subjects, since each set of subjects acts as a control on the other. Moreover, one more trial never hurt any experiment. The folks who urged us to test their product by spraying our right armpit with the deodorant we are then using and our left armpit with new whatever-it-was, relied on our gullibly assuming that both sides perspire equally. In order to squelch the challenge that probably most people perspire more on their right sides anyhow, and in order to produce a fair test, the new whatever-it-was folks need to have us compare their product against the competition by having us try it first on one side, preferably à side chosen at random, and then, in a later trial, the other.

Selecting Experimental Subjects If Johnny, age 5, gets cavities and his classmate Billy, age 5, does not get cavities, what can we conclude? Undoubtedly, Johnny and Billy have different heredity, diet, family situations, and who knows what else? That Johnny's *group* got cavities, however, while Billy's did not, is another matter. Groups can be chosen to avoid individual differences, or so that individual differences, statistically speaking, even out.

Obviously, groups which are to be compared must be comparable. How do researchers get groups which are truly alike? Perhaps the most widely used technique involves selecting *random* groups. Ideally, one would first "random sample" the parent group which one anticipates projecting to. The resulting sample would then be randomly split into two or more subsamples, one of which becomes the control. With samples of sufficient size, the probability of atypical items being distributed disproportionately thus becomes very small. The technique will be used where pretesting the samples would be impractical or would ruin the experiment. And if the original sampling, not just the splitting, has been conducted at random, the results will be fully projectable to the parent group. Where sampling the parent group would be impractical, techniques such as the following (in this case with a total group of 202) are typical.

> Patients were numbered sequentially as they volunteered for the study. The patient identification numbers were supplied to the Silford Hall USAF Medical Center pharmacy, who prepared the HCG or placebo during the first phase of the program according to a table of random numbers, and the investigators received the samples in vials identified with only the patient's number.[4]

Since obviously a drug study must use available volunteers, not a random sample, the investigators were able to compensate for loss of projectability in this random groups study by examining the patients in detail. Upon such examination, reasons, if any, to believe the patients atypical of the population to which the findings project, would usually surface.

Another technique for obtaining comparable groups is not to select the groups at random but to *match* them. One would examine a number of items, selecting pairs of items which were alike. The pairs would then be divided into subsamples composed of one member of each pair. (Which member went in which group might be decided by a random process.) Matched group studies include the so-called twin studies, in which one member of a number of pairs of identical twins, but not the other member, is subjected to some phenomenon, with the group consisting of the other members serving as the control. The following abstract describes such a study, and is worth quoting in full.

> Three different dosages of vitamin C, dependent on body weight, were administered to 44 school-age monozygotic twins for five months using a double-blind, co-twin control study design. The mothers recorded daily observations of cold symptoms, and multiple biochemical, anthropometric, and psychological measurements were made at the beginning and end of the study. Paired comparisons showed no significant overall treatment effect on cold symptoms, but the response was not uniform in all subgroups. Treated girls in the youngest two groups had significantly shorter and less severe illness episodes, and an effect on severity was also observed in the youngest group of boys. The seven treated twins in the latter group also grew an average of 1.3 cm more than their untreated co-twins during the five-month period of the study.[5]

Not all matched group studies use identical twins. In some matched group designs, numbers of volunteers are ranked according to their ability to complete some task or other, groups being chosen so that each member

---

[4] Robert L. Young et al., "Chorionic Gonadotropin in Weight Control," *Journal of the American Medical Association,* Nov. 29, 1976, p. 2495.

[5] Judy Z. Miller et al., "Therapeutic Effect of Vitamin C," *Journal of the American Medical Association,* Jan. 17, 1977. p. 248.

of each group has a counterpart with a similar ranking in the other group. Again, one of the groups will serve as test group, the other as control.

Like all techniques of this sort, the matched group technique has its advantages. Since the odds of getting one group stacked with atypical subjects does not need to be overcome, matched group studies require fewer subjects than would similar random group studies. Subjects readily available can be used—trees on the Capitol grounds, volunteers, all of a university's Chem. 1A students, etc.—no small advantage where collecting a random sample proves to be beyond the means available, or impossible, or simply not worth the effort. The vitamin C study required only 44 twin pairs. Also, since experimenters usually know more details about the subjects in matched-group studies, valuable peripheral phenomena occasionally come to light which might otherwise be lost.

Matched groups have disadvantages too, of course, foremost of which is loss of generalizability: what assurance is there that the groups are like whatever population the experimenter contemplates generalizing to? (To offset this disadvantage one might match a randomly selected group with non-randomly selected counterparts, gaining generalizability, the general conclusion being appropriately tentative. Was bias introduced in the matching process?) Another drawback of the matched-groups technique in some instances is that the act of matching may obliterate a contrast between the "before" and the "after," as in studies in which teaching subjects certain tasks in the process of matching the groups also gives them the ability to perform the related tasks in the study itself.

Significance Thus far we have simplified reality by limiting discussion to cases where differences between test and control were clear-cut or else turned out to be nonexistent. But much causal reasoning is a matter of degree. The Codys of this world neither miss them all nor get them all. In order to attribute causality, how many of them do they have to get? And in order to deny it, how many of them must they miss?

A result is said to be causally significant when the probability of its having occurred by chance, and hence not by the cause in question, falls below a certain level. Generally, significance will be higher the greater the difference between test and control results, the greater the number of individuals in the test and control groups, the greater the number of trials, and the less the inherent variability in the material. Many researchers and subjects choose a 5 percent significance level, meaning that on mathematical grounds the results could have occurred by chance in less than 5 percent of the cases. In research requiring more stringent significance levels a 1 percent figure is often used. Why 5 percent or 1 percent, and not 10 percent or .1 percent? And how is significance computed? Since answers to these questions get tricky both mathematically and philosophically, and since there exist many tests for different situations, let us pursue only the subject's more accessible and nonmathematical aspects.[6] For even here we laymen can often make a contribution. For instance, some newspapers featured a report alleging a connection between marijuana smoking and chromosomal defects. Far into the story, which carried a large headline and sensational lead paragraphs, were buried the details that one M.D. had examined nine patients who were regular marijuana users and nine who had never used the drug, finding chromosomal defects in seven of the users and in only two of the nonusers. We have here a prime example of an incomplete, hence in no way newsworthy, report. Aside from our having no reason to believe that the users and nonusers are at all alike, the difference between the two groups, for all we know, could have been due to chance. The following report embodies a related form of statistical incompleteness.

> Dr. Loma said the fetus of a heavy smoker can be damaged by not receiving enough oxygen from the mother's bloodstream. That oxygen is replaced by carbon monoxide. She reported that in a test of more than 2000 mothers in Washington State during a one-year period a higher incidence of spontaneous abortions, stillbirths, newborn deaths, and premature labor was noted among heavy smokers than among nonsmokers.

First, notice that the report mentions no controls. As far as we can tell, smoking mothers may have had more abnormalities for *any number* of reasons. Lifestyles of smokers, personalities and who knows what else probably differ significantly from those of nonsmokers. The main point here, however, is that although 2000 may seem an impressive figure, it may actually be inadequate: 2000 what? Mothers selected from the general population? If so, only a small proportion of these would conceive over the period of a year. And of those who did conceive, only a small portion would experience abnormalities of the sort mentioned. By "mothers" is probably meant those women who did conceive—2000 pregnancies. The trouble is, we are given no idea how many women of those 2000 experienced abnormalities. For all we are told the score could have been Smokers 2, Nonsmokers 1, or Smokers 101, Nonsmokers 99. Any such result would be insignificant.

[6] A straightforward presentation of a number of significance tests, and their applications, can be found in Russell Langley, *Practical Statistics for Nonmathematical People,* Dover, New York, 1971. For significance tests in cases such as the Cody incident, see M. Amerine and E. Roessler, *Wines: Their Sensory Evaluation,* Freeman, San Francisco, 1976—perhaps a less painful source than normal from which to acquire a working knowledge of elementary statistics, as well as techniques for testing a variety of substances and products.

CAUSAL REASONING AND THE IDEA OF CAUSE

This chapter began with a discussion of what we mean when we maintain that *A* caused or causes *B*. That discussion emphasized the connection between cause and control, between cause and our interests. Most attempts at causal argument accord with that connection. When they do not they will be more or less faulty.

Let us begin with the "more." A magazine advertiser once urged readers to send for a "Roach Killer. Only one moving part. Guaranteed 100% effective when used as directed." The device turned out to consist of two blocks of soft wood and the directions, "Place roach on one block. Smash with other." To those who squandered $3.95 this was no joke. The device cannot possibly be used as advertised. Therefore, the device cannot serve our interest in eliminating roaches. Therefore, the causal inference ("100 percent effective roach killer") cannot be justified.

Failure to do justice to the connection between cause and control faults many an argument. Let the following serve as touchstone for a whole category of mistakes. A commercial proclaims:

> Extensive tests at a famous hospital proved that two XYZ tablets give *twice* the pain relief of aspirin alone. Here, thirty women are taking two aspirin, and here an identical thirty women are taking two XYZ tablets. . . . Tabulated on this chart are the results thirty minutes later. You get twice the pain relief with XYZ. Twice the relief.

It turns out, however, in those "extensive tests," that XYZ exceeded aspirin by the stated degree *only* at the point one half hour after ingestion. The copy neglects to mention that at other periods during the test aspirin equalled or exceeded XYZ tablets in "pain relief." By selectively reporting results favorable to its side, the pitch thus engages in special pleading. (In fact, it seems to be a fault-finder's paradise.) The copywriters expect us to succumb to that form of oversimplification which consists of thinking that "before" and "after" in causal arguments are always simply two points in time. To serve our interests, however, a pain reliever must give results not only a half hour later but also after ten minutes, after an hour, in fact, continuously.

That causality is usually more than simply a "before" and an "after" matter, two points in time, seems to be missed by many people, at least in their more casual moments. They hear, for example, that the success rate at a smoking clinic is 80 percent. Now someone who invests agony, time, and dollars to quit smoking seeks something permanent. Most "cures" for smoking, however, have a high relapse rate. The same goes for a large number of enterprises which generate more hoopla, and funding, than genuine success—enterprises such as drug rehabilitation centers, alcoholism programs, "big brother" efforts for juvenile delinquents, behavior modification for the obese, shock therapy, or the latest cure for stuttering. Such enterprises *may* turn out to work, but only if their results last. Many of them have a placebo effect on their subjects. They work, for a while, until the excitement of newness wears off and old patterns resurface. Therefore, given a causal claim, questions such as, "How long does it last?" and, "What is the rate of relapse?" ought automatically to come to mind.

Many causal questions, perhaps most, are quantitative. We want to know not only if *A* causes *B,* but *how much A* causes *what degree* of *B* and *over what time span.* Qualitative connections are fine as far as they go, but quantitative breakdowns usually furnish more of what we need for control. Yes, alcohol causes traffic accidents, but what *proportion* of traffic accidents? And of that proportion how much alcohol was involved in 10 percent of the cases; how much in 50 percent; how much in 80? If one is going to drive at all after drinking, or if one is proposing responsible legislation, or enforcing the law, then the quantitative answers are the only useful ones.

Those testers of pain relievers attempted to quantify the unquantifiable, pain. Pain cannot be measured in percentage. But the researchers did at least sensibly plot relative effectiveness quantitatively—continuously against time—so that their chart (not the one shown in the advertisement) does depict the drugs' effects. Even when continuity is provided for one factor, however, continuity may be lacking for another. The following test will illustrate. The test features a device touted as "the effortless, no-nonsense way to increase bustline size." The argument provides "clinical proof," a thirty-day study of ten women, ages 19 to 58. Tabulated results, recorded after 1, 7, 14, 21, and 28 fifteen-minute daily treatments—enough of a continuity to show direction and rate of effect—do show increases in bustline measurement in nine out of the ten women, the exception having undergone a crash diet while the test was in progress. Scepticism about bust developers, and the ad's carnival-huckster tone (not to speak of elitism and anti-sexism) may lead us here to lose detachment. (Since our society's narrow ideals of human beauty are too entrenched and too widespread to be dismissed as stupidity, peoples' striving after such ideals must be taken as a datum just like anything else.) So let us assume that the results of the test are genuine. Even so, the test seems to be inadequate in many ways. There is no control group, and the researchers seem to have controlled for few variables, diet being the most obvious. Are there normal bustline fluctuations in women during the course of a month? Exactly how was the sample selected, exactly how were the measurements taken? Since the device consists of a hose which attaches to a household faucet, and a plastic cup attached to the hose (the water activating an impeller inside the cup which fits over the breast) maybe, just maybe, that stream does provide physical stimulation enough to cause the breast to swell. There could be a sort of order effect, moreover, according to which subjects over a period of days come to respond increasingly to that stimulation. Their bustline measurements would increase over that period of days, but only for a few minutes after each test. Women wishing to "increase bustline size," however, seek lasting results, not ephemeral ones. Therefore, if the device produces only ephemeral results it plainly does not work. The test should have included measurements before and on at least two occasions after each treatment.

The pain reliever test was typical not only in that it included multiple measurements after ingestion but also compared more than one dose of both drugs. The experiment was *factorial*, that is, it worked out relationships between more than two variables. Factorial designs not only express our need for quantified results but also are efficient in that numbers of questions can be answered by the same complex calculation or experiment: "How much recycled pulp and how little rag can we get away with in our product without reducing quality below an acceptable level?" "How much of what fertilizer will produce the best yields per dollar for these three varieties?" "What would it cost the Social Security System if the median age of death were to increase by one year; by two years; by five years—over a period of one year; of five years; of ten years?"

Let us examine one more way in which argument can go astray by ignoring the connection between cause and control. Recall the incident by which St. Augustine was able to debunk astrology, the case of his friend Firminus and the slave. Augustine's refutation succeeds because the horoscope cast for both infants had to augur well for both, or ill for both. Suppose that it had augured well: "The stars will cause anyone born now to have a bright career." The horoscope, if true, provides a distinction upon which action can rest. One would do well to befriend the slave and anyone born at that moment, to avoid competing for the same positions as the slave, to buy, or free, the slave, and so on. The horoscope makes a difference. In this straightforward version, however, the horoscope lies open to the sort of refutation Augustine supplies. Now sometimes astrologers and other explainers abandon straightforward versions in favor of sophistications which seems to insulate their contentions from falsification. "The little slave has grown up and remains a slave, you say?" we can hear such an explainer saying. "Oh, but when his horoscope was cast, it indicated that he would have a bright career. Well, he *was* a slave then, was he not? And he *has* had a bright career since, hasn't he, I mean, *for a slave?*"

Sophistications like this insulate at a price. The distinction on which useful action can be based has disappeared. If "bright career" could mean "wealth and power" *and also* mean "slavery," then action would be just a gamble—exactly what it would have been had no horoscope been cast at all.

As hedged, the horoscope may make *some* distinction; had the slave had a miserable career as a slave, then perhaps the horoscope could have been shown false. Some attempts at causal explanation seem able to explain *anything*. They gain unassailability, however, at the price of meaning. Underneath they make no distinction at all. Suppose that someone settles on the idea that because of a circumstance buried in his past, Frank is hostile toward his mother. Now plenty of behavior shows someone's hostility, but such behavior is scarcely mentioned. You protest that, on the contrary, Frank seems to be a loving son—does such things as visit his mother on holidays, help out with the rent, chide other relatives for neglecting his mother, and so forth. "Exactly," comes the reply, "Frank is merely compensating for the hostility he really feels." Now like the astrological sophistication, this explanation unfairly shifts ground. In skillful hands such sophistry can explain anything. But what distinction does it make about Frank? What are we, or what is Frank supposed to do? Again, the element of control having been omitted from the equation, the causal explanation suffers. Instead, the original explanation needs to be examined on its original grounds.

If the sophistications here under discussion seem to beg the question, it is because they do. Counterclaims get discarded illegitimately in terms of the very explanation they try to counter.

Examples and Comments

Using the ideas discussed in this chapter, and common sense, comment on the strengths and/or weaknesses of the following, sketching lines for improvement.

1 "Watermelon? gives me hives. Nothing else does. I love it. Tried it many times. Hives every time. So thanks very much, but I'll pass. . . ."

Comment This person's attribution of hives to watermelon is probably correct. There were probably enough trials and enough natural variation, even though conditions were, of course, not rigidly controlled. And the argument does contain a control—the (probably varied) similar situations in which, not having eaten watermelon, the person did not contract hives. If it mattered, two longshot aspects which could show misattribution might be followed up. Were those "too many times" also the only times at which *other* things also happened, or at which other foods are eaten? Some people eat watermelon and experience mosquitoes, or poison ivy, or sing-a-longs, only at Sunday school picnics. So, were those "too many times" various times? Second, hives being what they are, there could be a psychological element. Once a person has attributed hives to watermelon (perhaps after only one Sunday school picnic) this could be enough to bring on hives the other times.

2 "EDITOR: In over twenty years of general practice I have witnessed the effects of drug use. Long-term, heavy marijuana use ages the nervous system in somewhat the same way as Parkinson's disease. The brain itself is impaired. Don't risk this degeneration. Don't use pot. And above all don't legalize it." (James B. Haddon, M.D.)

Comment Patients who present themselves for treatment in doctors' offices provide representative samples for some purposes, but surely not for assessment of the effects of heavy marijuana use. Brain impairment from pot use could show up retrospectively only by comparing the brain function of a sizable group of users with that of an identical group of nonusers. (And even then there would be the question whether any differences might not be due to a propensity for those with less well functioning brains to become users.) Now nobody, especially a general practitioner, is going to be able to find identical groups of users and nonusers. Further, since heavy pot smokers would rarely confide the fact, how could a G.P. reliably discover who among his patients are and who are not users? A physician suspecting that use harmed the brain would tend to pursue the question to use with dull patients while never pursuing it with normal patients, who after all might be users too.

Next, suppose that by some technical device, or by clairvoyance, Haddon can detect brain impairment in known users. Even so, how could he attribute it to marijuana? Why not to degeneration due to years of directionlessness, or to loud music; why not to the use of other drugs, or to the adulterants in street pot, or to who knows what? He has no control against which to isolate a cause.

Finally, given the emotion expressed in the letter (and notice the blurring of the line between pot and other drugs), it might be difficult for someone, including Dr. Haddon, to say whether Haddon's passion is a cause or an effect of the "degeneration" he sees. It appears that Haddon has attempted to gauge brain impairment informally by behavioral criteria. If so, then one cannot help suspecting, since the behavior of those outside one's own culture often seems stupid, that what Haddon calls brain impairment may be little more than his incomprehension of an alien life-style.

3 "Women are entitled to these vital beauty facts! Synopsis of the nation-wide half-face test! . . . Who took part? 612 women, aged 17 to 55, from all walks of life—society matrons, housewives, clerks, factory workers, actresses, nurses . . . The test. For thirty days, under scientific supervision, each woman cleansed one-half her face by her accustomed method, and washed the other side with Visage Facial Soap. Supervised by 13 eminent dermatologists and their staffs. Reports checked and certified by one of the country's leading dermatological authorities. Results: Visage was more effective than other beauty methods in 106 cases of pimples; 83 cases of large pores; 103 cases of blackheads; 81 cases of dry skin; 115 cases of oily skin; 66 cases of dull 'uninteresting' skin." (Advertisement.)

Comment If there are flaws in the test they would most likely surface under the following lines of questioning. First, was the test "blind"? Most likely it was not, since each subject would have known which was the control, namely the half "cleansed by her accustomed method." In which case there could easily be "aim to please" bias in favor of the Visage folks. Second, were test and control parallel? It would be silly to compare a test material, which any competent dermatologist would have the subject apply thoroughly according to strict instructions, with a "control" material which was applied according to some uncontrolled, probably less than thorough, "accustomed method." And were the sides of test and control faces randomly varied? Assuming that answers to the above questions are affirmative, a crossover would strengthen the results. Third, there are questions about selection of experimental subjects; the authority of those "eminent dermatologists" and "leading dermatological authorities"; and especially about the precision, calculation, and meaning of the "106 cases of pimples," and "83 cases of larger pores," and so forth. Any of these questions could be pursued along lines sketched in Chapter 3 and 4. Finally, for a helpful comparison with this "half-face-test" argument, see example 14 below.

4   "Carefully controlled observations have shown no evidence that ascorbic acid has significant effect in preventing the common cold or affecting its duration. Dahlgren and Engberg carried out a mass experiment on 2500 army conscripts, randomly divided, with one half receiving 200 mg of ascorbid acid a day and the other half receiving placebos. No difference was noted in the frequency or duration of colds, fever, endurance tests, or diseases of any description in the two groups."

Comment The report omits some vital information. Over what period was the test run? If over a relatively short period, very few of either group may have contracted or fought off colds. Results, for all we know, could have been: control group, one severe and one minor cold; test group, one severe and one minor cold. Results even several times this order would not be significant enough to disprove effectiveness. We need to know the absolute numbers of colds for both groups.

Probably the researchers did run the test over a period long enough to generate a number of cases sufficient to disprove the hypothesis that 200 mg a day of ascorbic acid is useful against the common cold. That they did, however, in no way warrants the reporter's implication that ascorbic acid has been shown ineffective against the common cold. Such a conclusion would call for a study which was factorial. For one thing, recruits probably get a diet which is not ascorbic acid deficient: are there significant differences between their common cold incidence, severity, and duration and those of comparable groups whose diets are ascorbic acid deficient? If so, ascorbic acid *is* effective against colds. (If data on such comparable groups exist, a retrospective study would be possible.) For another thing, what about dosages *above* 200 mg? To test the reporter's hypothesis, since the experimenters seem to have all those tractable recruits available, 5000 recruits, let us say, could be randomly divided into a number of equal-sized groups, one of which would be the placebo-receiving control, the other groups getting controlled dosages of ascorbic acid ranging from deficient (perhaps in more than one degree) clear through to massive. Then if "no difference was noted" among any of the groups (assuming a large enough absolute number of colds) we could conclude, at least for that class of individual, that ascorbic acid is ineffective.

5 "Meat contains large amounts of cholesterol as well as saturated fat which stimulates the body to produce cholesterol. Vegetarian diets avoid this hazard. It follows that vegetarians should suffer less from heart diseases. In fact, a study of the dietary habis of the Seventh-Day Adventists, a sect whose members eat no flesh, found that the men suffered only 60 percent as much heart disease as other American males. If they did develop heart trouble it occurred much later in life."

Comment Of what this report implies we ought to be suspicious. The results should be preliminary at most. Seventh-Day Adventists and other "abstainers" do in fact provide controls against which researchers compare the indulgences of the rest of humanity. Such comparisons, however, must be made cautiously. Before being satisfied with what this argument implies we should demand indication that the supposed differences were not due to another factor or combination of factors. Why not to abstention from smoking and alcohol, for example, or why not to the Adventists' less stressful, regular, family-oriented habits? Comparison of Adventists with, say, Mormons, who eat meat but neither drink nor smoke and who lead similar lives, would be much better.

6 "Marijuana, as former President Nixon has said, is 'a halfway house to something worse.' While most marijuana users have not as yet tried heroin, a large fraction have and 1 to 2 million are now 'junkies.' Only marijuana users progress to heroin. Nonusers turn down opportunities to use heroin or LSD. The disastrous epidemic of new heroin addicts comes entirely from the ranks of pot smokers."

7 "Prohibition of cigarette advertising will not be the economic disaster to the tobacco industry which Tobacco Board spokespersons seem to fear. In Czechoslovakia, where there is no advertising, tobacco consumption has climbed at a rate very similar to that in the United States where hundreds of millions are spent on such advertising."

8 "Among the benefits which President Otsev attributed to his policies since taking over as head of State University were 'more stability, constancy, continuity. The university has more credibility; it's been a much more responsible institution.' "

9 "More doctors use and recommend Corngold than any other margarine. According to a recent survey, *twice* as many doctors personally use Corngold at home than any other brand. And *twice* as many doctors also recommend Corngold than any other *brand* to their patients. And in a separate clinical test, Corngold was part of a total dietary program along with reduced fats, fewer eggs, and skim milk that lowered serum cholesterol levels an average 17 percent. Shouldn't you serve your family Corngold? It's the only leading margarine made from 100 percent corn oil. Contains liquid corn oil."

10 "Two ads were prepared, set in editorial style with no pictures, two columns, 100 editorial lines. The last paragraph contained a phone number. Ad number 1 differed from ad number 2 only in headline. Number 1's read, 'It's not the heat it's the humidity. New room coolers dry the air.' Number 2's headline read, 'How to have a cool home. Even on hot nights.' Number 1 was run one Friday in May in the local daily (circ. 400,000) and number 2 was run the following Friday. Number 1 produced 75 calls, number 2 produced 160 calls. Obviously number 2 was the more effective at generating response."

11 "Vitamin C Passes Test. College City (PNS) Children taking big doses of vitamin C daily experienced fewer sick days than students taking fake pills, according to an Arizona study. For fourteen weeks half of 650 children who were aged 10–16 were given two-gram doses of vitamin C, and half were given inert placebos. Students receiving the vitamin C experienced 30 percent fewer sick days than their classmates."

12 "Mercury Link to Suicide? Temple University scientists are examining thousands of death certificates of dentists in an attempt to fathom why the suicide rate among dentists is double that of the general population. One explanation may be prolonged exposure to mercury, a substance dentists must handle daily. In studies of industrial workers exposure to mercury has been accompanied by acute anxiety."

13 "Teen Survey Links Smoking, Sex. Rochester (PNS) Recent surveys conducted by Kelly, Black and Bogdanovich, Inc. show that three of ten 16- and 17-year old youths of both sexes said they were current smokers. This was a rise of 5 percent for the girls since 1969 and a drop of 1 percent for the boys. Based on interviews of 250 boys and 250 girls, the surveys were reported at the opening of an American Cancer Society seminar here. The survey found that 57 percent of teenage boy smokers reported engaging in sexual intercourse compared to only 23 percent of the nonsmoking boys of the same age. Thirty-one percent of the girls who smoked had had sex, compared to 8 percent of the nonsmokers."

14 "Apparently estrogen hormone creams are of little or no value. A varied sample of twenty-seven women between 35 and 65 years old (mean age 52) most of them in or beyond menopause, were studied. Three well-known brands of hormone creams were tested, along with a control cream indistin-guishable from the hormone cream and like it except that it lacked estrogen hormones. Each woman was provided with two identical looking jars of cream, one hormone and the other a control (each marked with only code letters and the designation 'left' or 'right'), and was instructed to rub vigor-ously about ½ tsp. of each cream for 30 seconds on the side of the face for which it was designated. Neither subject nor dermatologist knew on which side of the face the hormone cream had been used. Observations and photographs of each side of the face of each subject were taken before the test, thirty days after the start of the tests, and again after three months. The dermatologist was able to detect no difference between the two sides of any face, although in a number of instances he found obvious improvement of both sides."

Applications

A Collect specimens of causal reports from several media sources—from example, from medical or popular science journals, from the tabloid scan-dal sheets sold in supermarkets, from business periodicals, or from a daily newspaper. Analyze the reports for adequacy and completeness. Could the report have been more meaningful in an equal or slightly greater amount of space?

B Are you sceptical about someone's horticultural, culinary, automotive, environmental, dietary, medical, or engineering claim? Do you have a pet claim yourself? Devise and defend an acid test of the claim.

C Using material collected in connection with this and other chapters, or collected anew, devise a *cumulative* "Examples and Comments" section (without your comments). Use it to test others, score it, and defend or discuss your scoring decisions.

D In the form of a report or essay, clarify or challenge this chapter's discussion of the alleged connection between cause and control, or carefully discuss another aspect of causality. Weigh pro versus con, anticipate and meet objections.

Index